D0583216

Classroom Teaching Skills

The Research Findings of the
Teacher Education Project

Edited by E.C. Wragg

First published 1984 by Croom Helm Ltd
Reprinted 1984 and 1986

Reprinted 1989, 1991, 1993, 1996 by Routledge
11 New Fetter Lane, London EC4P 4EE

© 1984 E.C. Wragg

Printed and bound in Great Britain by
Biddles Ltd, Guildford and King's Lynn

All rights reserved. No part of this book may be reprinted or
reproduced or utilized in any form or by any electronic,
mechanical, or other means, now known or hereafter
invented, including photocopying and recording, or
in any information storage or retrieval system, without
permission in writing from the publishers.

British Library Cataloguing in Publication Data
A catalogue record for this book is available from the British Library

ISBN 0–415–03939–8

Edge Hill College
Learning Resource Centre X

Author   WRAGG

Class No.   371.102

Book No.   593894

CONTENTS

TABLES

FIGURES

PREFACE

This book describes some of the research undertaken during the Teacher Education Project, a 4½-year research and development project funded by the Department of Education and Science, during which we observed over 1,000 lessons, interviewed more than 200 experienced and novice teachers, and developed sets of teacher training materials which were piloted and then published.

During the project we concentrated in particular on the development of teachers' professional competence, especially class management and control, the teaching of mixed-ability groups and the skills of explaining and questioning. Since the project was concerned both with research and development, the time and energy of the tutors and teachers involved was divided between both kinds of activity. The workbooks and other training materials produced during the project are listed in Appendix A.

The chapters in this book describe some of the empirical work undertaken in what became one of the largest studies of teaching skill based on the direct observation of secondary school lessons, ever undertaken in Britain. Even so, we were only able to scratch the surface of the vast and complex matter of studying and nurturing skilful teaching.

Professor E.C. Wragg
School of Education
Exeter University

ACKNOWLEDGEMENTS

We are grateful to the National Society for the Study of Education for permission to reproduce Figure 2.1 on page 22. In addition, we should like to express our sincere thanks to Pip Davis, Dick Madelin, Ned Colman and several others who assisted with data collection, Madeleine Atkins who commented on Chapter 5, countless colleagues at the Universities of Nottingham, Leicester and Exeter in particular, and in many other universities, colleges and polytechnics who collected data, tried out materials or commented on drafts, as well as hundreds of pupils, teachers, students, heads, advisers, Her Majesty's Inspectors and others who allowed themselves to be watched, interviewed or experimented with. Finally, our thanks are due to Tricia Bisley and several other typists who typed observation instruments, test materials, interview schedules, lesson reports and the manuscript of this book.

1 TEACHING SKILLS

E.C. Wragg

A Time for Skilful Teaching

Teachers have always been required to have professional skills, but there can have been few periods in our history when they have needed to display the degree of competence required in the uncertain world of the 1980s. In the nineteenth century training institutions were known as 'normal schools', on the grounds that there was some single 'norm' endorsed by society. The function of a training establishment was to perpetuate this stereotype, and the Master of Method was employed in the model school to ensure that each new generation of teachers was poured into the same approved mould (Rich, 1933). Today there are several factors which combine to require levels of skill, understanding, imagination and resilience from teachers which go infinitely beyond the rudimentary commonsense and mechanical competence fostered by the normal schools of the last century.

The massive explosion of knowledge gathering during the last 50 years has produced banks of data in such profusion that no human being is now capable of grasping more than the tiniest fraction of their contents. There are examples of computer-stored research data, such as the Lockheed Dialog system, which contain research reports in over a hundred fields, and the largest files in subjects like chemistry can disgorge in excess of 2½ million abstracts.

It is not only in the pure and applied sciences that this expansion has taken place, but also in many areas of human endeavour including the humanities, with thousands of new published books and articles in many fields being added each year. In addition to this formidable advance in the discovery of new information there has been a considerable development of new skills. Transplant surgery, for example, unknown only a few years ago, has become a standard part of many surgeons' professional armoury.

The implications for teachers of these rapid developments are clear. Given the tradition of localism in England and Wales, whereby individual schools have a considerable degree of freedom to devise their own curricula and teaching strategies, albeit subject to the scrutiny of their local authority, teachers need considerable skill to select topics, activities and ways of working from the vast array of possibilities. Furthermore, since their pupils can also acquire only a tiny fraction of the knowledge and skills currently available to humanity, teachers must develop teaching strategies which not only transmit information, but also encourage children to learn independently and as a member of a group. Although no committee would ever have composed Beethoven's Fifth Symphony, it is also unlikely that any individual could have sent a rocket to the moon. A great deal of human achievement will in future be the result of teamwork.

Alongside the demands placed on teachers by the expansion of knowledge and skills are those caused by the significant social changes in recent years which are taking place on a scale unparalleled in any period other than wartime. During the 1970s one million jobs disappeared from manufacturing industry in Britain, and another million had been obliterated within the first two years of the following decade. Most were unskilled and semi-skilled forms of employment which will probably never return.

Faced with youth unemployment on a large scale, many teachers, especially in inner-city schools, find that traditional forms of motivation, such as urging pupils to work hard at school so that they will obtain a good job, no longer have the appeal they once enjoyed. Disaffection over the apparent futility of learning reported by numerous adolescents offers another formidable challenge to the professional ingenuity of the teacher.

Employers, meanwhile, able to erect artificial barriers when applicants for jobs vastly exceed the actual vacancies, may require O levels for jobs previously taken by the less well qualified, A levels where O levels were once sufficient, and a degree in what was formerly a non-graduate profession. This spiralling demand for qualifications puts yet more pressure on teachers to use their skills effectively during the eleven compulsory years of schooling, or whenever else they have contacts with people who need to learn. In our increasingly technological and bureaucratic society those who leave school under-educated, for whatever reason, are at risk, likely to be unemployed, or fall victim to loan sharks and the other predators in society.

The more optimistic scenario, that labour will shift out of the factory and into the leisure industry, that people will have more free time in future and be relieved of the tedium of monotonous jobs, that early retirement will give a boost to community and life-long education, is no less demanding on teachers' skills. To enjoy leisure adults must have learned how to use it fruitfully, to be willing to learn throughout their lives it helps if they have been enthused rather than rebuffed and demoralised in school. The quality of personal relationships between teacher and taught, therefore, is a direct result of the interpersonal skill of the teacher, who usually sets the tone in a class, or has to take the initiative to improve relationships should they go awry. A notion of teaching skill that embraced only the transmission of knowledge would be a poor one in such a context.

A third factor to be considered is the development of new technology such as the micro-computer, forms of teletext such as the Prestel system, direct broadcasting by satellite and cable television. One important feature of some of the more recent forms of technological development is that the micro-computer, Prestel and cable television in particular, offer an interactive facility on a scale not previously available, changing the position of the teacher as the single authoritative initiator of or respondent to enquiry. Such developments test the flexibility and adaptability of teachers, who need to be able to modify their teaching styles to accommodate some at least of the many new developments which have a potential to improve learning.

A fourth factor requiring some degree of attention to improving teaching skill occurs as a consequence of the rapidly declining school rolls during the 1980s, especially in the secondary sector. The birth-rate fell dramatically from its 1964 peak until the end of the 1970s, and it was known in 1980 that for every four children in a primary school there would be only three by 1986, and that for every three pupils in a secondary school there would be only two by the end of the decade.

In inner-city and some rural areas the decline in pupil numbers has led to school closures and a loss of morale amongst a teaching profession used to extrinsic rewards, such as rapid salary and status improvements during the period of expansion of the 1950s and 1960s when the teaching force doubled in size. One way to reduce, if not avoid, falling morale when promotion prospects are less in evidence than they were formerly, is for teachers to take pride in honing their professional skills, and a number of in-service courses in recent times, especially certain school-based ones, have attempted to facilitate professional development and self-appraisal for experienced teachers. This theme will be taken up again in Chapter 10.

The 1983 White Paper *Teaching Quality*, though it did not give detail about all the factors mentioned above, recognised the importance to our society at its present state of evolution of having a highly skilled force of professional teachers who are able to nurture and facilitate learning for the next generation, as well as for adults who wish to continue their education. It was decided in the Teacher Education Project to study certain significant aspects of a number of skills displayed by teachers, and to develop training materials which would reflect what was learned from observing experienced practitioners, as well as stimulate trainee and experienced teachers to analyse and determine their own strategies.

Identifying and Defining Teaching Skills

There is less dissent about what constitutes effective teaching in discussion between people outside the profession than there is in the research and evaluation literature. Good teachers, it is commonly held, are keen and enthusiastic, well organised, firm but fair, stimulating, know their stuff, and are interested in the welfare of their pupils. Few would attempt to defend the converse: that good teachers are unenthusiastic, boring, unfair, ignorant, and do not care about their pupils.

Once the scrutiny of teaching is translated into the more precise terms demanded by the tenets of rigorous systematic enquiry, the easy agreement of casual conversation evaporates. The books and articles on effective teaching are numerous, and Barr (1961) summarising a massive amount of American research, concluded, 'Some teachers were preferred by administrators, some were liked by the pupils, and some taught in classes where there were substantial pupil gains, and generally speaking these were not the same teachers.' Biddle and Ellena (1964), reporting the Kansas City role studies, found that there was not even clear agreement amongst teachers, parents and administrators about the role teachers should play.

More recently, even the attempts to see consensus in the research literature have been criticised. For example, Gage (1978), summarising research studies which had attempted to relate teaching style to children's learning, concluded that in the early years of schooling certain kinds of teacher behaviour did show some consistent relationship to children learning reading and arithmetic. From this he derived a set of prescriptive 'Teacher should' statements, like 'Teachers should call on a child by name before asking the question', 'Teachers should keep to a minimum such activities as giving directions and organizing the class for instruction', or 'During reading-group instruction, teachers should give a maximal amount of brief feedback and provide fast-paced activities of the "drill" type'.

Critics of such prescriptions argue that much of the American research is based on short-term memory tests, that formal didactic styles of teaching appear to be more successful, and could too easily be perpetuated as the best form of teaching. Longer-term objectives which teachers might have are less frequently measured, so that the music teacher who hopes that children will have a lifelong interest in music is less likely to be investigated than the one who merely wants children to recall sonata form or define a triad in a short memory test.

There was once an interesting experiment at the University of Michigan which illustrates neatly the dilemma of trying to elicit what forms of teaching are most effective. Guetzkow, Kelly and McKeachie (1954) divided first-year students on a general psychology course into three groups. The first group was given a formal lecture course with regular tests, the second and third groups were based on tutorials and discussions. At the end of the course the lecture group not only out-performed the tutorial discussion groups on the final examination, but was also more favourably rated by the students. So far this represents a victory for lecturing and testing on two commonly used criteria: test performance and student appraisal.

The investigators discovered, however, that the students in the discussion groups scored significantly higher than the lecture groups on a measure of interest in psychology, the subject being studied. They hypothesised that though the lecture-group students gave a favourable rating of the teaching they had received, this may have been because they had less anxiety about grades for the course through their weekly feedback from test scores. It was decided to monitor the subsequent progress of all the groups. Three years later not one student in the lecture group had opted to study the subject further, but 14 members of the two discussion and tutorial groups had chosen to major in psychology. Thus, on short-term criteria the lecture method was superior, but taking a longer perspective the discussion method appeared to motivate students more powerfully, and ultimately some must have learned a great deal more.

Defining teaching skill in such a way that all would agree, therefore, is not a simple matter. If we were to say that teaching skills are the strategies teachers use to enable children to learn, then most people would want to rule out intimidation, humiliation, the use of corporal punishment or other forms of teacher behaviour of which they personally happen to disapprove. It is perhaps easier when seeking a definition of teaching skill to describe some of the characteristics of skilful teaching which might win some degree of consensus, though not universal agreement.

The first might be that the behaviour concerned *facilitates pupils' learning of something worthwhile*, such as facts, skills, values, concepts, how to live harmoniously with one's fellows, attitudes or some other outcome thought to be desirable. A second quality could be that it is *acknowledged to be a skill by those competent to judge*, and this might include teachers, teacher trainers, inspectors, advisers and learners themselves. We shall see in Chapter 4 that pupils can be shrewd in their appraisal of the teacher's craft, and that the ability to explain is often highly rated by them.

For it to be a recognised part of a teacher's professional competence the skill should also be *capable of being repeated*, not perhaps in exactly the same form, but as a fairly frequent rather than a single chance occurrence. A chimpanzee might randomly produce an attractive colourful shape once in a while given a brush and some paint, but an artist would produce a skilfully conceived painting on a more regular basis. Teachers who possess professional skills, therefore, should be capable of manifesting these consistently, not on a hit-or-miss basis.

One frequently cited observation on skills is that of the philosopher Gilbert Ryle (1949) who distinguished, in his book *The Concept of Mind*, between being able to state a factual proposition and perform a skilful operation. The difference between knowing *that* and knowing *how* is the difference between inert knowledge and intelligent action. Unfortunately, some competent teachers are not especially articulate about their skill, and it would be a mistake to assume that it is a prerequisite for skill only to be recognised as such if the person manifesting it is capable of explaining and analysing it in textbook language. The intelligence of an action may perfectly well be explained by another, and the behaviour is not necessarily unintelligent or shallow if its perpetrator is tongue-tied about it.

One problem encountered in defining teaching skills is that though in some contexts the term 'skill' has good connotations, attracts adulation, is a gift of the few, the result of years of practice or the mark of an expert, in other circumstances it is looked down upon, regarded as mechanical, the sign of a rude technician rather than an artist. We tend, for instance, to admire a surgeon's skill or that of a tennis player. Both may have had the same years of dedicated practice, but the intellectual nature of the knowledge and understanding required by the surgeon is vastly more exacting than that required by a sportsman.

Where the imagination is involved, even more fine distinctions exist. A sculptor would probably be disappointed to read a report that describes his latest masterpeice as a piece of skill. He would expect eulogies to contain words like 'artistic' and 'creative'. For those who liken teachers more to expressive artists than to surgeons, the very term 'skill' may be seen as belittling, reducing creative endeavour to mechanical crudity. It is difficult to dry-clean the term of these emotional associations with other kinds of human enterprise.

This uncertainty about the proper standing of the notion of skill when applied to teaching is partly explained by the varied nature of the teacher's job. Pressing the right button on a tape recorder, or writing legibly on the blackboard require but modest competence, and are things most people could learn with only a little practice. Responding to a disruptive adolescent, or knowing how to explain a difficult concept to children of different ages and abilities by choosing the right language, appropriate examples and analogies, and reading the many cues which signal understanding or bewilderment, require years of practice as well as considerable intelligence and insight. Although the term 'interpersonal skills' is now quite widespread, there is still some reluctance to classify human relationships in this way.

When children learn something there is often a magical quality about the excitement of discovery, the warmth of regard between teacher and taught, or the novelty to the learner of what is taking place, and the romanticism seems to be destroyed if teaching is seen as too deliberate, calculated, manipulated or over-analysed. Hence the debate, to which I shall return in Chapter 10, about learning to teach and whether the act of teaching should be seen as a whole or is at all capable of being separated into discrete if interrelated skills. My own view is that the extreme optimism of the supporters of the so-called Performance or Competency-based Teacher Education programmes fashionable in the United States during the 1970s was misplaced.

It was assumed that teaching would be broken down into hundreds and indeed thousands of particles, that trainees could learn each of these, and that they could be certificated on the basis of their proven ability to manifest whatever set of competencies had been prescribed. Lists of approved competencies were produced, such as the 1,276 compiled by Dodl (1973) under the heading *The Florida Catalog of Teacher Competencies*, and hierarchies were assembled with the skills required given a level. Thus, an operation by the teacher like 'form reading groups and give a good rationale for the grouping' was seen as being at a lower level than 'implement managerial procedures for efficient group operation'. There was an arbitrary quality to some of these hierarchies, and competency-based teacher education was criticised by writers such as Heath and Nielson (1974) for not being founded on any sound empirical evidence.

In selecting skills for study and development in the Teacher Education Project, we were conscious that the sustained debate about teaching itself and the education and training of teachers has not crystallised around any single viewpoint. Teaching and studying minute facets of behaviour like 'smiling' can soon become comical and divorced from overall reality, and at the other extreme constant denial that there is anything other than some global notion of 'teaching' which is sacrosanct, ethereal and must not be subjected to scrutiny, simply produces paralysis. The areas on which we chose to focus, class management, mixed-ability teaching, questioning and explaining, seemed, according to the tenets described above, to represent activities which required skill, intelligence and sensitivity from teachers. They were not so vague as to defy any analysis, nor so minute and piddling as to be silly. They were aspects of teaching thought by experienced professionals to be important both for experienced and trainee teachers. By studying these four aspects of teaching we inevitably left unstudied many other central skills, and even though we observed and analysed a large number of lessons we could still only hope to make a modest contribution to the understanding and nurturing of the teacher's professional art and craft.

Classroom Observation

Up to the late 1950s there were very few examples of research on teaching which had used direct observation of lessons. Many inferences about classroom life were drawn from interviews, questionnaires or from folklore, anecdotes and hearsay. During the 1960s and 1970s this situation changed rapidly, and hundreds of reports were published ranging from case studies of a single classroom to large scale observations of practice in hundreds of lessons.

There is not the space here to document the many forms of enquiry which have been undertaken nor the thousands of 'findings' reported in the literature around the world. These are in any case to be found in several standard reference books such as that by Dunkin and Biddle (1974), Delamont (1976), Wragg (1976), Cohen and Manion (1981) and many others.

There are considerable advantages and a few disadvantages to studying classrooms by observing what happens at first hand. The major disadvantage is that the presence of an observer invariably has an effect on what takes place, however slight, and there is no foolproof way of knowing what might have transpired had no outsider been there. Samph (1976) planted microphones in classrooms and then sent observers either announced or unexpected some weeks later. He found that teachers made more use of questions, praise and were more likely to accept pupils' ideas when someone was present. Teachers and indeed pupils may attempt to provide what they think the visitor expects, and this will vary according to the impression or stereotype they form of the observer concerned. They may be irritated by a visitor and behave differently from normal, hence the need for observers, where possible, to study a series of lessons rather than a single one.

Several traditions of observing classrooms have been developed. In the United States the great majority of published classroom studies have been based on a degree of quantification, often using some kind of category system. This tradition dates back to the attention studies of the 1920s and 1930s reported by Jackson (1968), and even earlier. It gained in popularity during the 1950s and 1960s, especially after the seminal article by Medley and Mitzel (1963) describing how to construct category systems. Some of the work is closely related to behaviourist learning theory; other studies attempt to relate measurements of the frequency of certain kinds of behaviour to tests of pupil learning or other estimates of outcome.

Since the hope of this kind of research was to establish a body of knowledge which would show some consistency about what successful teachers do, several writers have attempted to establish theories of teaching and learning based on systematic empirical enquiry. Techniques such as meta-analysis (Glass, 1978) have been developed which aggregate quantitative studies based on correlation coefficients, chi-squares, or analysis of variance, and determine an overall effect size. Thus, it is possible to calculate from several studies the average relationship between, say, the teacher's use of praise and pupils' learning. Although the apparent neatness of such an aggregation may appeal to some administrators looking for guidance from research, the proposition that fairly exact relationships can be discovered between what teachers do or are, and what pupils learn, has been criticised by several writers. Jackson (1962) described the findings of half a century of study on the relationship between teachers' personalities and pupil learning as 'so low in intellectual food value that it is almost embarrassing to discuss them.' Typically, small but significant correlations of around 0.2 or 0.3 have been commonplace, leaving a great deal still unexplained.

The more carefully conducted quantitative analyses of teaching have nevertheless yielded some useful and interesting information, even though much less has been delivered than was once hoped. For example, the extremely busy nature of the teacher's job is now well documented. Teachers may have up to 200 days a year with their classes, and various studies have shown over 1,000 interpersonal exchanges in a day (Jackson, 1962), teachers asking on average 348 questions a day (Floyd, 1960), some in inner-city schools spending up to 75 per cent of their time trying to keep order (Deutsch, 1960), or teachers allowing on average one second between a pupil answer and their own next statement (Rowe, 1972). It is quite clear that in the course of the millions of exchanges in which teachers may engage during quite a short phase of their career, they can find little time for a leisurely scrutiny of classroom processes.

Consequently, many teachers develop fairly fixed patterns of teaching which may well be laid down at the training stage. When new curricula, school reorganisation or other changes in circumstances come along, it is difficult to unlearn habits and strategies which have been rehearsed millions of times, even if they are no longer appropriate. Hence the criticism in Her Majesty's Inspectors' (HMI) reports of too much whole-class teaching with mixed-ability classes, or the difficulties experienced by teachers trying to use a fresh work scheme with old teaching methods.

Alongside these many quantitative studies has been a different style of enquiry based more on the pencil and notebook tradition used by anthropologists seeking to analyse human behaviour by recording phenomena in detail, and then inviting participants to explain them. Sometimes the investigator is also a participant, as in the case study by Hamilton (1975) of the introduction of integrated science teaching in two Scottish schools, sometimes a non-participant, like King (1978), who documented practice in three infant schools, and deliberately avoided becoming enmeshed in the life of the classrooms in which he spent many hours.

Incisive ethnographic accounts of classrooms often give intimate case details and interpretations which some of the quantitative accounts might have missed. The observations made in lessons by Ball (1981), who recorded how a ten-form-entry comprehensive school changed from a system of broad banding to one of mixed-ability classes, are quite close in tenor to those reported in the 1978 HMI paper on the same topic, which was based on evidence from the classrooms of several schools. The strategies employed by teachers of different subjects, the arguments underlying their behaviour and the reaction of pupils, however, are all described in much greater detail through the single case study.

Lacey (1970) taught twelve lessons a week himself, and spent another twelve lessons a week observing teachers and their classes in his study of Hightown Grammar. The result is an analysis of teaching and a description of individual pupils and teachers that set classroom processes in the wider context of the school in its social environment. A similar depth and breadth of insight was offered by Hargreaves (1967) in his study of Lumley Secondary Modern School.

In addition to the two major styles of enquiry there has been other research into teaching based on different procedures and traditions. Blurton Jones (1972) brought together a collection of research reports based on the ethological techniques used by students of the behaviour of animals, and Barnes (1971), Stubbs (1976) and Edwards and Furlong (1978) are amongst several investigators who have undertaken linguistic analysis of classroom transactions. Though verbal aspects of teaching and learning have commanded attention from researchers, increasing interest has been shown in non-verbal aspects of classroom communication by, among others, Argyle (1967), Knapp (1980), and Wilkinson (1975), the last of whom combined a variety of techniques for analysing both verbal and non-verbal behaviour.

Studying teachers and pupils by direct observation of what they do and say provides valuable information on which to base judgements about skilful teaching and intelligent action. There are many observation procedures from which to choose, each with their supporters and practitioners. It is a pity that the debate between proponents of various schools has occasionally been acrimonious. Attempting to decide whether, for example, quantitative studies are better than qualitative ones, is about as fruitful as trying to determine whether a black and white photo of the front of the building gives a more true representation of reality than a painting of the rear, a scale drawing or an aerial photograph, or, for that matter, whether bacon and eggs beats fish and chips.

Carefully undertaken studies of various kinds with their different ways of gathering data and explaining phenomena can enhance our understanding of teaching and learning. We decided in the Teacher Education Project that we needed to observe lessons at first hand as well as use other methods of acquiring information. This was not so that students or experienced teachers might merely copy current practice, in the tradition of the nineteenth-century normal school, but rather that we might add a little to what is known about classroom processes to help inform those who seek to improve their teaching or that of others, however improvement may be defined. We also decided to use a mixture of research methods rather than a single style of enquiry. Thus, some studies are highly quantified; others are more qualitative; yet others a mixture of both. In the chapters of this book are some of the inferences drawn from the observation of over 1,000 lessons given by teachers and students.

The Teacher Education Project

The Teacher Education Project was a 4½-year research-and-development project conducted at the Universities of Nottingham, Leicester and Exeter, and funded mainly by the Department of Education and Science (DES). Our principal intention was to undertake research and develop training materials which would help nurture the skills needed for class management, mixed-ability teaching, explaining and asking questions. There was no intention to produce a course as such, but rather to devise materials and ways of working which might help shift the balance of teacher training courses more in the direction of the development of professional skills for the reasons given earlier. A list of the teacher training materials we produced is given in Appendix A.

The project had only enough finance for one full-time appointment over the 4½-year period, that of Trevor Kerry the co-ordinator, and later for two years Kay Wood as a full-time researcher. Such was the enthusiasm of a number of teacher trainers and teachers, however, that we managed to obtain help from over 40 people during the life of the project, some conducting a single case study or a few interviews, others analysing transcripts, observing lessons or undertaking more substantial and sustained pieces of enquiry. There is a considerable curiosity about teachers' skills amongst teachers themselves and teacher trainers, and it is not difficult to capitalise on it.

When we began the project in the late 1970s there had been a decade of reports, comment and criticism of teacher training, as well as ten years of dramatic changes in schools, with comprehensive reorganis-ation, the raising of the school leaving age, major curriculum packages in most subjects, the spread of mixed-ability teaching and an increase in size and complexity of many schools. Teacher training had made some changes but not as many as critics like Dent (1971) would have liked:

> What they [the colleges] did not do, even in this period of extensive and intensive change, was to alter the basic pattern of teacher education. Despite all the modernisation and liberalisation that have occurred over the past century and a half, the 1814 pattern has persisted. Nearly everyone says it must be changed. One hopes the change will be for the better.

In Post-graduate Certificate of Education (PGCE) courses most of the recruits during the 1960s had entered grammar schools and were being trained by former grammar school teachers. As comprehensive reorganisation spread during the 1970s, the story changed rapidly. Nottingham University School of Education, with 250 students, illustrates the speed of this transformation. Around 1971 some 80 per cent of students undertook teaching practice, and subsequently obtained posts in grammar schools. By 1976 an analysis of posts obtained showed that over 80 per cent had done their teaching practice in comprehensive schools, and a similar percentage took their first post in such a school.

Thus tutors who themselves had taught only the most able found their students complaining about inadequate preparation for mixed-ability teaching, the use of workcards, teaching the less able or the very bright, handling difficult classes and the kind of assessment and record-keeping necessary when classes are of very heterogeneous ability and possibly engaged in individual or group tasks. The need for reform, the generation of good ideas and some research base for these was becoming crucial.

Although we began as a PGCE project, it was not long before considerable interest was being shown by tutors on BEd courses, particularly those planning submissions to the Council for National Academic Awards (CNAA). The story here was similar, but with some important differences. In some colleges strict demarcation existed between so-called 'subject' departments and 'education'. Many colleges were beginning to develop some kind of 'professional studies', but often the territorial problems were such that no-one could be sure at what points in the course and by whom students should best be taught professional skills.

Some college education departments were still set up on the foundation disciplines of sociology, psychology, history and philosophy. Subject departments meanwhile concentrated on the high level of subject knowledge required by the new BEd degrees. Students often complained that teaching skills were neglected, and one National Foundation for Educational Research (NFER) study by James and Choppin (1977) which polled 519 would-be teachers at the school level, found that even they, as yet uncontaminated by a training course, expected it to be more theoretical than they would like. In its extreme form a very bad professional training course in the early to mid-1970s was the medical equivalent of training surgeons by first giving them lectures on the sociology, psychology, history and philosophy of surgery, giving them each a scalpel and a few patients, and turning them loose in operating theatres with the hope that they would make sense of it all whilst engaged in the actual process. Next of kin would not have been too pleased.

We had no quarrel at all, it should be said, with the notion that student teachers should study such important aspects of education as sociology or psychology. It was rather that we felt first of all that study by itself did not necessarily make students operational in the classroom, and secondly that when students analyse classroom processes and work at their teaching skills, they become much more highly motivated to learn the kind of educational theory that informs practice. An inductive approach based on students' own professional experiences raises every conceivable issue in the traditional disciplines: how children learn, or fail to learn, what the purposes of education are, how factors in school and society affect learning, who holds power and how it may be used or misused, which teaching strategies are appropriate in what context, devising and evaluating a curriculum and a host of others.

Before long we discovered that the appetite of experienced teachers for information about and further training in teaching skills was just as voracious as that of trainees. An article in the *Guardian* (Wragg, 1978) about the project's research into class management, which described 56 case studies of student teachers thought to be good or poor at handling their classes, produced over a thousand requests for the trial version of a training booklet. Over half of these were from experienced teachers, heads, deputies, teachers' centre wardens or professional tutors. Many told the same story: that their own or their colleagues' training had contained little on professional skills, and that there was considerable demand from teachers, particularly those engaged in school-based in-service work, for suggestions about how they could learn to scrutinise and improve their own teaching skills. When the first set of training booklets, the FOCUS series, was published by

Macmillan in 1981 and 1982 on such topics as class management, questioning, explaining, group work, teaching slow learners and bright pupils in mixed-ability classes and group work, over 10,000 copies were sold within a year, and many of these were being used by experienced teachers.

Having identified topics of importance, we also had to select ways of working. We decided on the following:

Involve the Profession

Some teacher training procedures seemed traditionally to exclude classroom practitioners. We decided it was most important to involve heads and teachers: to solicit their views in interviews and questionnaires, to obtain descriptions of good practice, to do research into classroom behaviour, to use teachers to field-test training procedures with students on teaching practice, and to ask them to give a professional evaluation of our materials. It was equally important to involve the teacher training profession, and we decided that all the above should apply to them too.

Teachers Should Seek Their Own Styles

Although one can learn a great deal from intelligent current practice, any training materials based purely on what teachers are seen to do would be ultra-conservative. Had such a procedure obtained in the medical profession, doctors would still be using leeches. Teachers exercise skill and make their decisions in different contexts. In the absence of any single consensus about effective teaching, therefore, practitioners need to learn to use their senses to appraise situations and their intelligence and imagination to respond. On the other hand we can learn a great deal from our fellow human beings, and so the training materials we produced were devised in such a way that teachers could work together to analyse each other's teaching. Historically, teaching has been a far more isolated job than it needed to be. We shall return in Chapter 10 to a further consideration of learning from a professional partner.

Research and Development

Some curriculum development projects have no research base at all, and may be none the worse for it, depending more on the professional and creative wisdom of team members than some kind of systematic enquiry. We decided to combine research and development in the Teacher Education Project.

There are a number of difficulties involved in a research-and-development project. The first is that it is usually impossible to do a thorough enquiry first and then produce the programme afterwards. A proper research project takes about three years, by the time the design has been worked out, the fieldwork done and analysed, and the implications identified. If one starts development only at that stage, then circumstances may already have changed compared with when the research phase was undertaken. On the other hand if one starts with development, then research can only be *post-hoc* evaluations, and it may be difficult to incorporate findings once well-tested materials are in existence.

In view of this we decided that different kinds of research were needed. Some would be 'quick and dirty', for example a series of interviews or questionnaires with face validity, seeking opinions or describing practice with an opportunity sample, not the sort to win a Nobel prize, but essential if one is to have some fairly immediate, if imperfect, data on which to base planning. Alongside this there would be the longer-term, more painstaking building up of evidence, some of which would arrive too late to influence training materials, but which would be useful and more rigorously derived.

It would be foolish to try to base a curriculum-development project *entirely* on one's own or even other people's research. Perhaps the best example of the slavish application of research findings is programmed learning, which died during the 1960s partly because of the tedium experienced by those working through endless sequences of mind-corroding frames containing the classic ingredients of active-responding, small steps, immediate confirmation and high correct-response rates. We decided that our own and other researchers' findings would *inform* training materials, not *dominate* them.

Regular Field-testing

Some curriculum development has been improvised in an armchair, albeit by someone with a sound sense of what is appropriate. It was decided that all training materials and procedures would be field-tested several times, in different kinds of locations and with different sources of feedback. Most of the materials were tried in two experimental forms before the final drafts were produced. Indeed, it was most helpful to have a split-site operation at Nottingham, Leicester and later at Exeter, because large numbers of students and teachers connected both with the universities and local colleges were always available. Hundreds of tear-off feedback slips were collected from students, teachers, advisers, college and university lecturers, and their comments helped shape later and final drafts of materials.

Use Natural Language

It would have been easy to dazzle students with a mass of technical expertise and educational jargon. After all, some courses have been notorious for this, and one of the obligatory paper hoops through which BEd students in particular have traditionally had to jump, required an instant definition of such trigger terms as nomothetic, idiographic, norm-referenced, ethnographic, positivist or teleological. No materials can or should be jargon-free. Indeed, learning the professional vocabulary, whether in medicine or education, is an important part of training. No doctor would earn respect if he had to say 'funny piece at the end of the intestine' because he has not learned the word 'appendix'.

However, our intention was not, in some philistine or folksy way, to avoid coming to grips with the difficult issues involved, but to confine ourselves, wherever possible in the training materials, to the natural language used by teachers and understood by students, and only resort to technical jargon when necessary. In this research report there is, inevitably, some technical language. In conceiving training materials, however, it was certainly not our intention to replace existing courses in the theory of education by project materials, but rather to complement them.

Flexible Materials

Preparing materials and ideas for teacher training is not the same as developing a curriculum package for schools. In the latter case it is common practice to create a kit of some kind, or a set of books, and for teachers to buy the package and work systematically through it. Our intention was to influence practice in the training of teachers in professional skills by making it more classroom-oriented. We knew that some teacher trainers would want to work systematically through each exercise, but that others would be eclectic and take ideas to build into their own course. The materials had to be flexible, therefore.

It is interesting to note that within a few months of producing first-draft materials we had drawers full of letters and materials from tutors, advisers, heads and others telling us how they had modified the materials for experienced teachers. PE teachers, primary specialists or even deputy heads' courses.

Altogether some 23 research studies were undertaken during the 4½ years. The remainder of this book describes some though by no means all of this research work. Chapters 2, 3 and 4 recount the work on class management which I directed myself. Chapter 2 describes 56 case studies of student teachers thought to be good or poor at handling their classes, and 204 lessons given by 34 PGCE students on their one-term teaching practice. Chapter 3 is a study of first encounters, 313 lessons in all, which shows how 41 experienced teachers, BEd and PGCE students, behave when they first meet their classes. Over 100 lessons were observed, and each group and all participants were interviewed extensively. Chapter 4 considers the pupil's point of view, and contains an analysis of 200 pupil questionnaires and interviews with children who were in the classes of some of the teachers observed in the first encounters study.

In Chapter 5 George Brown and Rowena Edmondson report some of the work done on questioning when 36 teachers in five schools analysed the questions they asked in their own lessons. George Brown is also responsible for the experimental studies in explaining described in Chapter 6 when a group of trainee teachers were given a special training programme. The research describes the analysis of videotapes of their lessons as well as test scores obtained by the pupils.

Trevor Kerry and Margaret Sands present in Chapter 7 some of their findings about mixed-ability teaching based on 21 case studies of teachers, 40 studies of schools and concentrate on the use of group work by teachers. Trevor Kerry develops further the research he conducted into mixed-ability teaching in Chapter 8, where he analyses the demands made on pupils by the tasks their teachers set them.

Finally, in Chapter 9 Mick Youngman analyses the job done by student teachers on their teaching practice and in their early years of teaching by using a multi-item checklist, which is then subjected to cluster analysis. In Chapter 10 I myself look over some of the findings of the project and discuss the implications for teacher training.

The shortness of the chapter format does not, unfortunately, allow us to present as much detail as we should like, but we hope there is sufficient to convey the general flavour of what was found in each case. Regrettably, we did not have the time to embark on research in primary schools and so all the analyses are of secondary teaching.

Inevitably, in describing research we are caught in the usual dilemma of writing for three audiences: teachers and others concerned with schools in some professional way, researchers, and those lay people not professionally involved in teaching but nevertheless interested in education. Sometimes we do give tables based on cluster analysis or one of the commonly used statistical techniques like analysis of variance. Although researchers will be interested in these, other readers should not feel guilty if they skip over the detailed statistics and concentrate on the case material and summaries of findings.

References

Argyle, M. (1967) *The Psychology of Interpersonal Behaviour*, Penguin, Harmondsworth

Ball, S. (1981) *Beachside Comprehensive*, Cambridge University Press

Barnes, D. (1971) 'Language and Learning in the Classroom', *Journal of Curriculum Studies, 3*, 1, 27-38

Barr, A.S. (1961) 'Wisconsin Studies of the Measurement and Prediction of Teacher Effectiveness', *Journal of Experimental Education, 30*, 5-156

Biddle, B.J. and Ellena, W.J. (eds) (1964) *Contemporary Research on Teacher Effectiveness*, Holt, Rinehart & Winston, New York

Blurton Jones, N. (1972) *Ethological Studies of Child Behaviour*, Cambridge University Press

Cohen, L. and Manion, L. (1981) *Perspectives on Classrooms and Schools*, Holt, Rinehart & Winston, London

Delamont, S. (1976) *Interaction in the Classroom*, Methuen, London

Dent, H.C. (1971) 'An Historical Perspective' in S. Hewett (ed.), *The Training of Teachers*, University of London Press

Deutsch, M. (1960) *Minority Group and Class Status*, Society for Applied Anthropology, Monograph no. 2

Dodl, N.R. (1973) *The Florida Catalog of Teacher Competencies*, Florida Department of Education

Dunkin, M.J. and Biddle, B.J. (1974) *The Study of Teaching*, Holt, Rinehart & Winston, New York

Edwards, A.D. and Furlong, V.J. (1978) *The Language of Teaching*, Heinemann, London

Floyd, W.D. (1960) *An Analysis of the Oral Questioning Activity in Selected Colorado Primary Classrooms*, PhD dissertation, Colorado State College

Gage, N.L. (1978) *The Scientific Basis of the Art of Teaching*, Teachers College Press, New York

Glass, G.V. (1978) 'Integrating Findings: the Meta-analysis of Research' in L.S. Schulman, (ed.), *Review of Research in Education*, vol. 5, Peacock, Itasca, Illinois

Guetzkow, H., Kelly, E.L. and McKeachie, W.J. (1954) 'An Experimental Comparison of Recitation, Discussion and Tutorial Methods in College Teaching', *Journal of Educational Psychology, 45*, 193-209

Hamilton, D. (1975) 'Handling Innovation in the Classroom: Two Case Studies' in W.A. Reid and D.F. Walker (eds) *Case Studies in Curriculum Change*, Routledge, London

Hargreaves, D.H. (1967) *Social Relations in a Secondary School*, Routledge, London

Heath, R.W. and Nielson, M.A. (1974) 'The Research Basis for Performance-based Teacher Education', *Review of Educational Research, 44*, 4, 463-84

HMI (1978) *Mixed Ability Work in Comprehensive Schools*, HMSO, London

Jackson, P.W. (1962) 'The Way Teaching Is', *NEA Journal, 54*, 10-13
—— (1968) *Life in Classrooms*, Holt, Rinehart & Winston, New York
James, G. and Choppin, B. (1977) 'Teachers for Tomorrow', *Educational Research, 19*, 3, 184-91
King, R.A. (1978) *All Things Bright and Beautiful?* Wiley, Chichester
Knapp, M.C. (1980) *Essentials of Non-verbal Communication*, Holt, Rinehart & Winston, New York
Lacey, C. (1970) *Hightown Grammar*, Manchester University Press
Medley, D.M. and Mitzel, H.E. (1963) 'Measuring Classroom Behaviour by Systematic Observation' in N.L. Gage (ed.), *Handbook of Research on Teaching*, Rand McNally, Chicago
Rich, R.W. (1933) *The Training of Teachers in England and Wales during the Nineteenth Century*, Cambridge University Press
Rowe, M.B. (1972) 'Wait-time and Rewards as Instructional Variables'. Paper presented at the National Association for Research in Science Teaching, Chicago, April
Ryle, G. (1949) *The Concept of Mind*, Hutchinson, London
Samph, T. (1976) 'Observer Effects on Teacher Verbal Behaviour', *Journal of Educational Psychology, 68*, 6, 736-41
Stubbs, M. (1976) *Language, Schools and Classroom*, Methuen, London
Wilkinson, A. (1975) *Language and Education*, Oxford University Press
Wragg, E.C. (1976) *Classroom Interaction*, Open University Press, Milton Keynes
—— (1978) 'Getting to Grips with the Wild Bunch', *Guardian*, 14 March

2 CLASS MANAGEMENT DURING TEACHING PRACTICE

E.C. Wragg and P.A. Dooley

Ask student teachers before a block teaching practice to describe any
source of apprehension, and they will before long talk about some
aspect of class management, using terms like 'keep order', 'have class
control' or 'maintain discipline'. Tibble (1959) questioned a sample of
student teachers on a PGCE course and found that three-quarters were
worried about class control, though after teaching practice only half
felt their anxieties had been realised, albeit on a smaller scale than they
had envisaged. Wragg (1967) in a study of 90 PGCE students identified
the same kind of apprehension, and 'keeping order' was mentioned
most frequently when students were asked to reveal anxieties they felt
about their first few years of teaching.

Although class management is now a topic which increasingly
attracts research interest, it is a contentious field with disagreement
about what constitutes an effective classroom climate. Far more studies
of classroom interaction have been conducted in recent times than was
the case 20 years ago, but relatively little work has been published on
class management which was based on direct observation of lessons, and
there is almost nothing of this kind on student teachers.

The issues surrounding class management are complex, and Johnson
and Brooks (1979) have produced a useful model (see Figure 2.1)
which depicts the intricate nexus of relationships between the tasks
which society obliges teachers to perform, such as planning and organi-
sing lessons, the many kinds of setting in which teaching and learning
may take place, the values that teachers and learners may hold, and the
tensions between people and amongst roles.

For student teachers on teaching practice, as we shall show in
Chapter 3 when we describe the analysis of over 300 lessons given by
beginners and experienced teachers, the picture is much more confused.
In his classic text *The Theory of Social and Economic Organisation*
(1964) Max Weber observed that power in any social relationship is
reflected in the probability that one person will be in a position to
carry out his own will despite resistance. The apprehension of student
teachers before teaching practice is that they may not be able to fulfil

Figure 2.1: A Conceptual Model of Classroom Management

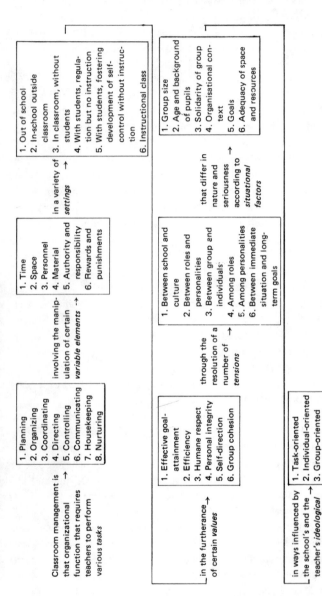

Classroom management is that organizational function that requires teachers to perform various *tasks* →

1. Planning
2. Organizing
3. Coordinating
4. Directing
5. Controlling
6. Communicating
7. Housekeeping
8. Nurturing

involving the manipulation of certain *variable elements* →

1. Time
2. Space
3. Personnel
4. Material
5. Authority and responsibility
6. Rewards and punishments

in a variety of *settings* →

1. Out of school
2. In-school outside classroom
3. In classroom, without students
4. With students, regulation but no instruction
5. With students, fostering development of self-control without instruction
6. Instructional class

in the furtherance of certain *values* →

1. Effective goal-attainment
2. Efficiency
3. Humane respect
4. Personal integrity
5. Self-direction
6. Group cohesion

through the resolution of a number of *tensions* →

1. Between school and culture
2. Between roles and personalities
3. Between group and individuals:
4. Among roles
5. Among personalities
6. Between immediate situation and long-term goals

that differ in nature and seriousness according to *situational factors* →

1. Group size
2. Age and background of pupils
3. Solidarity of group
4. Organisational context
5. Goals
6. Adequacy of space and resources

in ways influenced by the school's and the teacher's *ideological stances.* →

1. Task-oriented
2. Individual-oriented
3. Group-oriented

Source: Johnson and Brooks, 1979.

their own intentions, and that they will encounter resistance beyond their ability to cope.

Speculation by certain politicians and in press reports sometimes suggests that schools suffer from considerable disruption, and prominence is frequently given to reports of riots or violent behaviour when they occur. Systematic enquiry, however, reveals a less alarming picture. The survey of 384 secondary schools by HMI (DES, 1979) showed that only 25 schools, mainly, though not exclusively, in inner-city areas and older housing estates, reported serious problems of indiscipline, violence between pupils or hostility to teachers.

That serious indiscipline in tough schools can reduce the teacher's ability to teach and the pupils' opportunities to learn was underlined in an American study by Deutsch (1960). He studied classroom proce-dures in an urban school where teachers spent up to 75 per cent of their time trying to maintain order, with a consequent reduction to as little as 25 per cent being left for actual teaching and learning.

In the absence of any clear picture based on direct observation of how student teachers manage their classes during teaching practice, it was decided early in the Teacher Education Project to study a sample of trainees throughout their long teaching practice, and this chapter describes a 2-year enquiry into student teachers' class management which used a mixture of individual case study and quantitative analysis of classroom transactions.

Studies of Class Management

It is not possible to describe here more than a small amount of the research done in class management, but the field has been surveyed by several writers such as Dunkin and Biddle (1974) and Docking (1980). There is no shortage of 'how to handle classes' books for student teachers, often written by practitioners such as Francis (1975) and Marland (1975) or teacher trainers (Robertson, 1981). Some of the books and pamphlets on class management for teachers try to incorporate research findings, like *Maintaining Discipline in Classroom Instruction* (Gnagey, 1975) and the workbook *Class Management and Control*, which was field-tested as part of the Teacher Education Project by Wragg (1981).

Although a great deal of the research in the field has been under-taken in the last 20 years, American studies by Wickman (1928), who enquired into teachers' definitions of behaviour problems, and the so-called 'attention studies' of the 1920s and 1930s, when an observer sat at the front of the class scanning faces to assemble a simple measure of attentiveness (Jackson, 1968), show that interest in the topic is not entirely recent.

In Britain Highfield and Pinsent (1952) obtained estimates of what were perceived as pupil misdemeanours from a sample of 724 teachers. Restlessness and fidgeting, laziness and boisterous, noisy behaviour were seen as the most common forms of misconduct. During the last 10 years several surveys, some by local authorities or teacher associations, addressed the problem of more serious misbehaviour. Lowenstein (1975) intended to show trends in 'violent and obstructive behaviour', but failed to do so because, he claimed, there was a lack of objectivity and accuracy on the part of teachers filling in report forms and describing incidents.

Lawrence *et al.* (1977), in a detailed study of a boys' school, found similar difficulty in eliciting objective responses about misbehaviour. Events were most likely to be reported by teachers if they followed several similar happenings, and the investigator found that teachers tended to report incidents which interfered with their teaching, rather than violent or aggressive behaviour.

Hilsum and Strong (1978), in their study of the working day of 201 secondary teachers in 72 Surrey schools, found teachers averaged less than 1½ minutes of their day disciplining pupils, with a range of from twenty down to no instances per day, and an average of nine. They concluded, 'in the current climate of allegations of indiscipline in schools, one might have expected more instances of disciplining.' Teachers with less than 5 years' experience reprimanded pupils almost twice as frequently as their more experienced colleagues.

An interesting comparison with a parallel study of the primary teacher's day (Hilsum and Cane, 1971) which used similar methods of observation and analysis, shows that primary teachers were engaged on average in over four times as many disciplinary incidents each day. It is not clear from this type of study, however, to what degree teachers ignored misbehaviour, or how much 'indiscipline' has been subsumed under other categories in the observation schedule such as 'pupil organisation'.

A number of investigators, some through scrutiny of several teachers, others by in-depth case studies of individual classrooms or schools, have tried to map out the strategies which teachers use to control the behaviour of groups or individual pupils. One of the best-known and most influential series of research programmes was undertaken by

Jacob Kounin and his associates from the late 1950s to the early 1970s. Kounin concentrated on, among other events, the teacher's reaction to pupil deviancy, and studied the clarity, firmness and roughness of what he called 'desists', that is teachers' attempts to terminate behaviour of which they disapproved.

In a study of 49 teachers of grades 1 and 2 Kounin (1970) observed each for one whole day, and concentrated in his analysis of videotapes and transcripts on the techniques of group management each employed. He coined a set of somewhat off-beat terms to describe various kinds of teacher behaviour that seemed to be positively related to involvement of pupils in their work or to freedom from deviancy in the classroom. These involved the following:

Withitness Having eyes in the back of your head and thus picking up misbehaviour early

Overlapping Being able to do more than one thing at once, for example deal with someone misbehaving whilst at the same time keeping the children you are with occupied

Smoothness Keeping children at work by *not*
  (a) intruding suddenly when they are busy (thrusts)
  (b) Starting one activity and then leaving it abruptly to engage in another one (dangles)
  (c) ending an activity and then coming back to it unexpectedly (flip-flops)

Overdwelling Avoiding staying on an issue for longer than necessary

Momentum Freedom from slow-downs

Kounin found strongest relationships between 'withitness', the ability to scan the class, and pupil involvement and lack of deviancy, with correlations of from 0.307 to 0.615, depending whether children were working individually at their desks or engaged in whole-class activity, when the correlations were higher.

In an earlier set of studies Kounin and Gump (1958), looking at 26 kindergarten teachers, identified the 'ripple effect', that is, the impact of something the teacher does on pupils other than the target child, for example when a teacher says 'Haven't you started yet, John?' and other pupils nearby begin work because they read the signal that the teacher expects pupils to have commenced work. The findings were not entirely conclusive, though a later study suggested that the ripple effect made most impact on the highly motivated pupils, and that liking or disliking the teacher also influenced the degree of effect. It should be remembered that most of the Kounin studies referred to above were of 5 to 8-year-olds.

A number of significant case studies of class management have been reported and these will be discussed again in Chapter 3. Amongst the most notable are those by Woods (1979), who described 'mortification techniques' used by some teachers which strip the personality of certain pupils, as well as forms of fraternisation and negotiation which are often employed when other approaches fail. Hargreaves, Hester and Mellor (1975) analysed the rules of behaviour operating in two secondary schools during five different phases of the lesson. Other investigators have catalogued various 'coping strategies' witnessed during observation, including Hargreaves, D. (1975), Hargreaves, A. (1978) and Stebbins (1981). These include not only those described by Woods (1979), but also the use of promises, and keeping pupils busy so there is little time for deviance.

Freiberg (1983), writing about the notion of consistency in classroom management, cites a number of models of class management, including those that focus on psychological roles, methods of communication, the behaviour of the individual, pupil responsibility or rule-based models. A comprehensive summary of these has been produced by Charles (1981). Several of the models, notably those based on Skinnerian behaviourist theory using behaviour-modification techniques, have a sizeable, and in some cases controversial research literature attached to them. Others, like Rogers's (1970) influential writing on interpersonal relationships, or the proposals of Glasser (1969) for what he calls 'reality therapy', that is the involvement of pupils in decisions about rules and procedures, have produced some empirical research, but it tends to be less positivistic in style.

The Notion of Time Management

Brophy and Evertson (1976) in a correlational study of 7 to 9-year-olds, found that Kounin's categories of *withitness*, *overlapping* and *smoothness* were not only related to good behaviour, but also to greater pupil learning. Their conclusion was that the amount of time the pupil was engaged in the task was 'the key to successful classroom management' (p. 54). The notion of 'time on the task' or 'academic engaged time' attracted considerable research interest, and the California Beginning Teacher Evaluation Study (Denham and Lieberman, 1980) devoted much of its enquiry to the nature and amount of time spent by pupils on the task in hand.

Gage (1978) summarised some of the studies into academic learning time, and concluded that time was in itself 'a psychologically empty quantitative concept' (p. 75). What was needed, he argued, was a more refined analysis of the notion of time. In the California Beginning Teacher Evaluation Study such factors as allocated time and success rate were taken into account, but more value- and problem-laden concepts, such as the degree to which the tasks set were worthwhile, were not fully scrutinised.

Figure 2.2: Time Circles: a Model of Time Management (not to scale)

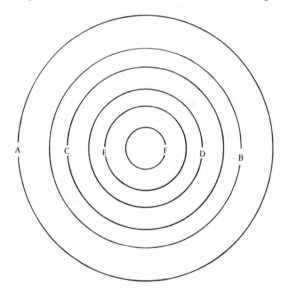

Circle A = all time   Circle B = time spent in school
Circle C = time assigned to a subject   Circle D = time actually spent on the task
Circle E = time on a worthwhile task   Circle F = with some degree of success

The apportioning and management of time may be seen as a set of concentric circles (Figure 2.2 not to scale), the largest, circle A, would be 168 hours per week, that is the total time available during seven days and nights. Inscribed within it, the next circle, B, would be quite small by comparison, only some 24 hours, being roughly the amount of time spent in school averaged over the year. This ranks in scale with some studies of children watching television which have shown an average of 25 hours per week (DES, 1975).

Circle C would show the amount of time assigned to the area under scrutiny, for example number work in the primary school or physics in the fifth year of secondary school. This would vary from school to school. In a subject like French in the third year of a secondary school the range might be from zero to 4 hours.

So far none of the circles is a direct reflection of the class-management skill of the individual teacher, since allocations are fixed by local authorities, heads and senior teachers. The size of the smaller circles, however, are indeed affected by the individual teacher's skill. Circle D would be the amount of time pupils actually spend on the tasks in hand. If the school had assigned 3 hours to French, then teachers with ineffective class management or very adverse circumstances, like some of those in the study by Deutsch (1960) cited above, might find pupils engaged in learning French for less than an hour. Other classes might spend over 2 hours. Totals for individual pupils, rather than class means, will show an even wider spread.

Circle E brings in the domain of 'worthwhile' tasks. Engaged time in a certain classroom might be high, but the task set might involve the equivalent of copying out telephone directories, so the concept of what is worthwhile, a major philosophical issue discussed by, among others, Peters (1966), is important but highly subjective and contentious. It must, however, logically be a subset of engaged time. Again, it will be a function of the skill of the teacher how much time is spent on worthwhile activities.

Finally, the concept of success at the task must be incorporated. If children spend time learning erroneous forms of French, their experience is less profitable than it would have been if they had learned correct forms. Thus, the final circle F encompasses that portion of circle E which is done with some degree of success. One operational definition of skilful class management, therefore, would be the extent to which teachers are capable of maximising circle F for each child, that is the amount of time spent on something worthwhile with some degree of success. The model is certainly not the only way of conceptualising time management; one could add such important aspects as enjoyment, but we offer it as a way of depicting some of the factors frequently mentioned when the matter is discussed.

McNamara (1981) has criticised the emphasis on time management in some studies, arguing that taken too far it can become an end in itself. It can also become a recipe for over-directive teaching. In our present study described later in this chapter, time-on-the-task constitutes but a small element, because it is one of the few outcome measures that can be appraised in different student teachers' lessons which is arguably of some significance. Our own analysis did not proceed beyond circle D, but in Chapter 8 Trevor Kerry moves to circles E and F.

Class Management on Teaching Practice

There have been few large-scale studies of students on teaching practice which were based on actual observation of lessons. The largest British study by Wragg (1972) documented 578 lessons given by 102 PGCE students during a ten-week practice, and showed that lessons at the end of term had a higher incidence of project-type activities, and that many students had fairly fixed patterns of teaching which hardly altered during their practice. This study was based on Flanders's (1970) categories of interaction, and paid only slight attention to class management.

Fink (1976), in an American study of 25 student teachers, used diaries, questionnaires and observations. She found that student teachers became more custodial towards their pupils as the teaching practice progressed. In a British study of discipline problems experienced by 100 PGCE students at Exeter University, Preece (1979) used self-inventories and tutor ratings. By means of a cross-lagged panel analysis he attempted to infer causal relationships between anxiety and disorder in lessons. He found that anxiety affected order for scientists but not for non-scientists, and that the general level of anxiety fell during the practice.

Dreyfus and Eggleston (1979) observed 44 science specialists who were PGCE students at Nottingham University, and found that early in their practice they employed similar strategies to those of experienced teachers, but that their teaching tactics bore less resemblance to experienced teachers as the practice progressed.

The evolution of styles of class management, student teachers' responses to pupil misbehaviour, the extent to which pupils are engaged in their task during lessons on teaching practice, all these matters are inadequately documented. It was partly because of this lack of a proper account that we decided to examine the field more closely. The remainder of this chapter describes a study conducted at Nottingham University as part of the Teacher Education Project.

The Pilot Study

Our research into student teachers' class management was in two parts. The first stage consisted of 56 case studies of student teachers thought to be good or poor at handling classes. Subsequently, the main enquiry analysed 204 lessons given by 34 PGCE students at six Nottinghamshire comprehensive schools, three in a city and three in other parts of the county.

In the pilot phase a case-study instrument was piloted and then mailed to a number of co-operating tutors who supervised PGCE students on teaching practice. Each was invited to select one student thought to be effective and one regarded as ineffective in the management of classes. Copies of the case-study outline were also given to the teacher in the school who had most frequent contact with the student. The sample was in no sense random, therefore, and was purely an opportunity sample of tutors and teachers willing to co-operate. The principal purpose of this preliminary exercise was both to collect useful case material and to prepare the ground for the main study.

The case-study instrument consisted of a booklet which the observer completed in a particular lesson during the second half of a block practice. The observer had to describe important aspects of class management, and to record up to three 'critical events' during the lesson which seemed illustrative of the teacher's good or poor handling of the class. Pilot work had shown that free-hand recording by experienced teacher trainers, or teachers not familiar with case-study research, produced too many generalities, such as 'kept class busy' or 'had a firm grip'. The advantage of the critical-event approach, based on the 'critical incidents' technique developed by Flanagan (1949), was that it compelled observers to describe some of the actual happenings in the classroom on which they based their judgement about whether the student was an effective or ineffective class manager. The observer was also asked to interview students after the lesson to elicit their own perception of the events recorded.

The case studies, mainly of science, English, maths and language lessons in the early years of secondary schooling, produced a rich set of insights, and included some 150 critical events. Two pairs of analysts worked independently of each other on the completed case studies. The first pair analysed all the lesson accounts, the critical events and the notes on interviews with the student teachers in order to distil features which observers reported as being illustrative of good class management. The second pair looked for the obverse: characteristics felt to be related to poor management. Finally, a third pair of analysts considered the analyses of the first two pairs, and selected illustrative case material from the case studies. The account of this final analysis is reported by Partington and Hinchliffe (1979).

The briefing notes to observers tried to explain clearly what constituted a 'critical event', but there were minor differences of opinion amongst them, some seeing it as unexpected or novel, others as more routine. It is not possible to draw too firm a set of inferences from subjective case-study data collected by observers other than oneself, even when these are fully documented, as one can only speculate on the quality or accuracy of someone else's insight; nevertheless, some interesting if tentative conclusions can be described.

Effective managers were seen as those who were well prepared, anticipated difficulties, and reacted quickly to disruption rather than allowed it to escalate. Teachers and tutors often highlighted good management which was executed with verbal deftness. There were usually affective messages in addition, such as briskness in the following physics extract, and humour in the English one:

> *Physics* The class asked, 'Why do we have to do this?' The student's response was that they had to do it because she was there and if they didn't pay attention they wouldn't learn anything. She was brisk, determined, earnest. The class sensed her purpose.

> *English* The theme for the session was 'Equality'. During discussion the problem of individual differences arose and she contrasted herself with one of the girls in the group (height, eye colour, age etc.) 'I'm better looking than you,' said one girl. Teacher smiled. Defused with ease. Decided that this was not threatening and came back rapidly with, 'Wait till you're my age and the wrinkles start to show.' Smiles all round and the discussion continued.

Many of the critical events highlighted aspects of management noted in research studies of experienced teachers. Successful student teachers usually arrived at the classroom before the pupils, personally admitted them to the room, established a presence, were seen to be in charge, but in a subtle rather than shouting or overbearing manner. Conversely, unsuccessful managers attempted to begin lessons before attention had been secured, and were not able to deal with simultaneous distractions like late arrivals, especially as these often coincided with the transition from an expository stage to a phase of pupil activity. The contrast between different degrees of social control achieved during lesson beginnings is shown in the following three extracts from accounts of critical events.

A. The student began the lesson before many pupils were paying attention and most were milling about. She attempted to give detailed instructions about the first class activity, but repeatedly interspersed rebukes to individuals and shouted orders. The general effect was of obscurity and confusion about what, if anything, was wanted.

B. The teacher began by giving out classwork books and collecting homework books. Teacher . . . to one of the boys

'This book's very thin.'
'Yeah, 'tis, i'n't it.'
'Why?'
'I've bin drawing in it.'
''E's bin usin' it for toilet paper, sir'. (Uproar)

There then followed a general argument about missing books with much shouting out from the rest of the class. The lesson proper got underway about 15 minutes late.

C. The tone of the lesson was set before the pupils entered the room. The teacher met them at the door and supervised their entry into the room. The teacher further reinforced his position by insisting on quietness and calm before attempting to start the lesson. In consequence the teacher was able to ensure that the lesson proceeded according to plan.

The observers themselves are an important consideration. Not everyone admired the more firmly teacher-controlled start, nor did every observer deprecate the kind of minor chaos amid which some student teachers learn their craft.

The pilot study also showed how personal relationships improve or degenerate during teaching practice. Events which in one classroom would be innocuous become magnified in lessons where the basic relationship between teacher and pupil had become sour. Windows are opened and closed during student teachers' lessons without incident in most cases, but the following extract, from the account of a critical event, reveals the potential for disarray in the most harmless-looking circumstances when interpersonal relationships have become poor:

Girl at back asks if she can open the window but is ignored.

'Get on with it!'

'May I open the window, sir?'

Half noticing, the teacher says 'O.K!'

Thereupon Carol opens the window fully. Gale blows in.

'Shurrit, yer fool!' says boy who is receiving the full force down his neck.

'Yeah, shu' it' says teacher.

But the window appears to have jammed.

'Can't move it, sir!'

A catch had stuck on the sliding window. Carol wrestles with window. Friend wrestles with Carol. Everyone gathers round. Work is abandoned. A milling struggle.

'Sit down! Sit down will you!' shouts teacher, but in vain. Pandemonium whilst teacher tries brute force on the window. Much advice from boys.

'We'll have to leave it', says teacher. 'Now get back to yer places!' No sooner have all resumed their intermittent labours when Carol quietly slides the window closed!

In their analysis of critical events and observers' interpretations of and comment on them, Partington and Hinchliffe summarised their conclusions about the constituents of effective management in student teachers' classrooms under five headings:

(1) *The establishment of good personal relationships* — learning pupils' names, getting to know individual pupils well during and outside lessons, responding to pupils according to what was known about them personally, rather than according to some general stereotype, using humour constructively.

(2) *Effective preparation* — knowing and feeling confident with the material of the lesson, appropriate organisation of material in the light of methods being used and time available, anticipation of conceptual, linguistic or practical problems and the devising of appropriate tactics to deal with them when they occur.

(3) *Organisation of materials and pupils' work during lessons* — which included the ability to decide when and how to use whole-class groups and individual work, to be aware of movement around or outside the room, and to recognise and work effectively within the location in which learning took place, gym, laboratory, drama studio or classroom.

(4) *Specific pedagogic skills* — the development of skilful explaining

and questioning, learning to read the myriads of cues about pupils' difficulties or moods and then making a suitable response.

(5) *Personal characteristics* — the qualities a student teacher needed for effective presentation of self. When certain students were observed failing to cope with their classes, whilst some of their fellow novices were more successful, it sometimes came down to aspects of personality, some of which may not be very amenable to modification.

The Main Study

In the light of this pilot work and after scrutiny of the literature we decided to conduct a systematic anlysis of the class management of a sample of PGCE students during their long block practice. An observation instrument, the Nottingham Class Management Observation Schedule (reproduced in Galton, 1978) was developed, and the emphasis in it was on pupil deviance and teachers' responses (see Appendix B).

The first step was to extract from the pilot case studies described above, from accounts of other observations of lessons of students undertaken during the pilot phase, from interviews with two classes of pupils seen individually or in pairs, and from the research literature, a set of over 200 statements related to the discrimination of effective and ineffective class management. Each piece of classroom behaviour was then noted on a separate card, as suggested by Berliner and Tikunoff (1976), using, wherever possible, the natural language employed by observers, respondents and people interviewed. Examples included the following:

Effective Teacher	Ineffective Teacher
82 Responds immediately when rule broken	Responds only when deviance is widespread or serious
85 Avoids threat/ultimatum	Threat/ultimatum frequent
92 Confrontation rare	Confrontation frequent
94 Sees pupils privately now or later	All investigations, etc. conducted in public

Similar and overlapping statements were eliminated, and the number was thereby reduced to 120. These were then put into groups and used to determine the final form of the schedule which fell into four major sections. Section 1 consisted of background information such as the name of the school, student teacher, class, subject, the predominant lesson activity and the degree of task involvement. Section 2 described the deviant act, whether it involved noise, interruptions, damage, movement, non-verbal factors, and the degree of seriousness of the deviancy. Section 3 recorded the student teacher's response, including such verbal factors as orders to cease, reprimands, threats, statements of rule, humour, praise or encouragement, non-verbal elements like gesture, facial expression, proximity, that is moving towards pupils, punishments of various kinds, whether the response was to a named pupil, to a group, whether the target was correct or incorrect. Finally, section 4 showed the pupils' response and whether deviancy lessened or increased.

In addition there was a section in which individual pupils were studied one by one for 20 seconds in regular 'sweeps' of the class to make a judgement about the extent to which the pupil observed appeared to be (a) on or off task, and (b) engaging in mild, serious or no deviancy. These data were used to compute an on-task and deviancy index, which gave a rough-and-ready picture of the overall amount of on-task and deviant behaviour in the class during the periods of observation.

The final schedule was piloted in a school and on videotapes, and used by the two present writers and two other observers who were trained for several hours. There were extensive discussions about the categories in the schedule and, for the individual pupil 'sweeps', of what could be regarded as mild or serious deviancy and on- or off-task behaviour. A full account of all the procedures used can be found in Dooley (1982).

Three measures of observer agreement were taken, two were of inter-observer agreement, that is the degree of concurrence between all four observers before and after the research, and one of intra-observer agreement, that is the extent to which an observer agrees with himself recording data from the same videotape before and after the research. There is no single standard method of calculating observer agreement in classroom-observation research, though the matter has been discussed in most of the standard works on classroom interaction such as that by Medley and Mitzel (1963).

We decided to opt for a percentage agreement figure, though this would be open to criticism if a system contained many unlikely or infrequent categories, such as 'teacher flies through the window'. The present schedule does not have such bizarre categories. One further reservation about a percentage agreement measure is that it could hide consistent disagreement on one particular category. Close inspection of the trial data did not reveal any such inconsistency.

Agreement between observers was high. In the pre-test they range from 77 to 85 per cent, in the post-test from 80 to 86 per cent, and intra-observer agreement ranged from 78 to 90 per cent. Deviancy level measures showed an agreement of 82 to 92 per cent, and task involvement from 65 to 83 per cent. The appraisal of whether pupils are on or off-task, therefore, is slightly less reliable than the other parts of the schedule, as one might expect. Although it is frequently self-evident whether pupils are engrossed in their work, there are several occasions when observers have to make a judgement on inadequate evidence, hence the slightly higher amount of disagreement on this aspect.

The arguments for and against the use of observation schedules have been well rehearsed (Delamont, 1976), but we decided that the instrument we had devised would provide a great deal of useful quantified descriptive and correlational information about student teachers' handling of their classes which was missing in the literature. A sample of 34 PGCE students in six comprehensive schools was selected. Though it was not, strictly speaking, a random sample, being rather all the students doing their teaching practice in six large comprehensives, it did not seem to be unduly biased. There were 17 science and 17 non-science students, and 20 of the sample were male and 14 female. The schools were commonly used teaching practice schools in city and county, and were regarded as 'typical' of the spread of schools in the area, in the judgement of tutors.

Wherever possible, first, second or third-year classes were watched. Each student teacher was observed for six lessons during his or her one-term block teaching practice, which came in the second term of their one-year PGCE course, following a term in which they had spent a whole or half-day per week on school experience. Two lessons were observed in the first third of the term, two in the middle period and two in the final third. In each lesson five successive 3-minute lesson segments were recorded on the schedule, followed by a sweep of every individual child for the deviancy and task involvement measures, and freehand notes were written. In summary, the study provided data from 1,020 segments in 204 lessons given by 34 student teachers in six schools.

Findings of the Main Study

Pupil Deviancy

In the event the 204 lessons observed were distributed as shown in Table 2.1

Table 2.1: Distribution of 204 Lessons Observed

Year	Percentage
1st	32
2nd	37
3rd	24
4th	7

The type of teaching which occurred during the 1,020 lesson segments, normally observed during the first 20 to 25 minutes of any lesson, consisted mainly of pupils working and teacher monitoring, 38 per cent of the time, and public teacher-pupil interaction for 30 per cent.

In 76 per cent of lesson segments some deviant act was recorded, and in 50 per cent of these cases five pupils or more were involved. Analysis of the kind of deviancy noted reveals a predominance of minor pieces of naughtiness. The most commonly recorded kinds of misbehaviour are shown in Table 2.2. In each case they are percentages of all 1,020 segments in which the particular piece of misbehaviour occurred.

Table 2.2: Most Common Forms of Misbehaviour Observed

Misbehaviour	Percentage
excessively noisy talk	38
non-verbal behaviour not appropriate to task	24
irrelevant talk	23
inappropriate use of materials/equipment	20
illicit eating/drinking	12
movement at the wrong time	11
fidgeting	9
provoking laughter (derision, not shared humour)	6
teacher interrupted (excluding normal exchanges)	5
physical aggression	2
damage to materials/equipment	1.5
disobeying teacher	1.5
cheating	1.5
pupil insulted	1.5
teacher insulted	1

All these categories, as in any observation schedule, require subjective judgement by the observer, and what is 'excessive' or 'inappropriate' for one person may not be so for another. However, student teachers themselves often reinforced the judgement of the observer, as will be seen in the section below, by saying 'there's too much noise' or 'don't bend the ruler like that'.

That most of the deviance reported was irritating rather than alarming, is shown by the high frequency of general noise, off-task gossip and minor jostling recorded, and the infrequency of damage, insult to teacher, or downright disobedience of a request or order. Physical aggression to other pupils was also rare, and there was no example of physical aggression to the teacher. The nearest to this occurred in only one confrontation: when a teacher asked a pupil to move to another seat, the pupil refused and the observer felt that physical violence by the pupil seemed likely until the teacher backed away. Unexpectedly, at this flashpoint the pupil did then move as requested.

Observers were also asked to make a subjective judgement about the degree of seriousness of misbehaviour which occurred. Their ratings in Table 2.3 revealed that approximately five out of six pieces of deviancy were regarded as mild.

Table 2.3: Observers' Ratings of Mildness/Seriousness of Misbehaviour

Rating	Percentage
mild	83
more serious	15
very serious	2

The Student Teachers' Responses

In 71 per cent of the lesson segments where deviancy occurred the teacher made some response. The kinds of reaction given in Table 2.4 are expressed as percentages of the 543 lesson segments in which a response to deviancy was noted.

Physical punishment was noted only on one occasion during the whole research. Punishment was threatened ten times more frequently than it was actually administered. Typically, therefore, the response was a statement to cease, a reprimand or a reminder of a rule, occasionally a threat, rarely an actual punishment. In those classes where there was a persistent buzz of noise 'stop talking', 'there's too much noise', 'pay attention John', 'if you don't work quietly you'll be kept in' became part of the landscape. In 84 per cent of segments the response was brief rather than sustained.

Several other characteristics of the student teachers' responses were

coded. Observers were asked to judge the timing of responses in relation
to the escalation of deviance. Table 2.5 shows that nearly three-quarters
of reactions to misbehaviour occurred before it had escalated, leaving
slightly over a quarter taking place afterwards.

Table 2.4: Student Teachers' Reactions to Misbehaviour

Reaction	Percentage
order to cease	61
reprimand	25
statement of rule	24
proximity (moving towards pupils)	20
involving pupils in their work	16
threat	10
facial expression	8
dramatic pause	7
gesture	5
pupil moved	3
humour	2
touch	1
ridicule	1
punishment	1

Table 2.5: Timing of Response to Deviance

Teacher responds to escalation of deviance	Percentage
before	73
after	27

This failure by some to nip misbehaviour in the bud produced class-
control problems, whilst those who were prompt in recognising and
responding to deviance had less difficulty.

Table 2.6 reveals that most responses were made to the whole class,
followed by reactions to groups and individuals in roughly equal
amounts.

Table 2.6: Target of Teacher's Response

Teacher's response to	Percentage
whole class	44
group of pupils	27
individual	29

In some 39 per cent of cases a pupil's name was used. Table 2.6

denotes the principal target of the teacher's response, so there were some cases when an individual pupil was named during a reaction aimed primarily at a group or the whole class.

It is sometimes speculated that student and experienced teachers accuse the 'wrong' pupils, that they, for example, turn round from the blackboard and name someone who was not actually guilty of misbehaviour. Observers recorded whether in their view the 'incorrect' culprit had been accused, and this happened on nine occasions out of 1,020 lesson segments analysed, which at less than 1 per cent, seems lower than one might have predicted from a group of novice teachers.

The student teachers were generally calm in their manner, but in just over one-fifth of all the events studied they appeared angry or agitated as Table 2.7 shows, though this quantifies only the observer's view of external characteristics. Whether the anger was feigned, or whether external calm masked internal rage is not revealed.

Table 2.7: Student Teachers' Manner

	Percentage
calm	79
agitated	16
angry	5

Pupil Responses and Behaviour

Once some kind of misbehaviour had taken place and the teacher had made a response, observers were asked to record whether, in their view, the deviance escalated, stayed the same, reduced or ended. Table 2.8 shows that in just over half the cases deviance ended, and in nearly a third of cases it lessened. It was only rarely that it actually increased.

Table 2.8: Outcome After Teacher Intervenes Over Deviance

Deviance	No. of cases
ends	53
lessens	30
sustained	15
escalates	2

The most common result, on 80 per cent of occasions, was that pupils fell silent or appeared to accept the teacher's reaction. In 9 per cent of cases there was some kind of altercation between teacher and pupils.

The individual pupil data, that is the aggregated 20-second 'sweeps' of the class, were used to compute a deviancy and involvement index which ranged from 0 (no-one deviant or no-one involved in the task) to 100 (everyone engaged in serious deviancy or everyone highly involved in the task). The deviancy-index scores for all 204 lessons showed a mean of just over 10, which might typically represent, for example, six children engaging in what the observer regarded as mild misbehaviour out of a class of thirty. The overall involvement-index scores produced a mean of 60, which could, in a class of thirty, for example, consist of a distribution such as twelve pupils highly involved, twelve medium involved, and six barely or not at all involved in their task task.

Scores for individual student teachers showed quite a wide range, with deviancy spread from a low of 4 to a high of 37, and involvement from a low of 26 to a high of 81.

When deviancy and involvement scores were computed for three different phases of the teaching practice as shown in Table 2.9, there was little significant difference in the means other than a small increase in involvement, though some individual students showed more marked changes over the term.

Table 2.9: Mean Deviancy and Involvement-index Scores During Early, Mid- and Late Teaching Practice

	Deviancy Index	Involvement Index
early	10.5	57.5
mid	11	60.5
late	10.5	61

Bivariate and Multivariate Analysis

Group Comparisons. A number of further analyses of the data were undertaken using the PMMD program CATT (Youngman, 1976), including certain group comparisons where the sample size justified them. Comparisons of lessons given by male and female student teachers revealed few differences other than might have occurred by chance. Women teachers showed a slightly higher incidence of pupil interruption, talk provoking laughter and fidgeting, all significant at the 0.05 level on a 't' test for planned comparisons.

When the lessons of different year groups were compared using the same program with linear and non-linear trend tests, Scheffé's group atypicality test and the Tukey test for unequal-sized groups, some significant differences did emerge, full details of which are described by Dooley (1982). The most significant were a marked increase in deviancy of certain kinds with older age groups, especially talk irrelevant to the task, talk provoking laughter and physical aggression to other pupils.

The deviancy-index scores show an increase each year significant at the 0.01 level, but the involvement-index scores decline slightly, before moving sharply up at fourth-year level, one guesses because most classes at this stage are in public examination groups, though caution must be exercised because the fourth-year sample was much smaller than the rest.

Table 2.10: Deviancy and Involvement Scores for Different Year Groups

Year	Deviancy Index	Involvement Index
1st	8.46	60.51
2nd	9.78	59.05
3rd	12.59	56.10
4th	12.86	73.57

Teachers' responses to older pupils also show some changes. As pupils grow older there is less use of reprimands, threats and statements of rule, though humour is used more frequently, and observers' notes confirm a more subtle, more adult response to older classes.

Correlational Analysis. With so many variables in the schedule it would be easy to produce a huge product moment and biserial-correlation matrix and give prominence to any significant correlation, when one knows that by chance several values significant at the 0.05 and 0.01 level can be obtained with such a big matrix. Some correlations are of special interest, however, including the relationship between deviancy and involvement, and that between classroom behaviour and measures of teaching competence.

Predictably, the correlation between involvement and deviancy measures is a large inverse one (more involvement means less deviancy, and vice versa). The actual value was $r = -0.48$ which is significant beyond the 0.001 level, and would have occurred by chance, therefore, less than one in a thousand times. On the other hand it is well short of perfect agreement, and this reveals that involvement in the task and mild deviancy can, and frequently do, coexist.

Other highly significant correlations of over 0.5 showed that pupils were more likely to be named during more serious misbehaviour (r = 0.66), and the more serious the deviancy the more likely the teacher was to make a response (r = 0.91). These findings accord with common sense, but the size of the correlation coefficient is of interest.

The supervising tutors of each student were asked to rate them for general competence as teachers, and also to record on a seven-point scale their appraisal of personal relationships with the class, task involvement, the degree of interest aroused, and the amount they thought the pupils were learning. Given the complexity of teaching practice and the difficulty of measuring accurately student teachers' performance, this was the nearest we could obtain to measures of teaching competence and pupil learning.

Surprisingly, there was only a low insignificant correlation between tutors' appraisal of task involvement and our carefully collected observation data (r = 0.13). This low agreement is not easy to explain. Tutors do not, of course, attempt specifically to analyse the involvement of every pupil in a systematic way as we did; they might indeed get a rude shock sometimes if they did. On the other hand they do, albeit in an *ad hoc* way, make judgements about pupil involvement. Furthermore, observers and tutors never observe the same lessons. Perhaps this partially explains the lack of significant agreement; but some degree of mystery remains.

On the other hand there was greater congruence between tutors' appraisal of the amount pupils were learning and several of our measures, notably task involvement (r = 0.37*), and deviancy (r = -0.46**).

Finally, the lessons were analysed according to the type of lesson activity in progress. Deviancy was highest during a transition from one activity to another, being noted in 61 per cent of the transitions when movement took place. This compares with 50 per cent during periods of teacher-pupil interaction. Involvement in the task was highest during teacher-pupil interaction at 89 per cent, compared with 79 per cent when the teacher was addressing the class.

Factor and cluster analyses were also performed of all 1,020 lesson segments. The factor analysis added little to what had already been learned from other analyses. A cluster analysis of several items on the schedule was performed using the PMMD CARM program (Youngman, 1976), and the six-cluster solution gave the clearest picture. Cluster analysis groups together those lesson segments which are most similar. The largest cluster consisting of 259 segments was characterised by noisy, disruptive behaviour with the teacher issuing orders to cease.

Another large cluster (243 segments) represented orderly periods with no disruption at all. A third cluster of 192 segments shows examples of behaviour inappropriate to the task, and inappropriate use of materials which attracts little or no response from the teacher.

Summary

This analysis of 204 lessons given by 34 PGCE students shows that most acts of deviance occurring in their lessons are of a minor nature, typically the buzz of chatter punctuated by requests or commands to desist. Few students had serious discipline problems, and almost no examples of severe disruption were observed, though many lessons sank into minor chaos and showed prolonged mild deviance. Most teacher responses were brief, and misbehaviour subsequently ceased or lessened.

Deviance occurred most frequently during transitions or change of activity, especially when movement occurred, and with third- and fourth-year pupils. Students showed a different style when dealing with older pupils, and involvement in the task was highest for fourth-year classes, though the sample was small. Students whose classes showed low deviancy and high involvement were more likely to be given a high grade by supervising tutors for the amount they thought pupils were learning, but there was only a small agreement between tutors' ratings of task involvement and the observation data collected systematically by the research team.

Those tutors and teachers who conducted case studies in the pilot stage tended to rate personal relationships highly, and students who had prepared well, organised their lessons and materials effectively, and developed the skills of explaining, questioning and using their eyes to read pupils' difficulties and anticipate problems, were thought to be more effective than those who were not able to do these things. Certain personal characteristics were also rated very important, and in the case of students who had poor class control there was some doubt whether their ineffective personality was always amenable to change.

Although a great deal of information was obtained in this study, many questions remained unanswered. Amongst these was the intriguing question of how student teachers compared with experienced practitioners, and it was to this matter that we next turned our attention in the study described in Chapter 3.

References

Berliner, D.C. and Tikunoff, W.J. (1976) 'The California Beginning Teacher Evaluation Study: Overview of the Ethnographic Study', *Journal of Teacher Education, 27*, 24-30

Brophy, J.E. and Evertson, C.M. (1976) *Learning from Teaching: A Developmental Perspective*, Allyn & Bacon Inc. Boston

Charles, C.M. (1981) *Building Classroom Discipline from Models to Practice*, Longman, New York

Delamont, S. (1976) *Interaction in the Classroom*, Methuen, London

Denham, C. and Lieberman, A. (eds) (1980) *Time to Learn*, National Institute of Education, Washington

DES (1975) *A Language for Life* (The Bullock Report), HMSO, London

—— (1979) *Aspects of Secondary Education in England*, HMSO, London

Deutsch, M. (1960) *Minority Group and Class Status*, Society for Applied Anthropology, Monograph no. 2

Docking, J.W. (1980) *Control and Discipline in Schools*, Harper & Row, London

Dooley, P. (1982) *Class Management and Control by Student Teachers*, MPhil. thesis, Nottingham University

Dreyfus, A. and Eggleston, J.F. (1979) 'Classroom Transactions of Student Teachers of Science', *European Journal of Science Education, 1*, 3, 315-25

Dunkin, M.J. and Biddle, B.J. (1974) *The Study of Teaching*, Holt, Rinehart & Winston, New York

Fink, C.H. (1976) 'Social Studies Student Teachers – What Do They Really Learn?' Paper presented at the Annual Meeting of the National Council for the Social Studies, Washington, November

Flanagan, J.C. (1949) 'Critical Requirements: a New Approach to Employee Evaluation' *Personnel Psychology, 2*, 419-25

Flanders, N.A. (1970) *Analysing Teaching Behavior*, Addison-Wesley, New York

Francis, P. (1975) *Beyond Control?* Allen & Unwin, London

Freiberg, H.J. (1983) 'Consistency: the Key to Classroom Management', *Journal of Education for Teaching, 9*, 1, 1-15

Gage, N.L. (1978) *The Scientific Basis of the Art of Teaching*, Teachers College Press, New York

Galton, M.J. (ed.) (1978) *British Mirrors: A Collection of Classroom Observation Systems*, University of Leicester

Glasser, W. (1969) *Schools without Failure*, Harper & Row, New York

Gnagey, W.J. (1975) *Maintaining Discipline in Classroom Instruction*, Macmillan, London

Hargreaves, A. (1978) 'The Significance of Classroom Coping Strategies' in L. Barton and R. Meighan (eds), *Sociological Interpretations of Schooling and Classrooms: A Reappraisal*, Studies in Education, Nafferton, Driffield

Hargreaves, D.H. (1975) *Interpersonal Relations and Education* (revised student edition), Routledge, London

——, Hester, S.K. and Mellor, F.J. (1975) *Deviance in Classrooms*, Routledge, London

Highfield, M.E. and Pinsent, A. (1952) *A Survey of Rewards and Punishments in Schools*, National Foundation for Educational Research (NFER), Windsor

Hilsum, S. and Cane, B.S. (1971) *The Teacher's Day*, NFER, Windsor

—— and Strong, C. (1978) *The Secondary Teacher's Day*, NFER, Windsor

Jackson, P.W. (1968) *Life in Classrooms*, Holt, Rinehart & Winston, New York

Johnson, M. and Brooks, H. (1979) 'Conceptualizing Classroom Management' in D.L. Duke (ed.), *Classroom Management*, NSSE Yearbook 78, 2, University of Chicago Press

Kounin, J.S. (1970) *Discipline and Group Management in Classrooms*, Holt, Rinehart & Winston, New York
—— and Gump, P.V. (1958) 'The Ripple Effect in Discipline', *Elementary School Journal, 35*, 158-62
Lawrence, J., Steed, D. and Young, P. (1977) *Disruptive Behaviour in a Secondary School*, University of London, Goldsmiths College
Lowenstein, L.G. (1975) *Violent and Disruptive Behaviour in Schools*, National Association of Schoolmasters, Hemel Hempstead, Herts
McNamara, D. (1981) 'Attention, Time-on-task and Children's Learning: Research or Ideology?' *Journal of Education for Teaching, 7*, 284-97
Marland, M. (1975) *The Craft of the Classroom*, Heinemann, London
Medley, D.M. and Mitzel, H.E. (1963) 'Measuring Classroom Behavior by Systematic Observation' in N.L. Gage (ed.), *Handbook of Research on Teaching*, Rand, McNally, Chicago
Partington, J.A. and Hinchcliffe, G. (1979) 'Some Aspects of Classroom Management', *British Journal of Teacher Education, 5*, 3, 231-41
Peters, R.S. (1966) *Ethics and Education*, Allen & Unwin, London
Preece, P.F.W. (1979) 'Student Teacher Anxiety and Class Control Problems on Teaching Practice', *British Educational Research Journal, 5*, 1, 13-19
Robertson, J. (1981) *Effective Classroom Control*, Hodder & Stoughton, London
Rogers, C.R. (1970) *On Being a Person*, Houghton-Mifflin, Boston
Stebbins, R.A. (1981) 'Classroom Ethnography and the Definition of the Situation' in L. Barton and S. Walker (eds), *Schools, Teachers and Teaching*, The Falmer Press, Barcombe, Sussex
Tibble, J.W. (1959) 'Problems in the Training of Teachers and Social Workers,' *The Sociological Review*, Monograph no. 2
Weber, M. (1964) *The Theory of Social and Economic Organization*, Free Press, New York
Wickman, E.K. (1928) *Children's Behavior and Teachers' Attitudes*, The Commonwealth Fund, New York
Woods, P. (1979) *The Divided School*, Routledge, London
Wragg, E.C. (1967) *Attitudes, Anxieties and Aspirations of Graduate Student Teachers Following the Postgraduate Certificate of Education Course*, MEd. thesis, Leicester University
—— (1972) *An Analysis of the Verbal Classroom Interaction between Graduate Student Teachers and Children*, PhD thesis, Exeter University
—— (1981) *Class Management and Control*, Macmillan, Basingstoke
Youngman, M.B. (1976) *Programmed Methods for Multivariate Data* (version 5), University of Nottingham

3 TEACHERS' FIRST ENCOUNTERS WITH THEIR CLASSES

E.C. Wragg and E.K. Wood

Student teachers usually begin their school experience or teaching practice part way through the school year. By the time they arrive routines have been established which, for better or worse, will persist through the school year.

A chemistry graduate once arrived at his teaching practice school in January. Before commencing his own teaching he watched a third-year class's regular chemistry teacher take a double period of practical work. After a brief exposition delivered whilst seated on the front bench, one or two shared jokes and asides, the experienced chemistry teacher signalled the start of the practical phase with, 'Right 3C, you know what to do, so get the gear out and make a start.' The class dispersed briskly to hidden cupboards and far recesses for various pieces of equipment, and an hour of earnest and purposeful experimental work ensued.

The following week the chemistry graduate took the class himself, and began by lolling on the front bench in imitation of the apparently effortless and casual manner he had witnessed only seven days earlier. After a few minutes of introduction he delivered an almost identical instruction to the one given by the experienced man the week before, 'Right 3C, get the gear out and do the experiment.' Within seconds pupils were elbowing their fellows out of the way, wrestling each other for bunsen burners, slamming cupboard doors. He spent most of the practical phase calling for less noise and reprimanding the many pupils who misbehaved.

This true story illustrates the problems facing student teachers. What they have not seen is experienced teachers' first encounters with their classes in early September at the beginning of the school year, when rules and relationships are established. There are few studies available of teachers during their first phase of the year. Indeed a common response to a request to be allowed to watch lessons in early September is for the teacher to say, 'Would you mind coming in a fortnight when things have settled down?'

The research reported in this chapter followed that described in Chapter 2. We decided to observe and analyse the first lessons of a sample of experienced teachers at the beginning of the school year from the very first minute of the first lesson in early September, and compare these with the lessons given by a sample of third-year BEd. students at the start of their final teaching practice in October, and then with the first lessons given by a sample of PGCE students on their block practice in January. Over 100 lessons were observed with each of the three groups, and this chapter describes the 313 lessons and the interviews with the teachers concerned before, during and after the observation period.

First Encounters With a Class

A number of social psychologists have looked at first encounters between human beings in a variety of social settings. Goffman (1971) has described the process of impression management which commences at first meetings and continues through subsequent encounters:

> The individual's initial projection commits him to what he is propos- ing to be and requires him to drop all pretences of being other things. As the interaction among the participants progresses, additions and modifications in this informational state will of course occur, but it is essential that these later developments be related without contradiction to, and even built up from the initial positions taken by the several participants. (pp. 21-2)

Argyle (1967) has described the rapidity with which people reach conclusions about those they meet, the difference in sensitivity of acute observers, like Sherlock Holmes, and mental patients whose perceptions appear distorted, and the growth of relationships in the early period of acquaintance.

> A will categorize B in terms of social class, race, age, intelligence or whatever dimensions of people are most important to him, and this will activate the appropriate set of social techniques on the part of A. It is found that people vary widely in what they look for first in others. (p. 46)

It is not merely the individual personalities which are important when people meet. The social setting is also a powerful influence on events: whether one person meets another as a colleague, employer, supplicant, whether someone holds a certain rank or status, wears a uniform, whether the encounter is in private or in public, between two people or several, takes place informally on the street, in a home, or formally at a gathering, in an institution or work-place.

When teachers meet a new class of pupils, a variety of social, environmental and institutional factors are at work in addition to the effects of the several individual personalities involved. Teachers, whatever their individual style, are known to be legally *in loco parentis*. They are inescapably part of a national, local and professional culture, even if they personally reject a number of aspects of it.

When teachers have been in a school for some time their reputation will precede them, and pupil folklore will have told their new classes a great deal about what to expect. Experienced teachers who have moved to another school frequently express surprise during their first few weeks about the difficulty of establishing their identity in a new location after their previous school in which so much could be taken for granted. Supply teachers in particular have to become adept at managing first encounters in new and varying locations because they have so many of them.

It is not too surprising, therefore, that there has been relatively little research into these intimate first moments of contact between teacher and pupils. The success or failure of a whole year may rest on the impressions created, the ethos, rules and relationships established during the first two or three weeks in September, and that is one reason why many teachers see it as a private matter rather than something to be observed and analysed.

Evertson and Anderson (1978) studied 27 teachers of third-grade classes in eight American elementary schools for the first three weeks of the school year, followed by occasional visits later in the school year. They used a mixture of interviews and observations of lessons, concentrating largely on pupils' engagement in their task. Those teachers who secured highest pupil involvement as measured by their schedule showed more evidence of having thought in advance about rules and procedures, gave more time to clarifying rules and procedures, and introduced their pupils gradually to independent work. This kind of study is of considerable interest, but is sometimes criticised for being self-fulfilling, that is, by setting a premium on task involvement, finding that formal and carefully structured teaching is 'effective'.

Eltis (1978) in an Australian study, concentrated on the extent to which impressions formed in early lessons influenced subsequent events. He found that both experienced and student teachers' perceptions of pupils were influenced by speech, appearance, voice and written work. Pupils' accents were thought to be particularly influential on teachers' early and subsequent judgements. He also found that both beginning and experienced teachers were reluctant to discuss pupils' progress and attributes during this early phase.

Eisenhart (1977) concentrated on teachers' methods of establishing control in her 2-year study of fifth- and sixth-grade classes in a city in Southern USA. Most teachers assigned seats to pupils rather than let them choose, and several developed their own distinct style of control from the beginning. One teacher capitalised on the impending arrival of autumn by writing each pupil's name on a leaf which was pinned to a large picture of a tree. Children were exhorted to keep their leaf from falling, and miscreants found their personal leaf removed from sight.

Soar (1973) followed the progress of a cohort of children in 289 kindergarten, first- and second-grade classes for three years. In a smaller-scale study of 20 teachers who were especially high or low in class control, he found that teachers with a high degree of control had started by permitting little pupil freedom and then increasing it, and teachers with a low degree of control had begun with high pupil freedom which they then attempted to decrease.

Some investigators have concentrated on the establishment of classroom rules. Buckley (1977), in an ethnographic study of one classroom, identified 32 rules, of which 22 had been spoken of in some form by the teacher within the first six days of the school year. Of these 32 rules some 15 came from outside the classroom, mainly from the principal. A number of rules emerged after the initial period, such as when a pupil in the third week played in a certain courtyard during break and was told by the teacher on duty that this was not allowed, even though no formal announcement had ever been made. Some rules were established indirectly and by euphemism. For example, the teacher, rather than state that cheating was not permitted, proclaimed that some pupils 'had big eyes'. Duke (1978) analysed discipline matters raised at staff meetings in an American High School, and found considerable inconsistency in the establishment and enforcement of rules by different teachers.

Kelley (1950) looked at the effect of first impressions of teachers on college students. He distributed to the class information about their 'new' teacher which was identical except that half the group had the phrase 'a very warm person' and the other half 'rather a cold person' in one sentence. When members of the class were asked to give their first impressions of the teacher, those given the 'warm' message consistently rated him higher on characteristics such as sociability, modesty, informality, humour and popularity, even though they had been exposed to precisely the same lesson.

There is not, therefore, a well-documented literature on first encounters based on observation from the beginning of the school year. On the other hand there is a great deal of information about established classrooms from which one might speculate about first encounters. Woods (1979) has described the process of securing and maintaining dominance, which in some classrooms can be a harsh procedure, especially in traditional PE lessons where the more aggressive teachers strip the personality of their pupils as they coerce them through the changing room and into the gym, bark commands and finally drive them through the showers.

Several investigators into aspects of teacher or pupil expectancy and the way people typify each other have also identified factors which can be of concern during initial meetings. King (1978) observed infant teachers in three schools, and described how they typified children mainly from their own perceptions in the classroom rather than from written reports of other teachers, and how their typification changed as the school year proceeded. Nash (1973) used personal construct theory to study what constructs eight junior school teachers had assembled about the children they taught. He found that teachers based their perception of the children they taught largely in terms of personality and behaviour rather than ability. Hargreaves (1977) identified three models of teacher typification from the literature, an ideal-matching model whereby pupils are set against some imaginary paragon, a characteristic model which is like an identikit, and a dynamic interactionist model, favoured by symbolic interactionists, which tries to reflect the effects of context and the changes in perception which occur over time as a result of events.

The Preparatory Phase

We began our research into first encounters with a series of interviews with 20 experienced and 40 trainee teachers taking either a BEd. or a PGCE course. Three schools had agreed to co-operate in the sensitive matter of allowing us to watch experienced or student teachers from the first moments of their lessons with new classes, two of them were comprehensive high schools for 12 to 16-year-olds in a city, the third was an 11 to 18 comprehensive in a town. All were used regularly for both BEd and PGCE teaching practice. They were regarded as good schools of their kind, and were thought by tutors to offer a fair challenge to students on teaching practice rather than a particularly easy or especially difficult assignment.

The intention during this preliminary stage was to try to interview teachers in July who might agree to be observed in September, and similarly to interview second-year BEd. students who had already completed a phase of half or whole day per week school experience followed by a 6-week block practice, and who would be starting their 10-week final block practice the following October. The one-year PGCE students were interviewed during the first term of their course, when they too had a half or whole day a week in school, prior to their one-term block practice the following January.

The final sample of 60 was not a random one therefore, though there were 31 female and 29 male teachers, and 20 experienced, 19 BEd and 21 PGCE students. None of those approached refused to be interviewed. A semi-structured interview schedule was drawn up and piloted, and the interviews were all conducted by one of the authors in a confidential setting. Interviews with student teachers took nearly an hour on average, and those with experienced teachers approximately one and a half hours, though some were considerably longer. The interviews were not tape recorded, the interviewer noting down replies as they were given. A fuller account of the research described in this chapter can be found in Wood (1983).

In each interview respondents were asked to think of a class of mixed-ability 12 to 13-year-olds that they would be meeting for the first time. Everyone in the sample was asked a series of questions about how they would enter the room, what sort of topic they might begin with, what rules they might establish and how they would set about this, what kind of relationship they would like to see develop, what they would intend to be doing one day, one hour and one minute before their first lesson.

In addition they were shown four photographs: one of a girl staring at the teacher in a hostile way and refusing to move to another seat, another of five pupils splashing water at each other during a laboratory class, a third of a pupil launching a paper aeroplane across the room, and a fourth of a teacher reading to a class with several pupils showing signs of inattention. They were asked to say how they would respond, and this use of pictures turned out to be a most fruitful projective device for eliciting thoughts on class management. Experienced teachers only were asked questions about whether they behaved differently at the beginning of the year, and to comment on how their early behaviour compared with what happened later in the year. All the interview transcripts were then analysed by two readers selecting what they judged to be the main features of answers from the three groups under the six headings given below.

Information Prior to Meeting a Class

There was a marked difference between experienced teachers and trainees about the information they would need prior to meeting a class. The experienced teachers almost all stressed that, other than essential medical information over deafness, epilepsy or the like, they preferred to find out for themselves rather than take on the prejudices of others. Several said they might look up pupils' records later in the year. This experienced art teacher's was typical of most replies:

> I don't deliberately read anything that might be about their characters and background which might prejudice my judgement. Later on reading about them [the pupils] might throw light on some of my experiences with them.

Some teachers described how they had learned this the hard way and reflected back on their first year, like this experienced English teacher:

> I like to meet them without any preconceived ideas. I like to teach them first and then look up information about them after. Otherwise I think that they tend to live up to their reputations. I wasn't like that to begin with. Once I wanted to know all about them before I met them.

An experienced maths teacher described how she had been given information in her first year that turned out to be incorrect. She was told that one of her classes was an especially bright group:

> I assumed that this was a correct statement of their abilities and I taught at top speed. They weren't that good and I had to lower my sights with them. You've got to do the assessing yourself.

There were only one or two exceptions to this general tone. An experienced French teacher said he wanted to know who were the 'bad eggs' so that he could think about where to seat them, and one drama teacher was quite precise about his need to be able to observe a future class beforehand if possible to assess the likely atmosphere:

> I'd like to see whether there are any noticeable problems, like isolation or over-exhibitionism . . . I'd like to see how far they can concentrate and how far they are inhibited with movement. This finding-out process is very important, especially if they have previously been taught by untrained drama teachers.

Student teachers, in sharp contrast, are extremely anxious about their relative lack of knowledge about children generally, and the classes they will take in particular. Almost all expressed their needs quite differently from the experienced teachers, and most were predictably anxious about potential discipline problems. There were only 4 out of 40 students who, like the experienced teachers, wanted to know little in advance. The great majority echoed this PGCE geography student:

> I'd like to know if they are a disruptive class. If they do mess about a lot, I expect that the experienced teachers will know why and I'll be able to avoid it when it does occur.

The PGCE students also showed special concern over individual needs, typified by this science graduate: 'I'd ask the last teacher to talk to me about every individual pupil for a few minutes. I'd be more interested in the individual than his capability in the subject.'

The BEd. students, presumably because of their experience of their previous block practice, made much more reference to needing information about materials, resources and facilities. They also wished to know about school organisation, standards of work, punishment, discipline and the predominant system of routines and established signals used by the staff.

Thoughts on First Lessons

When asked to reflect on the day before, an hour before, during the walk down the corridor and upon first entry to a new class, there were again predictable differences between experienced and novice teachers. The experienced teachers were able to describe events with considerable precision and certainty. For them these first lessons were part of a taken-for-granted set of routines during which they established varying degrees of dominance by restricting pupils' movement, taking up a central position, clearly being 'in charge', and making use of their eyes, a feature mentioned by several:

'I'd make a point of not turning my back on them or taking my eyes off them. I would say that eyes are the greatest controlling factor' (French teacher, male)
'The amount of looking you do is important' (science teacher, male).
'I keep alert. It's very tiring, but I keep an eye on them all the time. I can keep this attention by staring a bit rudely for the first two or three weeks' (French teacher, female).

There was a larger-than-life quality as teachers spoke of how they exaggerated themselves, established rules by being more pernickety than normal, defined territory:

I walk up and down the gangways. I don't hide behind the furniture. If they ask to leave the room I try to discourage them by umm-ing and ah-ing. I take their names and the time they left the classroom. I don't allow queuing. I don't allow standing by the teacher's desk. They only come out when I tell them to. You [the teacher] give the directions. They don't touch windows or blinds (French teacher, male).

It was very much a personal matter, what an English teacher called 'my rules, for my room, for my area'. Almost all the teachers stressed that they would stand by the door and see the class into the room at the beginning of the first lesson and supervise their exit at the end.

By contrast the students were much more jelly-like in their apprehension and uncertainty. Far from using their eyes to establish presence, they were self-conscious about themselves being looked at. They spoke of thudding hearts and excitement, especially the PGCE students:

'I think I'd just be a mass of nerves. I don't really know how I'll react in a class situation, but . . . deep breath, plunge straight in' (history PGCE, female).
'I'd briefly look over my notes, limber up my mind, feeling of "help!" brush hair back, compose features, steady the nerves' (German PGCE, male).
'I'll be a bit apprehensive, what they'll be like. Will they be noisy? Will I be able to control them? Will they give me a hard time? I'll wonder if they'll compare me with their usual teacher. I wonder

how they'll measure me up. I'll wonder how they'll react as I go through the door. Will they all be making a great noise whooping around, or will they be sitting down waiting?' (geography PGCE, male)

BEd. students tended to show more uncertainty about subject matter and whether they were master of it than PGCE students who, so soon after graduation, claimed a degree of confidence in their subject knowledge.

First-lesson Content

Both experienced teachers and BEd. students described how they would outline work for the term. Postgraduates, surprisingly perhaps in view of their strong subject concern, hardly mentioned explaining their overall plan.

The most striking contrast between experienced and novice teachers was that for the former first-lesson content was almost irrelevant. They perceived this opening encounter largely in terms of management rituals: 'The lesson would be concentrating on establishing standards. The work wouldn't be the most important thing. It would be secondary. I would be setting up expectations of behaviour' (geography teacher, female).

Even with those teachers who had more firm intentions to make a start on their subject there was a need to establish some predominant image, as in the lesson of this male science teacher:

Right at the start of the lesson there must be something for them to do: games, workcards, anything, because they rarely arrive at the same time. I try to create an atmosphere in which they start science as soon as they come in through the door.

The work itself would be simple and unexacting, 'nothing too earth-shattering' in the words of one teacher, simply a means of keeping children busy whilst teachers gained some perception both of individual pupils and the likely chemistry of the class mix.

Student teachers gave a great deal of thought to lesson content and little to managerial aspects. About half were desperate to make an impact with 'something interesting', 'a game', 'something dramatic like a fountain', 'quite exciting', 'interesting and active', 'a magic poetry machine that would make them look forward to the next time'. They spoke of their eagerness to sell themselves, to get introductions over quickly by writing their name on the board, and then give a perform-ance that would sell themselves and their subject for the rest of term.

The other half were much more cautious, would adopt a lower profile, choose a topic that was 'safe' not risky, conservative rather than radical. One PGCE geography student described his approach to Australian grasslands:

> I'll introduce it and talk about it for a while, quite a conventional type of lesson, not flashy because it might go wrong and the kids will remember, quite a safe lesson, a good conventional approach. I'd leave the flashy things to later on when I knew them better.

The BEd. students, more aware from their previous practice of the possibility of topic and tone being determined in some cases by the supervising teacher, and also, in some cases, having tried without success the spectacular opener, were more cautious than PGCE students. One remarked ruefully that she wished 'someone had said use something very set like cards, a textbook or worksheets, so that they know where they are going'.

Mood and Image

The presentation of self in the first lesson was described graphically by all the experienced teachers in the sample. All stressed the projec-tion of some larger-than-life image, though the nature of that image differed from teacher to teacher. The importance of what, for most respondents, was described in terms analogous to an opening-night theatre performance, was summed up by an experienced English teacher when she said: 'I think the first lesson is vitally important. If you don't make your mark in the first lesson in the way you want to, you will never make it again.'

The varying kinds of image which teachers sought to project are shown by the responses of people from different subject areas. A drama teacher, even more prone than most, perhaps, to an opening theatrical style, described how he quite consciously generated a sense of mystery about himself:

> The first impression I try to give is of tight purposeful nervous energy. The children learn to expect this. I try to create a feeling that something's going to happen, even if I don't know what I'm going to do . . . It's important to be hard in the first lesson. By 'hard' I mean a body thing, creating a shroud of mystery. I don't allow the kids to pierce it thoroughly until later.

In their reflections on the type of image they sought to project, several teachers described an element of self-caricature, even a deliberate cultivation of the crackpot in some cases:

'I'm well known for being mad. I do daft things, but they cannot do as they like' (English teacher, male).
'They consider me weird . . . Everyone at school thinks of me as being a bit eccentric, a mad scientist. I play on this' (science teacher, male).

For experienced teachers the first lesson with a new class is a time when they are acutely conscious of the need to reinforce and indeed exaggerate whatever they see as the predominant features of their reputation in the schools. In some cases this reputation was thought to be fearsome:

'I have a reputation before they arrive here. They come in fear and trembling because they think I am severe . . . It's important to put on a bit of a front at the beginning' (French teacher, male).
'I'm very stern and very hard. I am consciously being a little harder than I am' (PE teacher, male).

The reactions of the student teachers on mood and change in first lessons were different from each other. The BEd. students' responses were much closer to those of experienced teachers, with emphasis on performance, the establishment of dominance, and even the exaggeration of eccentricity and 'character': 'I'd keep control in my hands by constantly stopping them' (BEd. drama, female).

Next time I'm going to be just as rough and aggressive as I was last time, scare the hell out of them at the beginning, it'll be alright afterwards. I shall say, 'I'm the new teacher. If you treat me fairly, I'll treat you fairly.' (BEd. PE, male).

I'd say, 'I'm going to be teaching you for the next x weeks. I've got a very funny name so we're all going to have a good laugh' . . . I'd ham this up completely . . . 'Everyone get ready to laugh'. The kids ask what it is. I say, 'You don't look ready to laugh.' (BEd. drama, female)

By contrast the PGCE students were quite different. Their emphasis was on being friendly and approachable. They identified much more with the pupils, saw themselves as reluctant to be socialised into the 'hard teacher' stereotype, regarded their class as a collection of thirty individuals, and spoke much more in terms of negotiation, 'appealing to common sense', not seeing them 'as a class to be lectured at', reluctant to alienate by coming on too strong or setting too much homework. Most had given little precise thought to the matter beyond recognising in general terms what they guessed might be appropriate:

> Ideally I'd like a fairly intimate relationship with the class, but I realise that requires drawing a line between intimacy and cheek, a fine balance I'd like to achieve. I don't know how. I haven't given it a lot of thought. It's important. I need to think about it. (PGCE English, male)

Establishing Rules

There were two major differences between experienced and novice teachers about the establishment of rules. The first was that experienced teachers were quite clear about which rules were important and how they would secure compliance. The second difference lay in the nature of the classroom rules by which each group would seek to live.

The most common rule mentioned by all groups was 'no talking when the teacher is talking' in public sessions rather than during private conversations with individual children. Everyone mentioned this in interview, though subsequently when teachers and students were observed there was considerable variation in the extent to which the rule materialised.

Apart from this universal rule there was a very noticeable distinction in the tone of rules mentioned by teachers and students. Experienced teachers frequently cited rules that governed territory (entering and leaving the room, who could move where and when), respect for property, work ethic (having the 'right' attitude to learning, homework, etc.) and safety. Teachers' responses made frequent use of words with a strong moral component, like 'right', 'proper', 'correct', 'suitable', a dimension that was rarely present in the interviews with students.

It was a moral tone that was set by the teacher, but most spoke of transferring responsibility to the pupil, in the class of the science teacher below through a little handing-over ritual.'They understand the course cost . . . All books are numbered and I check them. I say I hope they've got lots of pocket money for bills if they damage things' (business studies teacher, female).

> I give out exercise books and textbooks calling them out to fetch their books so as to identify them further, and also to stress that *I* have given them the book and it is *their* responsibility . . . for homework after the first lesson I tell them to cover books and look after them. I reinforce that the books are in *their* care (science teacher, male)

This greater moral certainty which distinguished so clearly between experienced and beginning teachers came out very clearly when interviewees responded to the four photographs of classroom scenes described above. Most experienced teachers took an immediate stance on each issue, and declared immediately who was right or wrong and what the teacher would do:

> 'She has got to be made to do it [move to another seat] because of the audience. If she has the "why?" look, I'd not give her a reason, I'd become very authoritarian' (English teacher, male).
> 'I'd go over to the group and say . . . "the rules say you shouldn't do this" ' (science teacher, male).
> 'Shout at them, particularly if I'm talking. It would be something short and sweet like, "shut up!" You need a mental sledgehammer' (science teacher, male).

Student teachers on the other hand usually spoke of treating the incident lightly, often identifying with the pupils and recalling times when they had behaved in a similar way: 'I'd treat it fairly lightly – "Oh yes, very funny, ha ha. Can we get on with some work now." Then they'd realise that it's a bit stupid' (BEd. drama, female).

Some teachers were extremely precise about their classroom rules, and one maths teacher listed ten rules immediately he was asked, without any hesitation. He was one of 7 out of the 20 in the sample who said he announced his rules in the first lesson. Other teachers 'discussed' the rules, though no-one claimed the pupils had any right to change them. 'Discussion' was really an alternative and more memorable way of communicating what were principally determined by the school authorities or the teacher, as one science specialist explained: 'I know what the rules are, but we establish them through discussion. I believe that they remember them better if they have helped formulate them.'

Almost all teachers said they made use of case law. Whether they announced or discussed rules, they would assume that pupils were likely to make an inference from the way the teacher behaved in particular instances. It was common to hear statements like 'you have to make an example of someone early on' (maths teacher) or 'I stop the song if they aren't joining in' (music teacher).

There was a sharp contrast between experienced teachers and students on the question of rules, especially, though not exclusively, in the case of PGCE students, many of whom were reluctant to speculate and felt that an intuitive approach was better:

'I'd make up rules as appropriate when I see them doing something wrong. It's difficult to see what this would be' (PGCE geography, female).

'I'd bring the rules out gradually and naturally. I'd offer explanations because I think it is simpler to understand' (PGCE history, female).

'I'd establish the rules as the problem arises' (BEd. English, female).

Most students were anxious not to hazard personal relationships by giving prominence to rules of behaviour: 'The Art Room should have a happy atmosphere, and if you start telling them they mustn't do this and they mustn't do that, it ruins the atmosphere' (PGCE art, female).

Personal Relationships

Almost everyone in the sample, teacher or student, declared in interview that personal relationships were important. It is a concept in teaching which it is, of course, hard to be against. Experienced teachers showed more awareness of contact outside the classroom than did trainees.

A lot of understanding occurs outside the classroom, walking down the corridor . . . I play the clarinet. I have just started to learn. I play with the fourth year and am not very good . . . I put myself in a learning situation, and they can see that I also make silly errors. (English teacher, male).

'I try to go on school hikes and camps. I get the kids away from the classroom. I always take my own kids along so that they [the pupils] see me in a different context' (science teacher, male).

Student teachers spoke mainly of relationships within the classroom and were again aware of the, to them, thin line between friendliness and over familiarity. This geography PGCE student's fear of loss of control was echoed by many: 'I'm in favour of developing personal relationships as long as I don't get down to the "friend" level. I don't want to get too familiar, otherwise they will take advantage of me.'

Experienced teachers wanted to talk more of the longer-term style of personal relationships with their class. It was almost as if what they had said about establishing dominance was in conflict with their subsequent aspirations. We shall return to all these matters in the next section below, which describes the observation study of 313 lessons.

The Observation Study of First Encounters

The main study in this research was of 313 lessons given by 41 of the 60 teachers and students in the three schools described above, except for one BEd. PE student who was observed in a fourth school, another 12 to 16 High School. The sample was not a random one. Not all the people interviewed could be observed, and constraints included whether they taught the principal target age range of 11 to 13-year-olds and the extent to which their teaching timetable allowed observers to watch their lessons at appropriate times. All 60 people interviewed had agreed to being observed should the need arise, and no-one subsequently refused.

Where choice permitted we tried to include in the sample teachers with varied views as well as different subjects and preferred teaching strategies. All observations were conducted by the two present writers and three observers who were trained on videotapes and in classrooms until a high level of agreement was obtained between all five. It was the view of all observers that the sample of students eventually observed was a fairly typical cross-section of trainee teachers. The experienced teachers were generally, though not exclusively, fairly competent, and it is not so easy to say how typical they were of teachers at large. Lest it be thought that only the confident, extrovert and successful agree to be observed, it should be said that some of the experienced teachers had discipline problems, as did a number of the students.

The 313 lessons observed were distributed as follows:

13 experienced teachers (7 male 6 female)	103 lessons
13 BEd. students (5 male 8 female)	106 lessons
15 PGCE students (10 male 5 female)	104 lessons
Total: 41 teachers (22 male 19 female)	313 lessons

As intended, we were able to observe most lessons, that is 96 per cent, with the 11 to 13 age range, and there was the following distribution over subjects, with the number of lessons observed in brackets: English (65), humanities (60), science (52), languages (45), arts (31), physical education (26) and maths and business studies (34).

The data from interviews, our own and others' previous studies, were used to construct and pilot an observation schedule which consisted of a mixture of quantitative and qualitative items. It was in five sections. The first section recorded preliminary data about the teacher, class and subject of the lesson. The second section was about the entry and beginning of the lesson, how the teacher secured attention, opening words, voice, posture, movement, use of eyes, facial expression, response and behaviour of pupils, and how the task was set up. Section three was the 20-second pupil-by-pupil involvement and deviancy 'sweep' described in Chapter 2. The fourth section contained a set of five-point scales on the teacher's style during the lesson, with the observer rating warmth, confidence, the extent to which the lesson seemed businesslike, stimulating, the teacher's use of eye contact, mobility and formality/informality. In addition there was space for freehand accounts of establishment and maintenance of rules, personal relationships and the behaviour during transitions from one activity to another, all of which had been regarded as significant classroom matters in our earlier enquiry described in Chapter 2. Finally, the observer was asked to record one critical event during each lesson according to the same format as had been used in our earlier studies. There was also a space for a freehand lesson account, and for the observer to record any other field notes about matters judged to be of significance, and any comments from interviews with teachers after their lessons (see Appendix C).

The five observers discussed and piloted the schedule, and observer-agreement tests were conducted in similar, though not identical ways to those described in Chapter 2, because this study made greater use of rating schedules and field notes. On all observer-agreement measures there was over 80 per cent agreement between observers, and in final tests based on videotapes of lessons all five-point scale ratings were within one point of each other.

To check whether there was agreement between what teachers said in interview and what they actually did in practice in their first lessons, one of the research team went through all the interview schedules and drew up a list of explicit intentions such as 'I'll introduce myself and write my name on the blackboard' or 'I'll deal with infringements straightaway'. At the end of the research all the observation schedules and reports were read through and the list of intentions was checked. There was exceptionally high accord, of over 80 per cent in quantity, between the experienced teachers' stated intentions and actual practice. Only one teacher out of 13 actually fell below this. He fulfilled less than half of his expressed intentions. Student teachers were much closer to this figure of a half, and in one or two cases there was little congruence between what was predicted and what ensued, especially amongst PGCE students.

On average each teacher was observed for the first eight lessons with the same class, but because of timetable clashes it was not always possible to see all of these first lessons in sequence. In the event, the maximum number of lessons seen was twelve in the case of one teacher, and the minimum four in the case of one BEd. student. Everyone else was watched for between six and ten lessons. Over 80 per cent of classes seen were of mixed ability, 10 per cent were of high ability and 7 per cent of average or low ability.

The quantitative data were transferred to punched cards, and the ethnographic data were analysed by two members of the research team. In the cases where ethnographic data were translated into coded form, or when lists were drawn up, systematic checks of agreement were taken and there was over 90 per cent agreement in the assigning of qualitative data to codes or headings.

Lesson Openings

It soon became apparent that serving teachers have several advantages, in addition to their previous professional experience, which are not available to students. The most striking of these is that they meet their class right at the beginning of the school year, before any class identity has been established, and can therefore be influential in shaping it. All three schools in which we observed in September made a massive communal effort at the start of the year with special assemblies, heads and senior teachers visiting all new classes, statements and re-statements about rules of conduct, dress, conventions, aspirations, expectations ('we're expecting great things from you', 'now that you've come to the senior school . . .') a buzz of excitement and busy chatter, a high degree of institutional control, an assertion of who was who and what was expected to transpire. Student teachers, arriving anonymously during the year, enjoyed none of this collective stamp of businesslike authority and had to join an enterprise which, for better or worse, had been functioning without them for some time.

Recording of actual opening words in lessons was not always possible as these were sometimes uttered in the corridor or were not audible. Analysis of the opening words in the 181 lessons where it was possible to note them showed that half of the first statements were directive, the most common words being 'settle down', 'be quiet', 'come in', 'sit down', 'stand up', 'do . . .' or 'don't . . .'. The next most common opening statements were the immediate introduction of the subject itself, ('Today we are going to look at matrices' etc.) which occurred in 13 per cent of lessons, and 'Is everyone here?' which happened on 10 per cent of occasions. About 7 per cent of lessons began with some form of criticism like, 'You don't call this lined up, do you?' LINE UP!'

Experienced teachers and BEd. students almost all introduced themselves in their first lesson, whilst a number of PGCE students, who had said in interview they would, tended to pass over without any introduction. Experienced teachers had usually made an effort to be present before the pupils arrived as they had said during interviews, and this occurred on 71 per cent of occasions compared to 61 per cent for all students.

There were some interesting variations in the methods teachers employed to secure attention. The use of voice was easily the most common, this being noted as a predominant feature in about half the lessons observed. Some teachers, however, preferred to make use of posture (hands on hips, leaning against blackboard, arms folded), facial expression (smile, scowl), scanned the class rapidly with their eyes, or simply waited expressionless until the level of noise fell, each of these being commented on by observers in about one-fifth to one-quarter of lesson openings.

Experienced teachers and BEd. students showed similar lesson beginnings. PGCE students on the other hand appeared self-conscious, often averted their eyes, made little use of commanding posture or gesture, and relied almost exclusively on voice. Observers' accounts of the lesson openings of experienced teachers echoed what the latter had said in interview: performances enacted centre stage, elaborate mannerisms, confident articulation, not much ambiguity at this point about who was in charge. The school staff were in their different ways writing the agenda for the whole year during the first few minutes of lesson one. The management and projection of image were striking features of almost every experienced teacher's first lesson.

By way of stark contrast the image on arrival part way through the school year of one modern-language graduate, who was by no means a 'weak' teacher by the end of his teaching practice, was described by the observer as 'injured caring':

> The teacher spoke with a soft voice which he didn't raise at all. Phrases like 'pay attention' are said apologetically . . . A hurt note sometimes crept into his voice. He mostly remained standing, and walked up and down behind the desk at the front of the room. When he walked round the room he did not appear to convey any impression that his walking was to much purpose. He made few gestures and could almost be described as overlookable.

Teachers' Manner During First Lessons

There were some quite notable differences in manner of the three groups as revealed by the summary of rating scales in Table 3.1. The five-point scales were based largely on what were regarded as important characteristics in our own earlier studies, but were also influenced by the work of Ryans (1960) and others. Table 3.1. shows the means of the three groups, and in each case the higher the score the more positively the members of the group were rated on what characteristic or behaviour. The range of possible mean scores, therefore, is from 1, if all were given the lowest rating, to 5 if everyone were accorded the highest possible point on the scale. We have not given analysis of variance or gap-test values, preferring, because of the sample size, to consider the raw data to see similarities and differences. Rank order is given in parentheses.

Table 3.1: Mean Scores and Rank Order of Three Groups on 8 Five-point Scales

Characteristic/behaviour	Experienced	BEd.	PGCE
Warm and friendly	3.67(1)	3.36(2)	3.14(3)
Confident	4.44(1)	3.68(2)	3.54(3)
Businesslike	4.26(1)	3.62(2)	3.59(3)
Stimulating	3.52(1)	3.10(3)	3.14(2)
Mobile	3.52(2)	3.62(1)	3.11(3)
Formal manner	3.04(3)	3.05(2)	3.11(1)
Eye sweep across the class	4.00(1)	3.56(2)	3.42(3)
Eye contact with individuals	3.68(1)	3.28(3)	3.45(2)

With between 13 and 15 people in each group one interprets differences with some caution, but it is notable that the experienced teachers tend to display distinctly more of most of these characteristics than do trainees, especially confidence, as one might expect. They are also rated more businesslike, stimulating, warm and friendly, and make greater use of their eyes than students. PGCE students seem to show less mobility than the other two groups, and are less likely to use their eyes to scan the whole class, though their eye contact with individual pupils is not very different.

Despite their greater identification with pupils during interview, PGCE students were not seen as more informal in their manner. The apprehension several expressed in interview that children might take advantage if they were too relaxed, seems to have ensured that they were on average fractionally more formal than either BEd. students or experienced teachers. Consequently, they were also seen as a little more aloof than the other two groups on the warm-and-friendly scale. This slight tightness might explain why they were also less mobile, tended to teach from a fixed central point, and were less likely to move around the class monitoring pupils' work.

Establishing Classroom Rules

Two members of the research team analysed all lesson observation data and assigned references to classroom rules, however these were established, to one of eleven categories. It took a long time and a great deal of discussion before we agreed about the number of categories of rule there appeared to be, and different analysts might have produced other formulations. Table 3.2 shows the number of lessons out of a total of 131 in which some aspect of the establishment of a classroom rule occurred, either because it was explicitly stated, or if an infraction was punished or commented on, or if the teacher communicated in some form, by action or response, that the rule applied.

Table 3.2: Frequency of Occurrence, out of 313 Lessons, of Eleven Classroom Rules

Rule	No. of lessons
1. No talking when teacher is talking (public situation)	131
2. No disruptive noises	125
3. Rules for entering, leaving and moving in classrooms	109
4. No interference with the work of others	99
5. Work must be completed in a specified way	84
6. Pupils must raise hand to answer, not shout out	55
7. Pupils must make a positive effort in their work	49
8. Pupils must not challenge the authority of the teacher	47
9. Respect should be shown for property and equipment	38
10. Rules to do with safety	26
11. Pupils must ask if they do not understand	8

The raw frequency count of rule mention does not, of course, reveal much about the effectiveness or appropriateness of the rules themselves. Some experienced teachers established a rule such as that forbidding pupils' casual chatter when the teacher is talking during phases of public exposition, by stating it quite explicitly in the first few seconds of their first lesson, punishing the first infraction moments later, and then fine-tuning the rule on perhaps one further occasion early in their second lesson. After three public references the rule was laid down and understood. In the lesson of one teacher in particular and some students, the same rule was stated frequently but rarely observed.

There were several differences between experienced teachers and novices. Observation confirmed what people had said in interview: experienced teachers made most of the exhortations to respect property, show a positive attitude to work and complete it in a specified way. One might infer that since these rules have been established by the class's regular teacher in September it is less likely that students will need to remind pupils later in the year, but observers' lesson accounts show this is not the case and that students appear less willing or able to enforce such rules. Most of the examples of rule statements about disruptive noises, the need to raise one's hand before answering and talking when the teacher is talking, occurred in students' lessons because some beginners were not successful in making the rule apply. Table 3.3 shows how the six most common rules were distributed across the three groups. Thus, of the 131 lessons when rule 1 occurred, 25 per cent were in the lessons of experienced teachers, 31 per cent in those of BEds and 44 per cent in PGCE students' lessons.

Table 3.3: Percentage of Occasions When Rule Mention Occurred

Rule	Experienced	BEd.	PGCE
1. No talking when teacher talking	25	31	44
2. No disruptive noises	19	39	42
3. Entering, leaving, moving	43	31	26
4. No interference with others	28	26	46
5. Work completed in specified way	56	17	27
6. Pupils must raise hand	18	38	44

Analysis of critical events recorded by observers shows the differences in style, degree of success and reasons for rules existing. If one takes the most common rule 'No talking when I'm talking', for most teachers, students and pupils this is a common-sense basic rule of discourse: that if one person is attempting to communicate something of interest or value, distractions prevent those who wish to listen from hearing and learning. For some on the other hand there is a wider social aspect, not merely to do with discourse, but with general respect and concern for others. One or two teachers and students saw the rule more as the embodiment of their personal authority, and reacted much more aggressively to infractions, as this extract from the observation of the second lesson of an experienced teacher reveals.

The teacher was talking to the whole class when two boys, one of whom was in the class for the first time, began to chatter. The teacher swung round rapidly, pointed and glared at the offending lad and barked out in a very loud and frightening voice, 'Did I ask you to talk? He paused for two seconds in the ensuing silence and stared. 'Well don't then.' The boys stopped talking, and the observer noted that the rest of the class appeared shocked. There had been a considerable change in the teacher's voice strength and tempo.

The use of voice and rapid movement into threatening social proximity to establish a rule were not unique to experienced teachers. Early in the lessons of a BEd. science student she explained that she would not tolerate talk whilst she was explaining something:

One of the girls in the class began to talk as she was saying this. The teacher paused, noted the pupil talking, swung round, put her hands on the desk and stared into the face of the offending girl. 'I will not tolerate (pause) talking at the same time'. The teacher's speed of movement and shortening of social distance had a frightening quality about it. The girl looked flushed and there was complete silence.

In the lessons of the less confident students, however, there are several accounts of the teacher repeatedly saying 'Sh . . . quiet please' with little appreciable difference in volume, exactly as reported in Chapter 2.

The territorial aspect mentioned in interviews was noted frequently in the descriptions of rules about movement, several of which related to the teacher's concept of territory, a phenomenon observed more rarely in the lessons of student teachers. Experienced practitioners spoke frequently of *'my* room', *'my* class', *'my* lab', emphasising the personal pronoun. They defined time as well as space, 'You go when *I* tell you to', 'The bell indicates only that the lesson *may* be ending'. Student teachers suffer from appearing later in the year when someone else has staked out the territory. Conscious that they are on another's ground, they frequently have to ask the pupils about the regular class teacher's rules, 'Does Mr Smith allow you to . . .?' It underlines to the class the alien and subordinate status of the student on teaching practice.

Establishing Relationships

The need expressed by many teachers to establish some set of rules of procedure, however benign, might appear to cut across their equally keen aspiration for amicable relationships with their classes. After all, most of the rules described above were usually expressed in prohibitive form: no talking, no calling out, no shirking, no disrespect for people and property. With so much limitation and restriction and with most of the decisions taken by the teacher, it does seem at first glance, that many classrooms are totally unlike A.S. Neill's Summerhill, where pupils and teachers shared equal voting rights on such matters as rules, but rather like Geoffrey Bantock's (1965) assertion that a superior-subordinate relationship is inescapable.

> The teacher, however much he may attempt to disguise the fact, must, if only because he is not appointed or dismissed by pupils, represent an authority. He must do so, also because he is inescapably 'other' than the children . . . Power is an inescapable element in adult life, to which we all at some time or other have to come to terms; and I deprecate a great deal of the current insincerity which strives to hide the true situation

Furthermore, as will be shown in the next chapter, children seem to prefer teachers who are 'in charge'. Yet a number of both inexperienced and practised teachers managed to establish positive and harmonious relationships despite their professed need to exercise authority. They employed a wide variety of ways to achieve this.

Praise and Encouragement. Quantified as a percentage of all classroom events, the use of praise occupies relatively little of a class's day, an average figure of around 2 per cent being commonly reported in the literature (Amidon and Flanders, 1963; Wragg, 1972). Teachers who practise systematic behaviour-modification techniques may make more extensive use of praise as a form of reinforcement, whilst those with an aversion to behaviourism may deliberately eschew praise so as not to condition and control behaviour so deliberately. Teachers using the Humanities Curriculum Projects materials developed by Lawrence Stenhouse in the 1960s were actively discouraged from saying 'good' or 'well done', on the grounds that this was not consistent with the role of 'neutral chairman'.

Lavish praise, encouragement and reassurance were significant features of the early lessons of some experienced teachers and BEd students, somewhat less so in those of PGCE students.

Aware that pupils feel apprehensive amid the pressure of their adolescent peers when faced with a new teacher, one BEd English student skilfully used praise to rescue a girl from public ridicule:

> The pupils had been making lists of the characteristics of the animals in *Animal Farm*. The teacher selects one person to read out her list. Amidst giggling the girl complies. The pupil appeared embarrassed at having to stand up. When she had finished reading the teacher said, 'Well done, that was very good.' She smiled encouragement at the pupil who smiled back and sat down.

Attention to Individual Pupils. Experienced teachers and students tried to make opportunities to go around the class talking to individuals, as if conscious of the somewhat stentorian style of their early addresses to the whole class. The PGCE students in particular preferred individual contact. One English graduate spent almost the whole of his first two lessons walking around and talking to pupils, reading their work carefully, engaging individuals in eye contact and speaking with a soft voice. He frequently crouched alongside pupils to bring his height down to their level.

Experienced teachers were more capable of splitting their attention between the individual they were with and the rest of the class, not afraid to break off and comment on something happening elsewhere in the room, whereas some student teachers became so engrossed in their private exchanges with pupils they sometimes lost their overall perception of what was happening in other parts of the room.

Apologies. When teachers behave in a dominant way during first encounters they sometimes make errors, accuse the wrong pupil or shout at someone who did not understand. Some teachers and students were confident and compassionate enough to apologise for their errors, and on the relatively infrequent occasions that this occurred it made a considerable impact on pupils who, according to studies which will be mentioned in the next chapter, appreciate fairness. One of the most striking examples of this came in an early lesson of a BEd. drama student when she noticed for the first time a boy standing by the door of the drama studio:

> The teacher looks stern and demands in an angry voice: 'Why are you late?' Everyone is quiet. The teacher is looking aggressive. The child goes red and says nothing. A couple of the class tell the teacher that the boy has been there all the time. 'Have you?' asks the teacher. 'I thought you'd just slid in. My humble apologies for embarrassing you.' The teacher hugs him in a mock show of concern and then pats him on the head. The boy grins and the class laugh.

Explanations of Classroom Events. Despite what both teachers and students had said in interview, there were surprisingly few explanations of what teachers did and why. Occasionally a rule was justified rather than explained. When explanations were actually offered they seemed to be appreciated by the class. In one science lesson pupils were given the county's rules of safety in the laboratory and asked to write under each one why they thought the rule was necessary. The rules were then discussed. Some of the other teachers simply gave out the rules with little or no comment.

It was equally appreciated when teachers occasionally addressed an explanation to a particular pupil who was confused but, in these early lessons, too shy to ask for help. One BEd. student asked his class if anyone needed the task explaining again.

> One girl said, 'Yes, me.'
> 'Don't you understand what I want?' 'Oh yes. I understand what you want, but I don't see why.'
> The teacher stood by her and explained fully and carefully that it was an exercise in relationships and shapes, one with another. He had noticed that people were making mistakes, did not know what to emphasise, were not looking carefully. The pupil listened attentively and, apparently quite satisfied, went on with her work, looking very carefully.

Offers of Help With Work. Rather than merely explain, some teachers responded to pupils' occasional uncertainties at novelty by making positive offers of help and then working alongside the pupil. This was most marked in the lessons of PGCE students and experienced teachers.

An extract from the lesson of an experienced business studies teacher shows how she was quick to help a girl who had arrived late.

> 'Ah, come in', said the teacher, 'you haven't missed much. I've done your folder for you.' She smiled at the pupil. 'Find yourself one of the seats. I'll help you get out your typewriter. We won't make her go through the embarrassment of trying to get it out herself. There.' The teacher got the typewriter out for her and returned to the front.

Children's Names and Target Pupils. With only a few exceptions, experienced teachers learned pupils' names more quickly and deliberately than students. One experienced maths teacher had learned every name of the class observed by the end of the first week. He made his learning of names a public matter, and included an individual response with each name, promising to penalise himself when he made an error, as in this incident when he was handing back their very first test paper:

> What's your name? Robert − good boy Robert. Good girl − what's your name? − Andrea. Good girl. Well done Annabel. What a lovely name − when I have a little girl I'm going to call her Annabel. Good boy Freddie, excellent, excellent. Jean . . . It's not Jean is it? . . . It's Jill, sorry, prize later for my getting your name wrong.

In some cases name learning was not so much related to making positive social relationships as to social control, in that it was easier to reprimand if the teacher could put a name to someone. Student teachers were more likely to address the whole class, 'Quiet everybody', 'Pay attention 3C', whereas some experienced teachers deliberately chose a target pupil. It was as if certain children were being stereotyped immediately as exemplars of a whole genus of pupils whose names were as yet unknown.

One of the most striking examples of this occurred in a science lesson with an experienced teacher. Billy became stereotyped as the bad boy in his first lesson. In each ensuing lesson the teacher used him as a target pupil. On one occasion he told the class not to collect equipment until instructed. Some seconds later about ten pupils began to move towards the equipment cupboards. His response was swift. 'Billy, I did say wait until I told you to move.' During the interview after the lesson he explained that the reason he had reprimanded Billy was because he was not very bright, his IQ was 'off the IQ scale' and he had to be watched. In other lessons Billy became a different kind of target. In another teacher's class he received frequent and fulsome praise from the teacher, who explained afterwards that she thought he was like a number of pupils who needed encouragement. Later in the year all his teachers were surprised to discover that Billy had become the mouse-breeding champion of a large part of the country.

Humour. One could write at great length about the use of humour, which is already well documented by several writers including Woods (1979). Humour may be destructive if it is sarcastic or deprecating, just as it may relieve tension if it is positive and warm. PGCE students made much less use of humour than experienced teachers. Men teachers in particular seemed to disregard the familiar tip not to smile until Christmas by engaging in banter and cheerful insults soon after the first lesson or two had passed.

An experienced science teacher, who had conducted a formal and quite stern opening lesson, began his second laboratory session by tempering the first image with a skilful mixture of humour, self-deprecation and a reminder that he too was human and had a family:

> I've got a son your age, and so when my wife and I were invited out to dinner the other night we tossed up to see who would stay at home babysitting, and of course I lost. I decided to watch 'Match of the Day' with my boy and the commentator began to use some very funny language − 'a square ball', 'the referee blew up', 'he left his foot behind' (laughter). Well, we have some special language that we use in science that you will need to learn.

In general, humour occurred most easily and naturally in the lessons of the experienced male teachers in the sample; one or two teachers and a number of students made little or no use of it, and there were only occasional examples of humour that was destructive or deprecating of individual pupils. The most striking aspects of humour were first, that it occurred so soon, frequently in the second lesson, despite a general impression in folklore that teachers prefer to suppress laughter and amusement for some considerable time, and secondly, that it seemed to be used to mitigate the more stern and austere initial impression conveyed during opening encounters in the very first lesson.

Most, though not all, of the examples given in this section on relationships have been of a positive kind, and certainly a predominant feature of the lessons of almost all students and teachers was the effort they made, despite their frequently expressed need to establish a fairly dominating presence, to bring about a classroom climate in which the conditions for learning were supportive. Sadly, some teachers and students, but only a minority, established negative relationships. Confrontation occurred from the beginning, and whereas similar incidents would have been less explosive in neighbouring classrooms, in the case of three teachers in particular, one experienced, one PGCE and one BEd student, the foundations for a sour relationship were firmly laid from the very first lesson. We shall return to this matter and to one of these three teachers in the next chapter when we consider the pupil's view of first encounters.

Pupil Involvement and Deviancy

Using the same procedures for calculating the rough-and-ready measure of deviancy and involvement described in Chapter 2, whereby a series of 'sweeps' of the class were made with every pupil being observed in turn for 20 seconds, giving a deviancy and involvement-level score ranging from 0 to 100, we made a number of quantified comparisons of the three groups. We again recommend caution in interpreting these data, which raise interesting questions and hypotheses but which are inevitably frail because of the difficulty of quantifying such complex matters as misbehaviour and pupils' involvement in their task. Although analysis of variance and Tukey gap tests showed that differences between groups cited below were statistically significant, we do not quote these as they might give a false sense of precision.

Table 3.4 shows the involvement-level scores for the first eight lessons, and there is a noticeable difference between the average involvement level of 90 measured in the lessons of experienced teachers and that of 81 and 80 in the case of BEd and PGCE students.

Table 3.4: Pupil Involvement-level Scores During the First Eight Lessons

Lesson	Experienced teachers	BEd. students	PGCE students
1	91	86	86
2	91	78	82
3	94	84	86
4	86	80	81
5	91	80	84
6	94	75	73
7	91	84	73
8	84	78	75
Average	90	81	80

Table 3.5 shows the levels of deviancy noted during the same first eight lessons, and again teachers' lessons show less occurrence of misbehaviour than those of either student group.

Table 3.5: Pupil Deviancy Scores During the First Eight Lessons

Lesson	Experienced teachers	BEd. students	PGCE students
1	0.4	8.3	2.8
2	0.9	9.4	3.4
3	0.3	7.7	2.2
4	2.8	9.0	4.5
5	0.6	9.6	4.7
6	0.2	9.1	5.7
7	1.0	4.2	4.5
8	2.0	5.4	5.3
Average	1.0	7.8	4.1

The differences between scores for experienced teachers and trainees cannot be explained solely in terms of individual competence. For reasons given earlier the massive collective effort by all teachers early in September, and the fact that many younger pupils find themselves in new and strange surroundings, produce a sense of awe, uncertainty and expectation which has largely evaporated by the time students arrive later in the year. Deviancy scores as low as those obtained by experienced teachers mean there was on average barely one pupil out of 30 mildly misbehaving during the period of observation. In the case of students, scores between 4 and 10 are obtained when about 3 to 6 pupils out of 30 misbehave.

The general climate even for students, therefore, is one of orderly involvement during the first few lessons, and it is only from the sixth lesson onwards that the level of pupil involvement begins to fall. It is not possible to make too many comparisons with the involvement level of about 60 and deviancy level of around 10 or 11 reported for the sample of student teachers in Chapter 2, because they were based on a whole term, included more lessons with older adolescents and were in large, Midlands comprehensive schools. It may be the case, however, that students on teaching practice enjoy a honeymoon period of about six lessons, though our analysis of observers' reports show that this was less in the few cases where the student's first lesson or two made a negative impression on the class.

Summary

This analysis of 313 lessons given by experienced teachers, BEd and PGCE students at the beginning of the school year and on teaching practice, shows the massive combined effort made by experienced teachers in September to establish a working climate for the whole school year, and the difficulties of students who arrive later when the territory has been staked out, rules and relationships have been developed and procedures established.

Experienced teachers seemed clear in their minds before the year begins how they would conduct themselves. What they described in interview was by and large fulfilled when they were observed in September. Most sought to establish some kind of dominant presence, usually though not always chose to make up their mind about children from their own experience rather than from a scrutiny of pupils' records, tempered any initial harshness with humour, and conveyed to their class that they were firmly in charge, using their eyes, movement and gesture to enhance what they were trying to do. There was a strong moral dimension to some of their classroom rules, and they strove to establish these substantially in the very first lessons.

Student teachers were less certain about their rules and aspirations, PGCE students in particular tending to identify closely with pupils and hoping that rules would become evident as the need arose. At the same time they were conscious of the difficulty they might encounter if they were too informal and were anxious about personal relationships with their classes.

Both student and experienced teachers were able in most cases to secure a high level of pupil involvement with little misbehaviour in their earliest lessons. Teachers were rated more businesslike, confident, warm and friendly than students, were usually more deliberate in their learning of children's names and male teachers in particular made use of humour from quite early in the year.

It would be wrong to infer, however, that the differences between groups described above persisted to the end of teaching practice. We did observe some lessons after the formal study of first encounters was over, but not on a scale or in a manner which would give a proper longer-term account. Much of the early rawness and uncertainty of PGCE students, for example, tends to diminish during the term.

So far our analysis of class management has concentrated on the student or experienced teacher, and pupils have been more in the background. In Chapter 4, therefore, we look specifically at the pupil's-eye view of class management and of some of the teachers who were described in the present chapter.

References

Amidon, E.J. and Flanders, N.A. (1963) *The Role of the Teacher in the Classroom*, Paul S. Amidon and Associates Inc., Minnesota

Argyle, M. (1967) *The Psychology of Interpersonal Behaviour*, Penguin, Harmondsworth

Bantock, G.H. (1965) *Freedom and Authority in Education*, Faber, London

Buckley, N.K. (1977) *An Ethnographic Study of an Elementary School Teacher's Establishment and Maintenance of Group Norms*, PhD dissertation, University of Houston

Duke, D.L. (1978) 'How the Adults in your Schools can cause Student Discipline Problems – and What To Do About It', *American School Board Journal, 165*, 6, 29-30, 46

Eisenhart, M. (1977) 'Maintaining Control: Teacher Competence in the Classroom'. Paper presented at the 76th Annual Meeting of the American Anthropological Association, Houston, Texas, December

Eltis, K.J. (1978) *The Ascription of Attitudes to Pupils by Teachers and Student Teachers*, PhD thesis, Macquarie University, Sydney

Evertson, C.M. and Anderson, L.M. (1978) *Correlates of Effective Teaching*, University of Texas, Austin

Goffman, E. (1971) *The Presentation of Self in Everyday Life*, Penguin, Harmondsworth

Hargreaves, D.H. (1977) 'The Process of Typification in the Classroom: Models and Methods', *British Journal of Educational Psychology, 47*, 274-84

Kelley, H.H. (1950) 'The Warm-cold Variable in First Impressions of People', *Journal of Personality, 18*, 431-9

King, R.A. (1978) *All Things Bright and Beautiful?* Wiley, Chichester

Nash, R. (1973) *Classrooms Observed*, Routledge, London

Ryans, D.G. (1960) *Characteristics of Teachers*, American Council on Education, Washington

Soar, R.S. (1973) *Follow-through Classroom Process Measurement and Pupil Growth*, Florida Educational Research and Development Council, Gainesville

Wood, E.K. (1983) *First Encounters between Teachers and their Classes*, PhD thesis, Exeter University

Woods, P. (1979) *The Divided School*, Routledge, London

Wragg, E.C. (1972) *An Analysis of the Verbal Classroom Interaction between Graduate Student Teachers and Children*, PhD thesis, Exeter University

4 PUPIL APPRAISALS OF TEACHING

E.C. Wragg and E.K. Wood

Whereas manufacturers of soap powder do not hesitate to solicit the views of the users of their product, relatively little educational research has employed pupil appraisals of teaching. The reasons are quite clear: some people believe that youthful consumers are not sufficiently mature to give a proper appraisal of quality or even utility; others are apprehensive about the effects on teacher-pupil relationships if pupils should be allowed to make a judgement about teaching, or even afraid that school discipline might suffer irrevocably if children are publicly permitted to flex their critical muscles.

Kurt Lewin (1943) claimed that children as young as 3 or 4 could be even more sensitive than adults to certain situations, yet a huge survey of 672 studies of teacher effectiveness by Domas and Tiedeman (1950) reported only 7 in which pupil ratings were used. In more recent times there has been some soliciting of pupils' views, but it is still the case that the production of many major new curriculum packages, the raising of the school leaving age, mixed-ability teaching and comprehensive reorganisation were all undertaken with little if any soliciting of pupil opinion.

Perhaps this is understandable. Most children have no experience of schools other than their own, have a restricted picture of what adult life or the next phase of schooling may hold for them, and often tend to favour the familiar. An educational system based entirely on pupil opinion would probably be ultra-conservative.

On the other hand although children of their own accord might never have designed a microelectronics program, there are many who are capable, from their reading and from watching television, of asking why such a subject is not on offer in their own particular school. Whilst few people would advocate basing teaching solely on pupil opinion, it is difficult to justify ignoring it completely, especially when such research as exists reports certain consistent findings.

It has commonly been found that pupils when given a list of teacher characteristics, rate most highly competence in key professional skills. In one of the earliest studies Hollis (1935) analysed the rank order of seven statements about teacher behaviour accorded by over 8,000 pupils. Highest esteem was given to the teacher's ability to explain difficulties patiently, though the format of this particular enquiry does not allow one to infer whether it was the explanation or the patience that was valued.

Taylor (1962) co-ordinated a group of 21 teachers studying part-time for an advanced diploma. Between them they analysed 1,379 essays written by primary and secondary school pupils on 'a good teacher' and 'a poor teacher', and constructed a checklist which was filled in by 897 children. About 40 per cent of their rankings were given to teaching skills and only about 25 per cent to personal qualities.

When Evans (1962) summarised research on pupils' views of teaching, she concluded that preferred personal characteristics included kindness, friendliness, patience, fairness and a sense of humour. They appeared to dislike sarcasm, favouritism, and domineering or excessive punishment.

In more recent times Meighan (1977) and Cohen and Manion (1981) have summarised enquiries into the pupil perspective. Research over the past ten years includes a well-known study by Nash (1976) in which he used a repertory-grid technique with a class of 12 to 13-year-olds. The constructs which emerged concerned discipline, the ability to teach, explaining, degree of interest, fairness and friendliness.

Furlong (1976) studied a single class for two terms, and reported how some of the 15-year-old secondary modern girls in it appraised their teachers and behaved towards them. Even some of the aggressive so-called 'non-academic' members valued teaching skill, and were prepared to learn in the lessons of those able to arouse interest. Gannaway (1976), in a small-scale study of one school, proposed a sequential pupil model of teacher evaluation which began with the question 'can the teacher keep order?' If the answer was 'no' he would be rejected. The model progressed through a further series of yes/no questions such as 'can he have a laugh?' and 'does he understand pupils?' It is difficult to demonstrate that pupil judgements about teachers occur in precisely the order Gannaway formulates, but he mentions characteristics which consistently appear in the literature.

The Present Study

We decided to solicit pupils' views about teachers and teaching in one of the schools which we used during the study of first encounters described in Chapter 3. It was decided to poll pupils' opinions through a questionnaire, and to interview a sample of children about some of the teachers we had observed. The data were collated by Ned Colman as part of his BEd. dissertation.

The school was a six-form-entry city comprehensive high school for 12 to 16-year-olds. It has a very mixed, well-established catchment area, partly drawing on a large, working-class estate, partly on a middle-class, privately owned residential area. The school is well regarded in the community and is one of the more popular choices amongst parents. The head and staff put a high value on both personal care and academic achievement.

A stratified random sample of 200 pupils was selected, 50 from each of the four year groups. Equal numbers of boys and girls were chosen, except in the second and fourth year where there were more girls than boys in the whole year group, so a 30/20 ratio was selected. As pupils come from 8 to 12 middle schools the new entrants are called second years. Details of the sample are given in Table 4.1

Table 4.1: Stratified Random Sample of 200 Pupils

Year	Boys	Girls	Total
2nd	20	30	50
3rd	25	25	50
4th	20	30	50
5th	25	25	50
Total	90	110	200

Each pupil completed a 39-item questionnaire related to some of the areas of concern of the Teacher Education Project. The first three items were in forced-choice format and were to do with first encounters with teachers: how the teacher should introduce himself, how he should dress and how he should behave in his very first lesson.

The next 32 items were all descriptive of teacher behaviour and were a modification of the pupil attitude instrument used by Flanders (1965) in his New Zealand study of teacher influence, pupil attitudes and achievement. They measured on a five-point, Likert-type scale aspects such as teacher enthusiasm, interest, use of praise, humour and teaching skills of various kinds. Items included such statements as 'This teacher would boss you about', 'This teacher would want you to help each other when working', 'This teacher would be enthusiastic in lessons', and 'This teacher would expect high standards' (see Appendix D).

The remaining four items concerned grouping by ability, who should run schools, what size of group was liked for small-group work and preferred ways of learning (using the library, practical work, listening to teacher, work cards, reading a book).

Pupils were given the instruction 'Imagine that the best teacher in the world has been sent to your school (it might be a man or a woman). In all the following questions please answer with this teacher in mind. Please remember that your answers should be about the best teacher in the world.'

Pupils' Views

The 200 questionnaire responses were analysed in a number of different ways. Means and standard deviations were calculated for all the five-point scale items as were product-moment correlations. Factor analysis is commonly used to reduce a large set of correlations and identify a smaller number of significant factors for better understanding of the relationships between sets of measures. A factor analysis was undertaken with rotation to simple structure according to the varimax criterion which maximizes zero and near-zero loadings. In addition, two-way analysis of variance was used to investigate sex and year-group differences.

The answers to the first three items on introductions, dress and style showed that 84 per cent expected the teacher to introduce himself with more than just his name, about half of these preferring details of his teaching and half personal details about interests and hobbies. On the matter of dress 48 per cent preferred casual dress, 33 per cent smart dress and 7 per cent very smart dress, with 12 per cent feeling that dress did not matter. From four different options about style in the very first lesson an overwhelming 75 per cent preferred 'understanding, friendly and firm' rather than the other combinations 'efficient, orderly and businesslike', 'friendly, sympathetic and understanding' or 'firm and serious but fair'.

The means of the 32 five-point scales are most interesting. Scores theoretically may range from 1 (everyone strongly agrees) to 5 (everyone strongly disagrees). The five items which attracted strongest agreement are shown in Table 4.2.

This confirms the findings of some of the enquiries cited above. As in the Hollis (1935) study the ability to explain is most highly valued. Statements in second, third and fifth place seem to stress good sympathetic personal relationships.

Table 4.2: Five Statements Showing Strongest Agreement

Item	Mean score
1. This teacher would explain things clearly	1.46
2. This teacher would call you by your first name	1.61
3. This teacher would help the slower ones catch up in a nice way	1.65
4. This teacher would help you learn a lot in every lesson	1.66
5. This teacher would be a good listener	1.86

At the other end of the spectrum the five statements attracting greatest disagreement shown in Table 4.3 are also illuminating.

Table 4.3: Five Statements Showing Strongest Disagreement

Item	Mean score
1. This teacher would hit you	4.37
2. This teacher would boss you about	4.28
3. This teacher would sometimes be too busy to talk to you	3.71
4. This teacher would let you mark your own tests	3.55
5. This teacher would do something else if that's what the class wants	3.52

What is noticeable here is the pupils' rejections of child-centredness in statements 4 and 5. One would expect the condemnation of physical aggression and an over-authoritarian approach in the two statements in first and second place, though Nash (1976), using the rep-grid technique, reports Scottish children's views which seemed more accepting of corporal punishment. Nevertheless, it always seems disappointing to the liberally minded when pupils appear not to wish to make decisions about their work and its assessment, seeing this as a central part of the teacher's professional job.

Analysis of variance of all the 32 five-point scales produced an astonishing lack of difference between sexes and between year groups. On some items the mean in each of the eight cells (four year groups and two sexes) was almost identical.

Some responses were, however, strikingly different. Older children claimed to be less hostile to being told off publicly, as the means in Table 4.4 show, where the year-group effect is significant at the 0.001 level.

On the question of response to pupils' wishes there was both a sex and a year-group difference, with girls more likely than boys to disagree that a good teacher would do something else if the class wanted (0.05 level) and 4th and 5th years significantly more hostile to this than

2nd and 3rd years (0.01 level) as Table 4.5 shows.

Table 4.4: Responses to Item 12 'This teacher would tell you off in front of the rest of the class'

Year	Boys	Girls
2nd	4.09	3.45
3rd	3.72	3.60
4th	2.99	3.22
5th	2.92	3.00

Table 4.5: Responses to Item 22 'This teacher would do something else if that's what the class wants'

Year	Boys	Girls
2nd	3.00	3.76
3rd	2.96	3.52
4th	3.44	3.53
5th	3.88	4.04

A varimax factor analysis of the 32 five-point scales produced six factors which between them accounted for 42 per cent of the variance. The strongest factor accounted for 14.5 per cent of the variance, and was characterised by interest and enthusiasm, loading on items such as 'This teacher would be interested in what you do outside of school as well as in it', 'This teacher would be enthusiastic in lessons' and 'This teacher would be a good listener'.

On the remaining items there was one very significant finding. When offered a choice between streaming, setting and mixed-ability classes, all of which were explained, 72 per cent opted for setting, 19 per cent for mixed-ability and 9 per cent for streaming. Although the first two years were spent mainly in mixed-ability groups and the final two years were in sets, there was no significant difference between year groups: all heavily favoured setting.

The item on favoured small-group size produced a mean of about 4 with no significant differences between year groups. Girls, however, preferred larger groups (mean 4.22) than boys (mean 3.87) a difference significant at the 0.01 level.

When asked to evaluate on a five-point scale different ways of learning, the rank order was:

1. Practical work	1.89
2. Listening to the teacher	2.29
3. Reading a book or using the library	2.36
4. Work cards	2.91

The questionnaire data provided interesting information about pupils' views of teaching. There is a degree of congruence between the pupils' expressed preference for teachers who are understanding, friendly and firm, and both the teachers' views in interview and their behaviour in the lessons observed and described in Chapter 3, which showed that they tended, on the whole, to establish a climate of businesslike firmness at the beginning of the school year, but with a tempering of warmth and humour.

On the other hand there are important points of difference and some warning signs. The pupils clearly dislike over-bossy and aggressive teachers, and it is the younger children, especially boys of 12 or 13, who are most hostile to being told off in public. Teachers who begin their year in an over-dominant manner with younger groups may not be able to redeem the situation subsequently.

Pupils' responses to the questionnaire items also explain some of the problems experienced by student teachers. It was shown in Chapter 3 that PGCE students in particular identified with pupils, though they were well aware of the difficulties an over-familiar approach might cause. They frequently expressed a wish to accommodate pupils' wishes in their teaching, yet the children's rejection of items such as 'this teacher would let you mark your own tests' and 'this teacher would do something else if that's what the class wants' confirm that considerable negotiation and exploration will be necessary when teachers wish to share decision-making in their classrooms, skills that novice teachers may not possess at the beginning of their career.

Pupils' apparent need for compliance is sometimes difficult for those student teachers with discipline problems to understand. On the one hand, it would seem, they wish to be told what to do, on the other they are not willing, in the lessons of those with poor class control, to do as asked, a paradox which we could only partially explain in Chapters 2 and 3. The pupils' overwhelming endorsement of setting, for example, caused little overt resentment of the school's policy of mixed-ability teaching in the first two years, probably because personal relationships between teachers and children were in general sound.

Interviews With Pupils

The Teacher Education Project ended two years after the first encounters study described in Chapter 3 had begun. The final phase of enquiry in the class management studies was a series of interviews with groups of either two or three pupils, a total sample of 25, about teachers who had been observed during the first encounters study. There were 14 girls and 11 boys in the sample and each group was interviewed for about an hour. The interviewer was one of the present writers, and a semi-structured interview schedule was used. The interviews took place in the school, were informal in manner, and were not tape recorded, the interviewer noting down as accurately as possible what was said. There is a loss of exactitude in this procedure, but pupils are understandably anxious, and may be less than frank if their conversations about their teachers are recorded.

The pupil sample was not a randomly chosen one, but rather a group of second years who had been taught by a sample of the teachers we had observed the year after our fieldwork. No pupil approached refused to co-operate. The semi-structured interview schedule was in three parts. First of all the pupils were invited to recall their very first lesson with each teacher, then they were asked to talk generally about him or her, finally they were shown the four pictures of classroom misbehaviour used in teacher interviews as described in Chapter 3, and asked how each teacher would react if such an incident occurred in his or her lesson. Pupils' reactions to two of the teachers are described, the first was successful in establishing harmonious relationships with his classes, the second was not. Most teachers in the sample in their different ways did secure positive relationships, and the unpopular Mr Baker was one of the very few students or teachers who aroused hostility from the beginning. Pseudonyms are used for both teachers and pupils in the descriptions given below. A fuller account of the interviews can be found in Wood (1983).

Mr Abel

Mr Abel is a science teacher in his mid-thirties. He was described by the observer who saw the first nine lessons with his mixed-ability, second-year class as 'relaxed and pleasant with a slightly disconcerting grin'. In interview he had been extremely precise about what he would do in his first lesson, how he would see the children into the room, give out the books, write his name on the board and spend most of the first lesson on laboratory and classroom rules. When observed he had fulfilled everything he described to the letter. Sixteen statements were elicited for the purpose of verification from his interview as described in Chapter 3, and he accomplished 14 of them in the view of the analyst.

During their interviews all the pupils recalled with remarkable vividness what had taken place. Their account matched in every important

ant respect features recorded by observers:

> 'We did the lab. rules. There were fifteen. They told us what to do and what not to do in the lab . . . We thought of rules like: Don't run in the lab, go in without a teacher, no eating or chewing, tie back long hair, don't suck or blow tubes.' (Alison and Beryl)

> 'He gave us a sheet on lab rules and a blue sheet where we had to spot the mistakes. The rules were that you were not to eat in class; you don't put things near the edge of the table; you don't muck about with the burners; you report accidents; you don't let the chairs stick out; baggage must be under the table; do not run or fool in the lab; don't enter the lab without the teacher's permission; always ask if you're not sure.' (Charles and David)

Mr Abel was keen on lesson and lab organisation, did not like pupils where he could not see them or those who sat with their back to him when he was explaining, and described in interview how he liked to surprise pupils. Science, he felt, was a mixture of excitement, unease and potential danger, and he had to keep pupils on their toes. Part way through the third lesson observed he had demonstrated how to use a fire extinguisher, and sprayed freezing-cold carbon dioxide at two boys who had turned their backs to him. They were temporarily shocked until Mr Abel made a joke of it. Usually Mr Abel's jokes were shared, but three of the girls took a different view as exemplified by the following statement from one of them:

> 'He likes to play tricks on people, especially the girls. He dropped a model of a bird-eating spider in front of me. I shrieked. He does this kind of thing mostly to the girls because he says they need toughening up. They're too soft.' (Elizabeth)

Mr Abel recognised that his unpredictable style might be a little frightening occasionally, and had described in interview how he would diminish this effect with humour, support and mild flirtation. His view of himself was very close to that expressed later by his pupils:

> 'He looks like Bodie in 'The Professionals'. He's sexy. He's not too strict but he can be when you misbehave, like when you break more than two lab rules in any day or when you mess about with chemicals or break the test tubes. He asks those who break them to pay

for them. He shouts then as well. Mr Abel's alright. He's not too strict and he's not too gentle.' (Frances and Gail)

During interviews pupils were shown the picture of pupils splashing water in the lab to which their teachers had reacted during their own interview. Mr Abel had been prompt in his own response to this particular picture:

'He's turning the tap around. I think it calls for an unofficial thick ear. Shock situation, surprise. There are too many people around the bench. The picture is an organisational mess. The fact is that the situation should not have occurred. That boy has a pen in his mouth. He's in trouble.'

The pupils, asked in interview to guess how Mr Abel might react to the situation in the same picture, were astonishingly close to his own reaction:

'Mr Abel would give a detention. You're not allowed to have bags on the table and that girl behind has. He would really shout. He would ask who started it first. That boy chewing his pencil, he'd get it. He'd tell the girl to tie her hair back. He'd say, "You don't come in here to squirt water, back to work." They'd have to clear up. Smashing things is wrong and Mr Abel worries about the cuts.' (Hilary)

Mr Abel used his voice quite deliberately when misbehaviour occurred. 'I'm fortunate to have a deep voice. I can stop someone dead in their tracks by a quick sharp word', he had said in interview. An incident from the sixth lesson observed in his laboratory illustrated this. Early in the lesson he heard a test tube being dropped. 'Oi!' he shouted loudly in contrast to the low-key, benign voice that characterised most of his teaching, 'Did I say get your test tubes yet? Go back to your seats please. Go and stand where you are going to work. Right, one member from each group to fetch the test tubes.' It was the firmness in his voice and the insistence on his procedures being followed that led to compliance.

On another occasion in the eighth lesson observed he again used case law to illustrate his control and to define the limits within which pupils should operate. Two girls entered the classroom during the lesson. One had previously been given permission to go to the toilet. 'Where have you been?' Mr Abel asked in a loud and stern voice. 'To the loo', they replied. 'Where?' he persisted with by now the whole class watching. The girls repeated their answer. 'What both of you? You never go out of the room without permission.' Having established his point Mr Abel went over to the girls within a short time and talked in a very friendly manner with them about their experiment. It seemed a deliberate act on his part.

In interview Peter and Richard amongst others, reacting to the picture of pupils splashing water in the lab, described Mr Abel's loud voice. 'He'd shout at us to stop. 'Oi you − stop it' (imitating Mr Abel's public voice). He'd probably give us a detention.' Alison recalled his friendly humour and ready response to pupils' work:

'We once made a mobile. Mine was very funny. It wasn't good. We both laughed at it. Richard he calls Noddy because he's always nodding his head when he is talking to you. We all think it's funny, so does Richard.'

The girls seemed to know precisely how to handle Mr Abel, what to do, what not to try, and when to flirt back with him. Shown the picture of the girl who refused to move when asked by the teacher, two replied as follows:

Mr Abel would shout and say ' "Come on you've got to move" and she will because it's Mr Abel, because he's nice and a laugh. We wouldn't like to see him cross. He understands us and we want to keep it like that.' (Iris)

'She'd say "Oh sir, please can I stay here. Give us a chance." He would probably let her. She would move if he really wanted her to though.' (Alison and Beryl)

Analysis of the observation data for Mr Abel showed that he was rated extremely high by the observer on confidence, being businesslike, mobility and warmth. In his earliest lessons he also had a very high degree of eye contact with individual pupils. Pupil attention was high and misbehaviour almost non-existent. He knew how he wished to be perceived by his pupils, and they, in turn, apart from an occasional misunderstanding over one of his sudden surprises or jokes, reported a very similar impact to the one he intended.

Mr Abel demonstrated many of the characteristics used by other teachers in the sample to establish benign control: a brisk businesslike manner, high eye contact with individual pupils, quick reaction to the first signs of misdemeanour before it escalated, clearly defined rules about behaviour, devoting much of his first two or three lessons to these, a clear staking-out of the territory over which he had control. His ready humour, use of surprise, and interest in pupils' work, especially after they had been reprimanded, established very positive social relationships with his pupils who showed an incisive understanding of the processes which had been at work when interviewed two years later.

Many of these characteristic pieces of behaviour have been described by other researchers studying the establishment of teacher-pupil relationships. Stenhouse (1967) and Ball (1981) in his study of Beachside Comprehensive have described how children test the limits until the parameters of control are established. In Mr Abel's case any ambiguity was dispelled within the first three lessons, and pupils were clear both at the time and in retrospect what was permitted and what proscribed. Several writers, including Gannaway (1976), Woods (1976) and Willis (1976), have referred to humour and 'having a laugh'. In Mr Abel's case the purpose was not so much for 'being one of the lads' as described by Willis, but sometimes explained by Woods' proposal that a type of gallows humour can permit pupil and teachers an emotional escape from tension, and on other occasions offering a challenge to pupils to operate at a high level of arousal and attentiveness.

All the pupils interviewed were clear about Mr Abel: they knew where they stood, they respected and liked him, and they described his classes with affection. They were equally united in their view of Mr Baker, but this time for quite different reasons.

Mr Baker

Mr Baker was an older teacher whose reputation had preceded his first entry to his classes. Even pupils from the primary feeder schools knew about him and looked forward to their first encounter with a mixture of fear and excitement, as these pupils recalled in interview:

> 'Everyone warned us about him. We knew all about it before we got here. Our brothers and sister are in the fourth year and they told us what it would be like.' (Janet and Kate)
> 'Nobody likes Mr Baker. We stood outside the library door and waited. I was excited to see him.' (Hilary)

Mr Baker was observed teaching his first eight humanities lessons with a class of 13-year-olds. His own view of first encounters had been very clearly expressed in interview. He stressed that he would be firm but consistent:

'I try to get over that you are God, the paternal figure. You need to get them screwed down a bit. It takes about two months to get them in order. When they arrive they stand outside the door. I would stand in the door and say "Fill up from the front of the class first." Then they'd fill up the next row till it's all squared up. I look at the room and put their names on my plan. I might get them to sit in alphabetical order. Afterwards I put them in order of merit. It's a good idea to get people to sit according to their ability. I think mixed-ability teaching is inefficient. I would say, "You call me Mr Baker or sir, and I'll call you by your christian name. I'm the boss and I give the orders.'

Whereas Mr Abel explained his classroom rules and even invited pupils to devise their own on occasion, Mr Baker saw no room for pupils to express a view or have rules explained. Many of the analogies he used in interview were expressed in military language. He spoke of his 'forays' into the classroom, children's 'mutinies', and felt that sarcasm was one of his chief 'weapons' in the 'classroom war '. He was at odds with his colleagues, whom he thought soft and with poor standards. In terms of the distinction made by Woods (1979) between social control and situational control, where the former describes teachers' obligation to society to raise well-behaved citizens, and the latter is concerned with handling day-to-day problems which occur in a particular classroom, Mr Baker saw himself as responsible for social control, a front-line defender of standards not just in the school but in society at large. To achieve this he was prepared to provoke conflict:

'I believe in confrontation. It is an attempt to maintain standards. Most people just operate a policy of containment. To do this is just to cause problems for others. You have to remember that to clash with you is to clash with the school, the culture and ultimately with society. If they get away with it in school then they will end up as troublemakers in the unions and responsible for wildcat strikes.'

His first few lessons were punctuated by lengthy monologues about pupils' behaviour saturated with statements about the importance of authority and obedience. Pupils tended to listen in silence and then resume their minor misdemeanors when he eventually ceased. In his fifth lesson a pupil was thought to be chewing and his ensuing monologue reveals the general tone of such addresses to the class.

'Are you eating? Well stop moving your jaws. Sit still. Some of you should be in strait-jackets. If you don't work then you'll have to copy out of the book. You are going to conform to my standards which are not in any way abnormal. In this life there are some people who want to work, there will be six million unemployed in the 1980s – none of you has convinced me that you are in any way employable. I'm in charge here. I can enforce it and I will. It's as simple as that (bangs fist on table). Sooner or later someone will get physically hurt. Don't push me too far. We're all human, boys and girls alike. You are my family. It's my legal right to punish you. Don't forget that.'

The pupils' response to Mr Baker was almost universally negative. They all commented on his lack of humour and the unremitting tedium of his lessons. This confirmed the classroom data collected during observation where the ratings of the observer were the lowest of any person, teacher or student, on the stimulating-dull scale, lower than most on warmth, and, despite his apparently firm manner, lower than many teachers on pupil attention to the task and higher on pupil misbehaviour. He was rated high on confidence, but this reveals the frailty of rating scales in the appraisal of teaching. Analysis of critical events and transcripts of some of his exchanges with pupils seem to show that, underneath the rhetoric about himself being in sole charge, lurks a considerable anxiety about loss of control and lack of rapport for which he attributes blame to the pupils and the corruptness of his colleagues.

His lack of any rapport with the pupils was confirmed in all the interviews with them, as was the message he had given them about their likely unemployment:

'He gave out the books. He told us we were going to go through this book very fast. I didn't like it at first but you need to do well at school to get a good job so I got used to it later. Every day I was scared. He was firm and never laughed with us. He never forgot anything. I told my mum I wouldn't get used to him and I didn't. He didn't get better. He thinks he's soft on us!' (Mary)

'He's too strict. He says he treats us like he was taught at school. He never does anything interesting. He makes the book a lot harder. He leaves the interesting pages out. He skips them and then goes back to the beginning again. He goes over and over the boring bits.' (Stephen and Tom)

One or two pupils who were highly motivated were resigned rather than hostile to a certain degree of pain in their learning, were prepared to consider the possibility that effective teachers may not always be popular or good-humoured and vice versa. Even they, however, were easily dissuaded by their colleagues as the following conversation between William and Andy during their interview reveals:

William: He may be a good teacher, but pupils do not find his methods enjoyable. In fact they leave something to be desired. It all seems boring.
Andy: We learned it thoroughly though, didn't we? I mean we went over and over it much more than the other classes did.
William: Yes, but they all did much better than us in the test. It didn't do us much good, did it?

The interviewer recorded 'gloomy acceptance' of William's point by both Andy and Caroline, who were being interviewed together.

When the pupils looked at the pictures used in the interview there was again an astonishing concurrence between what Mr Baker had said and their own reactions. When considering the picture of a girl being asked to move by the teacher and refusing, Mr Baker's response was that it offered a confrontation he would relish:

'I have dragged another girl across five desks in this situation. I'd say, "Go to the year head." If she refused I'd dispatch another child to fetch the year head. You could push it to the pont of confrontation.'

All the pupils used the same kind of language to predict what would happen in Mr Baker's lessons if someone refused to move. There was no dissent from the view that his reaction would be quick and aggressive:

'He would shout. He'd go mad, out of this world. He'd drag her to the next place. He's too strict. He has no sense of humour.' (Charles and David)

'He'd kick up a stink. He'd kill her. He'd give her everything – in at break, dinnertime to do jobs. He'd have blown his top, grabbing her by the ear and picking her up.' (Graham)

Whereas Mr Abel had a picture of himself that was close to that of his pupils and field notes made by the observer of his lessons, Mr Baker's view of himself is not supported by others. Indeed, of his intentions stated in interview fewer than half were fulfilled in the view of the analyst who scrutinised lesson accounts. He saw himself as consistent, yet his reaction to pupils was erratic:

'He told me that if I made a mistake to correct it underneath. So I did that. When he took our books in he forgot that he had said that and he did a line under it and shouted at me and told me that I should have done it on top. He changes his mind.' (Stephen)

He also said that he liked some laughter though not too much, but laughter was absent from his lessons and several said that if pupils smiled he told them to stop smiling. One expressed it much more strongly:

'If anyone laughs or talks then they have to stand up for the rest of the lesson. He said, "Smile and work well and you'll be alright." I tell you if I saw Mr Baker smile then the next thing you would see would be a pink elephant.' (Graham)

It is beyond the scope of this short chapter to explain why Mr Baker behaves as he does. The simple explanation that he is out of touch with modern youth will not suffice. There are plenty of teachers whose own ideology is not that of their pupils who are nevertheless successful at working with them. Despite his insistence that he stood for the defence of high standards of work and behaviour he achieved success in neither. Although he aroused fear in some children his lessons actually became the war game in which he saw himself engaged. His seeking of confrontation, belittling of pupils and inconsistency provoke the very disobedience he seeks to avoid. Even apprehensive pupils described how they joined in the vengeful conspiracy to frustrate him:

'I once threw something on to his desk. He wasn't sure who had thrown it. He didn't do anything. He just glared at me. I like getting him stewed up. I don't know why. It's fun, but sometimes he frightens me too.' (Alison)

These two brief descriptions of Mr Abel and Mr Baker do not permit many generalisations about how pupils perceive their teachers, or how other teachers establish relationships with their classes. What they do show is that pupils have a clear and consistent understanding of classroom events which often coincides with that of their fellows. They tended to give the same view of each teacher they discussed with very few dissenting voices. They also understood how teachers define or fail to define rules of behaviour, knew exactly how their teachers would respond, even in some cases using identical words and metaphors to those used by the teachers in their interviews.

They also understand how case law is used by teachers to establish limits, and are able to make inferences, not so much from the teacher's stated intentions, but rather from his or her interaction with individuals. Furthermore, this study confirms many of the findings of earlier enquiries. The pupils in the sample liked teachers who were firm but fair, consistent, stimulating, interested in individuals and had a sense of humour, and they disliked those few who showed the polar opposite of these characteristics. Although there have not been too many published studies of pupils' views of their teachers, the results of those available are remarkably consistent.

Thus, the first impression teachers make on their pupils when they encounter each other for the first time is crucial. Those who wish to make a firm start and establish control should recognise that, whilst pupils can see the need for and even expect such a beginning, if they are over-bossy, fail to temper their authority with humanity, they may never secure a positive working relationship with their class. Part of Mr Abel's success with his pupils was that he was quick to work alongside pupils after he had needed to reprimand them. For teachers who wish to involve pupils in sharing decision-making from the beginning, it is also clear that this is often contrary to their expectation and may even confuse and irritate them, so considerable thought must be given to explaining and winning support for this way of working.

References

Ball, S. (1981) *Beachside Comprehensive*, Cambridge University Press
Cohen, L. and Manion, L. (1981) *Perspectives on Classrooms and Schools*, Holt, Rinehart & Winston, London

Domas, S.J. and Tiedeman, D.V. (1950) 'Teacher Competence: an Annotated Bibliography', *Journal of Experimental Education, 19*, 101-218

Evans, K.M. (1962) *Sociometry and Education*, Routledge, London

Flanders, N.A. (1965) *Teacher Influence, Pupil Attitudes and Achievement*, US Office of Education, Research Monograph 12

Furlong, V. (1976) 'Interaction Sets in the Classroom' in M. Stubbs and S. Delamont (eds), *Explorations in Classroom Observation*, Wiley, London

Gannaway, H. (1976) 'Making Sense of School' in M. Stubbs and S. Delamont (eds), *Explorations in Classroom Observation*, Wiley, London

Hollis, A.W. (1935) *The Personal Relationship in Teaching*, MA thesis, Birmingham University

Lewin, K. (1943) 'Psychology and the Process of Group Living', *Journal of Social Psychology, 17*, 113-31

Meighan, R. (1977) 'The Pupil as Client: the Learner's Experience of Schooling', *Educational Review, 29*, 123-35

Nash, R. (1976) *Teacher Expectations and Pupil Learning*, Routledge, London

Stenhouse, L. (ed.) (1967) *Discipline in Schools*, Pergamon, Oxford

Taylor, P.H. (1962) 'Children's Evaluations of the Characteristics of the Good Teacher', *British Journal of Educational Psychology, 32*, 258-66

Willis, P. (1976) 'The Class Significance of School Counter Culture' in M. Hammersley and P. Woods (eds), *The Process of Schooling*, Routledge and Open University Press, London

Wood, E.K. (1983) *First Encounters between Teachers and Their Classes*, PhD thesis, Exeter University

Woods, P. (1976) 'Having a Laugh: an Antidote to Schooling' in M. Hammersley and P. Woods (eds) *The Process of Schooling*, Routledge and Open University Press, London

—— (1979) *The Divided School*, Routledge, London

5 ASKING QUESTIONS

G.A. Brown and R. Edmondson

Questions are as old as speech itself, and the use of questions in teaching is at least as old as classrooms. Studies of questions may be traced from pre-Socratic philosophers through till modern times. In the nineteenth century questions were much discussed by school inspectors (Macnamara, 1980) and in the twentieth century there have been several studies of questioning. The first of the twentieth-century studies was probably by Stevens (1912), who reported that teachers in her sample asked about 395 questions per day. Similar results have been reported by Corey (1940), Floyd (1960), Flanders (1970) and Wragg (1973). Generally speaking, it seems that teachers spend about 30 per cent of their time asking questions. In other words they may ask about 100 questions per hour. There are wide variations in rates of asking questions, depending on the subject, the ages and abilities of the pupils and the experience of the teachers.

In this chapter we do not propose to review all the research literature on questioning. Useful reviews may be found in Gall (1970), Turney *et al.* (1973, 1975), Hargie (1978), Wragg (1980) and Hargie, Dickson and Saunders (1981), and guidelines on asking questions in classrooms may be found in Taba (1966), Brown (1978) and Kerry (1982). Instead, we propose to explore some of the problems underlying the study of questions, to discuss some of the relevant research, and to describe the findings from a small study of teachers' questions which was carried out as part of the Teacher Education Project. The study was concerned with the questions teachers ask and their reasons for asking them. Thirty-six teachers drawn from five schools and representing all subject areas, were invited to complete a booklet on questions and tactics and sequences of questions.

There were 11 teachers of English, 9 of science and mathematics, 4 of second languages and 4 of history and geography. The remainder were from art, craft, home economics and PE. They were asked to provide examples of questions phrased in the way they used them with first- or second-year secondary classes. Examples of questions, reasons given and to whom addressed were collected as well as questions to quicker learners and slower pupils. The sample was also asked to offer comments on teaching quicker and slower pupils and suggestions on questions and questioning to student teachers.

The teachers' responses to our questions provide the framework of this chapter. The responses also provided us with data to explore. In no sense do we claim that the data we present are a definitive account of the questions teachers ask. The results should, instead, be regarded as a set of tentative observations and hypotheses based in large measure upon teachers' own reports of their use of questions.

What is a Question?

At first glance questions are easy to define. They are merely requests for information. In practice they are not so easy to distinguish. Consider, for example, the two statements which are provided as examples of questions by teachers in the sample,

'Put up your hands if you know why we count in tens?'
'How are you getting on Gary?'

The first is expressed in command form, yet it contains an implicit question. The second is expressed in question form, yet it contains an implicit command. Which is a question?

Statements expressed with inflections may be used as questions:

'You are *sure* that Brisbane is the capital of Queensland?'
'The answer is twenty-*four*?'

and occasionally a statement without inflections may be used deliberately as an implicit question. 'I watched "Brideshead Revisited" yesterday . . .' Such statements may evoke responses and questions in discussion classes, provided that the pupils feel secure enough to respond. Grunts, gestures, facial expressions and even physical contact may be used as questions. To complicate matters further, can one decide whether a question is a question by examining only the intentions of the teacher? If a question does not evoke an answer, is it a question? The question 'What is anaphoric etic pronominalisation?' is likely to evoke stunned silence from most first-year pupils. If the teacher intended someone else to answer the question and no one did, was the question a question?

A way out of this impasse might appear to be to consider the answers received. If the answers received to a question are incoherent or irrelevant, one might say the question was incoherent to the pupil. On the other hand it may have been answered incoherently because the pupils' intentions were to disrupt teaching. A related difficulty is that the teacher may ask a question beyond the level of most pupils, yet one knowledgeable pupil answers it. Does the pupil's answer then set the level of the question asked, or is the level estimated by other means? Clearly there are dangers in using intentions, in using pupils' answers, and in assuming that a pupil's answer is representative of the whole class.

We raise these issues here to remind readers that deciding what counts as a question in the classroom may be less easy than first appears. The operational definition that one adopts influences the data collected and the results obtained from studies of questioning – or indeed any topic. Our working definition of a question in the classroom is:

Any statement intended to evoke a verbal response.

We therefore do not attempt to distinguish between commands requiring verbal responses and questions, but we do separate questions from commands involving other responses such as, 'Would you mind shutting up?'

In the survey reported in this chapter we asked teachers to provide examples of their questions, and thereby adopted their implicit definitions of a question. Phenomenological approaches are sometimes useful for avoiding problems of definition. But as one teacher wrote in the 'open comments' sections of the survey,

I consider it almost impossible to define questioning. The techniques change with the mood of the teachers and class. The ability level, the subject, the personality of the child, the time of day, where the lesson is being held etc., influence the questions we ask.

Why Ask Questions?

Granted that questions are statements intended to evoke verbal responses, it seems appropriate to consider why teachers ask questions. Turney (1973) lists twelve functions and these are shown in Figure 5.1. Pate and Bremer (1967) asked 190 elementary school teachers to each provide reasons for asking questions. In their statements 69 per cent emphasised the use of questions to check understanding and knowledge to aid teaching, 54 per cent were concerned with diagnosing pupils' difficulties, 47 per cent stressed the recall of facts, and only 10 per cent stressed the use of questions to encourage pupils to think. Thanarrootoo (1981) asked 25 experienced teachers why they asked questions and when they asked pupils questions. All the teachers indicated that they asked questions to gain information, but they asked questions of pupils either to test knowledge or maintain control.

Figure 5.1: Functions of Questions

To arouse interest and curiosity concerning a topic
To focus attention on a particular issue or concept
To develop an active approach to learning
To stimulate pupils to ask questions of themselves and others
To structure a task in such a way that learning will be maximised
To diagnose specific difficulties inhibiting pupil learning
To communicate to the group that involvement in the lesson is expected, and that overt participation by all members of the group is valued
To provide an opportunity for pupils to assimilate and reflect on information
To involve pupils in using an inferred cognitive operation on the assumption that this will assist in developing thinking skills
To develop reflection and comment by pupils on the responses of other members of the group, both pupils and teacher
To afford an opportunity for pupils to learn vicariously through discussion
To express a genuine interest in the ideas and feelings of the pupils

Source: Turney (1973)

As Delamont (1976) puts it,

> It is rare to demand of people . . . 'How do you spell rhododendron?' . . . unless you really do not know the answers. Cross-questioning, checking up and interrogation are rude in everyday life, but the staple of classroom life. (pp. 102-3)

In other words, teachers have different intentions when asking pupils questions and when asking others questions. Role demands shape intentions.

Reasons for Asking Questions

The specific reason for asking a particular question at a particular time is also relevant here. We asked the sample of teachers to provide us with a set of five questions they had asked in a lesson that day, and then to provide the reasons for asking them. We developed a classification system of reasons from their responses and used this to code the reasons given. The classification system and the results are shown in Figure 5.2. In effect the system is a summary of the reasons given by the teachers; it is not a set of mutually exclusive categories.

The most common reasons were encouraging thought, checking understanding, gaining attention, revision and management. The teachers who provided samples of questions from high ability classes used 'G' (gain attention) and 'U' (understanding) most frequently. Teachers of medium-ability classes reported more checking (Ch) questions and revision (R) questions, whereas teachers of low-ability classes tended to stress understanding (U) and management (M). Teachers of mixed-ability classes tended to stress understanding, gaining attention, to move towards teaching point, management and revision.

Figure 5.2: Teachers' Reasons for Asking Specific Questions

		N
U:	encouraging thought, understanding of ideas, phenomena, procedures and values	33
Ch:	checking understanding, knowledge and skills	30
G:	gaining attention to task. To enable teacher to move towards teaching points. In the hope of eliciting a specific and obscure point to enable the teacher to move towards a teaching point. As a 'warm-up' activity for pupils	28
R:	review, revision, recall, reinforcement of recently learnt point. Reminder of earlier procedures	23
M:	management. Settling down. To stop calling out by pupils. To direct attention to teacher or text. To warn of precautions	20
T:	specifically to teach whole class through pupil answers	10
J:	to give everyone a chance to answer	10
BP:	ask bright pupil to encourage others	4
D:	to draw in shyer pupils	4
Pr:	probe children's knowledge after critical answers. Re-direct questions to pupil who asked or to other pupils	3
O:	to allow expressions of feelings, views and empathy	3
Ø:	unclassifiable, unreadable, incoherent	2

Note: This is a classification of the reasons given by the teachers. If a teacher said 'To check understanding and knowledge' it was assigned to Ch. It does not follow that a teacher's statement is exclusive of other categories, nor that the reasons the teacher gave are the only reasons.

Amongst the English teachers in the sample the most common reasons were gaining attention and management, whereas for mathematicians and scientists the most common reasons were checking understanding and encouraging thought. The practical arts and second-language teachers gave more revision and checking reasons, whereas history and geography teachers provided more encouraging understanding and gaining attention. On the basis of this small sample the evidence suggests that teachers' reasons for asking questions, not surprisingly, vary according to the subject being taught and the class.

A teacher's reasons for asking a specific question are not always discernible in the content of the question. For example, one teacher asked the question 'What are we trying to do when writing descriptively?' His reason for asking it was 'I ask such a question to a boy I know will answer well as an illustration to the others. I then might ask others'. Other teachers provided instances of questions which as far as content was concerned were to encourage thought, but in fact were used to regain attention.

Some teachers also used questions ostensibly concerned with management to encourage pupils to think about their actions. 'Why did you hide Sharon's purse, Dean?' The reason given for asking this question was 'I want him to consider his motives', not as one might expect 'to reprove or reprimand him'.

It seems then that questions asked and reasons given are not always congruent, and one should be cautious about drawing inferences from questions uttered. The reasons given may reflect the teacher's perception of the individual pupil or the class, as well as the underlying teaching objectives.

It is also likely that questions are multiply determined, that is to say that there may be many reasons for asking a question of a particular pupil or class. Furthermore, the reasons given for asking a question may not be *the* reason. Who is to decide: the teacher, the observers or the pupils? How can we know? Ultimately, perhaps, there is no such thing as a 'true' account of a classroom event.

Classifying Questions

Questions may be classified in terms of the *mode* of delivery, such as threatening, neutral, encouraging; according to *target*, whether to particular individuals, groups or the whole class; in terms of the degree of *clarity* of the question and, according to the *type* of question asked, whether the question is primarily cognitive, affective or procedural. In addition there are the various tactics of questions, such as prompts, probes, leading questions and double-barrelled questions (see Brown, 1978).

Every system of classifying questions presents problems to its user. What may appear to be a neutral question to an observer may feel threatening to the recipient of the question. A question stated ostensibly to the whole class may be directed at a particular pupil. An unclear question to an observer may be perfectly clear to a participant and vice versa. A question may have the form of an affective question, yet require a pupil to think deeply.

Two consecutive questions may be thought to be connected. One of the teachers gave these two consecutive questions. 'What is the sound?' 'What is the matter?' The second question was not a question on physical materials through which sound may be transmitted, but a management question. A question may appear to require thought, but may require recall only because the pupil asked had already thought out the answer.

The complexities of classifying questions have not prevented researchers or teachers from attempting to use their classifications to study classroom discourse. The most common classification systems are 'open-closed' and 'recall-thought'. Open questions permit a wide range of responses including usually the expression of feelings, empathy, intuitions and values. 'What would happen to us in Britain if there were no bridges?' is an example of an open question. Closed questions have one correct or 'best' answer or one from a narrow range of responses. Barnes (1969) suggests a third category in the open-closed dimension: the 'pseudo-question', which is apparently open, but which is used where the teacher is seeking one particular reply. One teacher in our sample provides evidence for extending the concept of the 'pseudo-question' to closed questions, in which the one obviously correct reply to a question is rejected in favour of the less obvious alternative. The question was 'What time do we leave school?' The teacher reported that after asking the question five times with a low-ability group she got the answer she wanted: '16.00 hours' (not 4 o'clock). She was lucky.

Recall questions require pupils to recall existing information, whereas thought questions require pupils to use their existing information to create new information. Recall questions are the most common type of questions asked by teachers.

Generally speaking, over 60 per cent of teachers' questions are concerned with the recall of facts (see Gall, 1970; Hargie, 1978). The reasons for this are not hard to find. Information has to be known before it can be applied; curricular objectives and examinations often stress factual content, and to ask higher level questions requires preparation, thought and perhaps training. Not surprisingly, the evidence on the use of thought questions and subsequent pupil achievement is mixed, (Rosenshine, 1971; Dunkin and Biddle, 1974; Turney 1973). In so far as there is a trend it is that higher-order questions and the use of probing questions can raise the level of class discussion but not necessarily performance in examinations. This may be because examinations are testing low-level skills, and because higher-order questions have a differential effect upon pupils of different abilities. It is also likely that questions demanding complex types of explaining are likely to yield incoherent answers, thereby generating confusion. Thought questions require thought by the teacher as well as by the pupils. Wragg (1980) summarised research into questioning by saying that for every five questions asked, three required data recall, one was managerial, and one provoked higher-order thinking.

The open-closed and recall-thought continua are not identical nor are they distinct. A recall question may permit several responses; a thought question may have one best answer or many. Barnes (1969) attempted to avoid the problems of overlapping continua by using the categories 'factual', 'reasoning', 'open but non-reasoning', and 'social' including control. He too observed in his study that 'Since most questions in the sample were closed-ended, pupils were seldom invited to think about, to generate new sequences of thought, to explore implications.'

The most widely adopted system for classifying cognitive questions is that of Bloom (1956). His major categories are 'recall', 'comprehension', 'application', 'analysis', 'synthesis', 'evaluation'. These categories represent, roughly, a hierarchy or pyramid of question types. Whilst his general classification is a useful guide, one should be cautious in using his, or indeed anyone's system of classifying questions. These remarks apply also to the system described in Figure 5.3.

The primary reason for caution is that what may be one type of question in one context may be another type in another context. The question 'What do you think of Proust?' may require the use of evaluative skills by a lower-sixth-former; it may require only recall by an undergraduate who has just taken finals. Furthermore, 'What do you think of Proust?' and 'What do you think of eggs for breakfast?' might both be classed as evaluative questions but, for most of us, Proust is harder than eggs.

The Problem of Classifying Questions

These observations may appear frivolous, but there is a deep problem underlying them: the problem of classification in context. The problem may be stated thus: How can one compare data from different contexts when the classification system itself varies in different contexts? In so far as the system remains constant across contexts then one can make generalisations. In so far as it is context-dependent one cannot legitimately make generalisations — but one can, of course, make legitimate observations about the specific context.

This problem is at the heart of the controversies between phenomenologists and experimentalists, and between those who prefer case studies and those who prefer surveys. Indeed, the problem may be at the root of literary and scientific modes of knowing.

We do not pretend to have solved this problem. We raise it here because it is one of the central questions in classroom research, and because it is crucial in the problem of classifying questions.

Our system of classifying questions is given in Figure 5.3. It is based partly on the work of Bloom (1956), Tisher (1970) and Smith and Meux (1970), but it is also rooted firmly in the responses given by the sample of teachers.

Figure 5.3: Types of Questions

Cognitive level
1. Data recall including recall of task, procedures, knowledge, values. Naming. Observing. Classifying. Reading aloud. Providing known definitions
2. Simple deductions based usually on data provided. Comparing. Providing simple descriptions and interpretations. Providing examples of principles given
3. Providing reasons, causes, motives or hypotheses which do not appear to have been taught in the lesson
4. Problem solving. Sequences of reasoning
5. Evaluating a topic, set of values or one's own work

Speculative, affective, management
O Speculative, intuitive guesses, creative, open
F Encouraging expression of feelings and empathy
M Management of class, groups, individuals, including directing pupils' attention, control, checking that task is understood, seeking compliance

The system divides questions into cognitive levels or into speculative (O), affective (F) and management questions. The system was developed from the samples of questions provided by the teachers, and then used also to classify their samples of questions to fast and slow learners and to the sequences of questions.

Frequencies of Question Types

Table 5.1 sets out the distribution of questions according to subject groups. Sixty seven per cent of all questions were of types 1 and 2. Less than 20 per cent required complex responses, and the remaining 13 per cent were concerned with speculation, feelings or management. Whilst this tendency to ask relatively simple questions was apparent in teachers of all subjects, it seems slightly less true of arts subjects than of science or practical subjects. A striking exception to this generalisation of arts teachers were the questions asked by second-language teachers who tended to demand only type-1 responses. This is likely to be because second-language teachers are more concerned with basic linguistic competence. Hence, a different system of classifying second-language questions may be required to reveal their approaches to questioning as evolved in the Project's subject-specialist booklet by Partington and Luker (Appendix A).

Table 5.1: Types of Questions and Subjects

Type	1	2	3	4	5	O	M	F	Total
Subject									
English	13	10	7	2	2	2	6	2	44
Foreign languages	13	4	—	1	1	—	—	—	19
History/Geography	6	10	4	1	3	—	—	1	25
Practical/arts	19	6	2	2	1	—	6	—	36
Maths	22	7	4	1	1	1	4	—	40
Science	5	3	3	—	—	—	2	—	13
Total	78	40	20	7	8	3	18	3	177

The table of results of subject and type of question also raises a further problem of classifying questions. We grouped history and geography together, as most people, except historians and geographers, tend to do. However, it is likely that in a detailed survey of questions across subjects there would be marked differences between all subjects in the curriculum. In other words we are suggesting that every subject is likely to have its own characteristic modes of questioning.

The comparison of types of question against type of class suggests there were no major differences in questions asked according to ability.

Mixed and middle-ability classes had similar question distributions. The high-ability classes did receive fewer level-1 and level-2 questions and marginally more levels-3 to 5 questions than the other classes. More management questions were provided by teachers of middle, mixed and low-ability classes than of high-ability classes. Evaluative questions were more common in the low or mixed-ability classes than in the high or middle-ability classes. However, the numbers involved in the sample are small, so one should be wary about generalising to other contexts.

Table 5.2: Types of Questions and Classes

Class ability	Type of question								
	1	2	3	4	5	O	M	F	Total
High	4	5	3	1	0	0	1	2	16
Middle	35	11	6	3	1	1	5	1	63
Low	19	9	4	1	4	1	6	0	44
Mixed	20	15	7	2	3	1	6	0	54
Total	78	40	20	7	8	3	18	3	177

There appeared to be no discernible relationship between the target (class, groups, individual) and the type of questions asked. What was interesting was that the first question provided by 35 of the 36 teachers was at level 1.

The other teacher commenced his samples with a level-2 question. The patterns of the questions provided suggests that teachers store sub-routines or sequences of questions on topics which they can then generate in different contexts. This notion of stored sub-routines might be worth pursuing by those interested in teachers' cognitive processes in the classroom.

Questions to Bright and Slower Pupils

We asked the teachers also to provide us with samples of questions they might use with quick learners and slower pupils and with a general comment on the differences. Table 5.3 summarises the results.

As one might expect when asked questions on fast and slow learners, the sample provided proportionally more type-1 and type-2 questions for slower learners and more 3, 4, 5 and 'O's for fast learners. However, as one history teacher observed, 'My aims in teaching them (quick and slower pupils) are the same. It's just that one has to take longer on the

Table 5.3: Quick and Slower Learners

Subject	Quick									Slower								
	1	2	3	4	5	O	M	F	Total	1	2	3	4	5	O	M	F	Total
English	2	5	2	6	3	2	0	0	20	10	9	1	0	1	1	0	1	23
Foreign languages	0	5	0	0	1	2	0	0	8	2	9	0	0	0	0	0	0	11
History/geography	1	2	8	1	3	0	0	0	15	4	6	3	0	1	1	0	0	15
Practical/arts	2	6	3	4	4	2	0	0	21	14	3	1	0	1	1	0	0	20
Maths	0	4	1	4	0	0	0	0	9	3	6	0	8	0	0	0	0	17
Science	1	6	0	0	1	1	0	0	9	4	3	0	0	0	2	0	0	9
Total	6	28	14	15	12	7	0	0	82	37	36	5	8	3	5	0	1	95

Total 177

early stages with slower pupils'. His view was shared by three other teachers, and it is reminiscent of Taba's (1966) observation that one has to extend children's learning at one level before lifting it to the next.

The comments on teaching quick learners and slower pupils contained many suggestions and observations which may be of interest to young teachers as well as to researchers. Examples of the comments are given in Figure 5.4. Much of the advice offered for slow learners may well apply to quick learners and vice versa. Involvement, motivation, confidence and the use of concrete examples are more frequently mentioned in teaching slower pupils, whereas deeper, thoughtful approaches are mentioned more frequently for quicker learners. Open questions are suggested for use with both quick and slower pupils and leading questions for use with slower pupils. One of the teachers commented that 'We "place" lower kids and don't stretch them. Stretch them with a bit of help and some guarantee of success'.

All the examples of questions provided were of type 1. Reality and rhetoric may not always be congruent. Another teacher provided a sensible reminder about quicker learners. 'But do remember they are not *that* bright. They need encouragement too, so don't use language and ideas which are well beyond them.' The terms 'quicker learners' and 'slower pupils' may themselves have contributed to the differences in questions and comments provided by the sample. There is a wealth of evidence on the effects of question phrasing on answers received (see Hargie *et al.*, 1981). For example, in a study of eye-witness accounts, two groups of subjects were asked, 'How fast was the car going when it *smashed*?' and, 'How fast was the car going when it collided?' The estimates of speed were significantly different. Sometimes one cannot avoid asking questions involving value-laden terms. If one does ask them, one should bear in mind that the answers evoked are only as good as the questions asked.

Tactics of Questions

We asked teachers ten questions (A-3) on tactics of questioning. Five required responses ranging on a five-point scale from 'strongly agree' to 'strongly disagree', and five required them to make estimates of frequency of usage. The results are shown in Table 5.4.

Most teachers agreed that teachers should nominate pupils to answer and to use rephrasing rather than redirection. They were less certain about using other pupils to correct a pupil's answer: they tended to disagree with the view that teachers should know the answers to questions

Figure 5.4: Teaching Quicker and Slower Pupils

Quicker Learners	Slower Pupils
I use more complex open free-er questions (English)	Use revision questions not only to make sure they have not forgotten, but to create a sense of well being that they know and are getting praise for knowing (English)
Be aware of danger of boredom and frustration. Give everyone a chance. Set and mark follow-up work carefully (English)	Use specific concrete experience and carefully planned questions to keep them encouraged. Use leading questions to aim to get them to same place as brighter ones (English)
I have questions here which only fantastic, bright geniuses can answer. They like this and usually rise to the challenge (French)	They must feel involved and not get the impression that they are being fed questions for the stupid. The questions should be difficult enough to provide sense of achievement, but not too difficult to discourage. Success is important to maintain involvement (French)
Shock them with apparently impossible questions so they are forced to think and have the pleasure of achievement. Widen outlook. Get them to look at work as a series of problems to be solved. Remember, some problems transcend age and ability barriers (art)	Use step-by-step approach. Use question/answer as a game. Teach via entertainment. Instil confidence. In art something to be said for asking fewer questions. The medium is often the answer (art)
Use simple questions but go deeper. Don't ask too challeng-ing questions too quickly. Remember able children need success and encouragement as well, but let them go off at tangents and explore ideas (science)	Simple questions — simple answers. Use reiteration and rephrasing. Break question into parts. Suggest one or two probable answers in your question (science)
	They prefer to do and talk rather than think and write. Bear this in mind . . . (craft)
Explain more abstract concepts. Be precise and accurate. Use sequences of questions to show logical development (maths)	Explain patterns underlying methods. Make some concepts not cluttered with difficult numbers. Use concrete examples, simple step-by-step approaches (maths)

Figure 5.4: (contd) Teaching Quicker and Slower Pupils

Quicker Learners	Slower Pupils
Expect recently acquired knowledge to be more retained by brighter pupils (French)	Ask open-ended questions which most pupils can answer. Direct some at individuals you know have special interests (French)
Ask for more reasons. Ask them to apply their knowledge (German)	Ask them questions which narrow down alternatives. Is it . . . or . . . Don't teach differently just take longer over it (German)
Ask deeper questions and more open questions — but this can be overdone. Get them to organise evidence and factors. I try to make them realise there are causes and effects beyond the obvious (history)	Use simple language. Include answers in the question or lead the pupil. Help them to realise they can get the right answer and spot their own mistakes. Get some idea of what they already know. Use questions to build up a picture of the facts (history)
I mixed-ability classes ask bright pupils so they can lead slow pupils. But bright pupils are often shy and less forthcoming (geography)	My desire is to keep them involved or they switch off (geography)

Table 5.4: Tactics of Questioning

	Mean
A) During whole-class teaching the teacher should nominate pupils to answer, not just rely on volunteers	1.83
B) If a pupil gives an incorrect answer it is best to ask someone else in the class to correct it	2.97
C) Teachers should not ask a question unless they know the answer	3.57
D) If a pupil does not understand a question it is better to rephrase it for him rather than put the same question to another pupil	1.69
E) The important questions have to be set and answered in written form rather than discussed orally	4.06
(1 = strongly agree, 2 = agree, 3 = neutral, 4 = disagree, 5 = strongly disagree)	
F) I address questions to the whole class	2.63
G) I call on a pupil by name to answer question	2.57
H) I praise correct answers	1.54
I) I get children to ask each other questions	3.91
J) I ask questions systematically around the class calling on each pupil in turn	4.11
(1 = always, 2 = frequently, 3 = about half the time, 4 = occasionally, 5 = never)	

asked, and they disagreed with the view that the important questions have to be answered in written form. The sample reported that they praised answers frequently; they estimated that they addressed questions to the whole class about half the time and called on pupils about half the time; they occasionally got children to ask each other questions, and they very rarely asked questions to each pupil in turn. There were no significant differences between teaching subjects on these items.

Targets of Questions

It is interesting to compare the teachers' responses to the items on tactics with the examples of questions that they provided. The sample reported that they used questions to the whole class about half the time. Of the questions they provided 113 were directed at the whole class, 9 at groups and 48 at individuals. Whilst questions to the whole class may more readily spring to mind, one might expect that if the teachers did use questions to the whole class for only half the time, then they would have provided more group and individual questions.

Table 5.5 sets out the questions grouped in terms of targets and classes. Teachers or researchers who expect to find fewer whole-class questions and more group questions amongst mixed-ability classes will be disappointed.

Table 5.5: Targets and Classes

	High-ability	Middle-ability	Low-ability	Mixed-ability
Whole class	12	49	23	29
Group	0	2	4	3
Individual	3	13	17	15

The distribution of questions amongst classes, individuals and groups suggests there was a slight tendency for the teachers to ask more type-2 questions of specific individuals, but fewer questions requiring other forms of thought. Management questions towards individuals are more frequent than to the whole class.

Table 5.6: Targets and Types of Questions

	1	2	3	4	5	O	M	F	Total
Whole class	56	21	14	6	6	2	6	2	113
Group	2	3	3	0	0	0	1	0	9
Individual	16	15	3	0	2	1	10	1	48
Total	74	39	20	6	8	3	17	3	170

Sequences of Questions

Studies of sequences of sections of lessons are relatively sparse (see Dunkin and Biddle, 1974). In the United States, Smith and Meux (1970) have explored sequences in transcripts of lessons and Wright and Nuthall (1970) in a study in New Zealand of teaching and pupil achievement used their notions to study sequences and questioning levels. They noted that the use of open questions leading to more specific questions was a successful strategy, that summaries and mid-lesson summaries were significant correlates of pupil achievement, and that the use of open rather than closed questions aided pupil achievement on tests requiring thought. Their definition of 'open' and 'closed' is very similar to the term 'recall' and 'thought' used in this chapter. In this country there have been no published studies of sequences in lessons, but Chapter 6 provides details of sequences or units of lessons used in the detailed studies of explaining undertaken in the Teacher Education Project.

In this study of questioning we did not attempt to identify sequence throughout a lesson. Instead we asked the teachers to provide us with examples of sequences of questions that they used and the context in which they used them. We classified the sequences in terms of types of question and searched for simple patterns to describe the sequences.

The most common sequence was 'extending and lifting'. One such sequence included the questions:

	Type
When people are afraid what do they look like?	2
When people are happy what do they look like?	2
When people are violent what do they look like?	2
(Continue questioning along these lines)	

Now, imagine you have painted a picture of someone looking sad. What would you have done to the picture to make him look sad?　　　　　4*

(*We classified this as 4 — problem-solving rather than 'O' — open since the teacher was looking for specific techniques.)

The teacher wrote of this sequence, 'Good response to my questions. There was much face-pulling to remind ourselves of what one looks like. Answers to the last question showed they had begun to analyse the usual characteristics of human emotions and feelings'.

Eight of the teachers provided this sequence of extending and lifting, and seven provided examples of 'extending'. That is to say they used questions all of the same type, for example, 1, 1, 1, 1, 1, or 1 (to gain attention) followed by 3, 3, 3, 3, in a search for reasons. Five teachers began their sequence with an open question which led to either recall or simple deduction (1 and 2) or to problem solving and reason giving (3 and 4). One teacher posed a problem, encouraged speculation and then narrowed the question down to simple deduction (4, 0, 3, 2, 2, 2, 2, 4). Another teacher posed a problem, and then asked several simple recall questions and then re-posed the problem. Three teachers moved steadily from types 1 to types 4 and 5, and two teachers moved from types 5 to types 2 and 1. One teacher began with an evaluative question and went straight to recall. She reports that the strategy was not successful. The remainder of the sequences did not appear to have a pattern. The sequences identified are described briefly in Figure 5.5. All the sequences may be disrupted by management questions.

Figure 5.5: Some Sequences of Questions

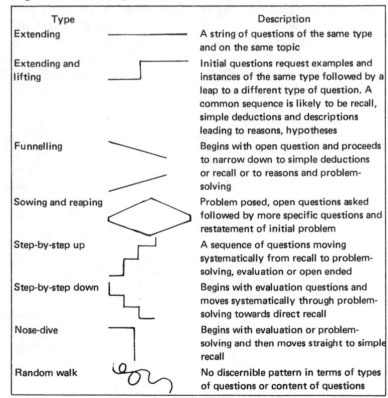

Type	Description
Extending	A string of questions of the same type and on the same topic
Extending and lifting	Initial questions request examples and instances of the same type followed by a leap to a different type of question. A common sequence is likely to be recall, simple deductions and descriptions leading to reasons, hypotheses
Funnelling	Begins with open question and proceeds to narrow down to simple deductions or recall or to reasons and problem-solving
Sowing and reaping	Problem posed, open questions asked followed by more specific questions and restatement of initial problem
Step-by-step up	A sequence of questions moving systematically from recall to problem-solving, evaluation or open ended
Step-by-step down	Begins with evaluation questions and moves systematically through problem-solving towards direct recall
Nose-dive	Begins with evaluation or problem-solving and then moves straight to simple recall
Random walk	No discernible pattern in terms of types of questions or content of questions

The sequences identified could provide the basis of a more detailed study of patterns of questions used in classrooms. These could be used to draw out the implicit psychological models of learning which teachers adopt.

Advice to Young Teachers

Teachers were asked to specify the sorts of mistakes made by students who were not particularly good at asking questions, and to indicate what they do to help students improve their questioning. Responses to both these questions were classified using a common system. One category − 'Methods of improving questions' − was included for advice which was not specific to students' errors in questioning. The classification system used is shown in Figure 5.6.

Figure 5.6: Classification of Student Teachers' Errors and Teachers' Advice

1. Delivery of questions
   e.g. clarity, volume and speed of speech; failure to look at pupils while asking questions
2. Structure of questions (affecting clarity of demands made of pupils)
   e.g. vocabulary used; length and complexity of questions
3. Level of questioning (pitch)
   − questions too easy/too difficult for the pupils asked
4. Target of questions
5. Background in which questions are set
   − putting questions in the context of a lesson; problems of sequencing questions
6. Handling answers
   e.g. accepting only expected answers; allowing insufficient time for answers
7. Discipline and management
   e.g. ensuring all pupils can hear both questions and answers; avoiding mass shouting-out of answers
8. Methods of improving one's questioning technique
   e.g. by observation of experienced teachers; by discussion and feedback; by practice

Twenty-seven teachers gave responses to these two items (the remaining 9 teachers had little or no experience of working with students and so could not reply). Most of the teachers gave more than one example of the types of error made and of the sort of advice/help they would give. Table 5.7 shows the number of teachers who mentioned the different *types of errors* and/or offered different types of advice. The advice offered tended to reflect the kinds of error which these teachers described, although several teachers (10) did give advice of a more general nature such as, 'talk to them and . . . try to get them to realise for themselves their mistakes' and 'Discuss better techniques and ideas. Watch as wide a range of teachers as possible'.

Table 5.7: Number of Teachers Mentioning Different Types of Error and Offering Different Types of Advice

Category*	Errors	Advice
1	4	1
2	14	13
3	6	1
4	6	3
5	7	8
6	11	10
7	7	3
8	—	10

*See Figure 5.6

The most commonly mentioned errors were concerned with presentation of questions. Some teachers mentioned students' errors in actual delivery of the questions (e.g. 'They don't look at the pupils; speak too fast; wrong volume; lack of clarity of speech'), but more teachers concentrated on the structure or fabric of the questions themselves. Students' questions were criticised as being complex, ambiguous and lengthy, and to contain vocabulary beyond the comprehension of the pupils concerned. It should perhaps be noted that the frequency of occurrence of different criticisms of students' questioning does not necessarily reflect the frequency with which students actually make these different types of errors. The large number of comments about presentation of questions may be because faults in presentation are relatively easy to detect and, possibly, easy to point out to the student in a non-threatening way.

The second most commonly mentioned type of mistake was the way students handle the replies they get to their questions. One particular fault mentioned by a number of teachers was that of accepting only those answers which the student had wanted or expected. As one teacher put it, 'They ask too many questions with one specific answer in mind and do not expect or accept many or any alternatives'. One way of dealing with this particular type of mistake is to incorporate questions in the lesson plan and, at this, the planning stage, to 'try to write as many "correct" answers to the question . . . as they can'.

Category 5 (background in which questions are set) deals with the use of questions as part of a lesson. One teacher commented that students 'do not really know why they are asking a question at all, except that it seemed a good idea at the time'. A common criticism of students was their failure to provide background information. Students 'do not provide enough source material for answers, either from pupils' previous experience from books, maps, etc.' Another criticism was of the lack of a logical sequence in a series of questions, so that questions are 'disjointed – jumping quickly without linking ideas, making a point or discussion too difficult to follow'. Suggested solutions to such problems tend to be to do with careful preparation of lessons, e.g. 'Prepare questions before – write them down. Are they logical? Will they occur at the correct point in the session?'

Teachers' comments relating to the target of questions tend to suggest that students are prone to focus their attention on a small group of individual pupils and to ignore the rest of the class. As one teacher put it 'They become obsessed with a few pupils and ignore the rest of the class'. One teacher, on the other hand, pointed out the dangers of the other extreme: 'They ask the whole class and some pupils go to sleep; others don't bother.' Adams and Biddle (1970) showed that teachers tended to interact with children sitting in a V-shaped wedge in the middle of the room.

Some Comments on Questions Asked

In this chapter we have discussed some of the problems of studying questions, outlined some of the earlier research on questioning and reported on the questions provided by a group of 36 teachers and on their observations on techniques of questioning.

The responses of the teachers in our modest investigation were reported and set in the context of earlier research. The system of classifying questions that we developed was based in large measure upon the questions provided by the teachers. In common with many other researchers we found that the questions asked tended to be predominantly factual or require only simple deductions or descriptions. This is not a criticism of teachers, least of all of the teachers in our sample, so much as a comment on existing curricula. Factual questions and simple descriptions are the main ingredient of the school curriculum. Even in enquiry-based approaches, factual and simple thought questions should not be neglected. But changes in the curriculum and in training in questioning are necessary if teachers are expected to use more thought, empathic and open questions.

There appear to be some differences in types of questions asked across the curriculum and across classes of differing abilities. High- and low-ability groups seem to receive more thought questions than middle or mixed-ability groups. The examples of questions provided to quick learners contained more thought questions than the questions provided to slower pupils. This may be because some of the teachers were thinking of quicker and slower pupils in the same class. Motivation of slower pupils was an overriding concern of this sample of teachers.

The most common errors of student teachers were, according to this group of teachers, the structuring of questions and handling pupils' answers. The advice given on these matters was essentially to plan and think before you question. To this we would add specific training in using questions and handling pupils' answers. We have ourselves developed a 3-hour workshop on questioning which is designed to help student teachers improve their questioning and responding to pupil answers.

In the study of sequences of questions we have identified tentative patterns which might well be explored further. Sequences of questions are an important but neglected aspect of questioning. It would be interesting to know what types of sequences of questions are in general used in classrooms in different subjects, how useful such sequences seem to be, and the implicit models of learning on which they are based.

Finally, we should like to draw the attention of the reader to some of the complexities of studying questions. Classifying questions entails the problems of intention and definition, and the deeper problem of comparing types of questions across different contexts. Systems of classifying questions are inevitably modified by the context in which they are used. The meanings of questions are influenced by the context and the intentions of teachers and pupils. Answers by pupils are not always a good guide to the type of questions asked. The reasons for asking questions are not always congruent with the type of question asked, and the reasons may not be inferrable from the content of the question, or even, occasionally, the context in which the question was asked.

Despite these complexities, questioning is such an important and ubiquitous activity in the classroom that one should not shirk the task of studying questioning – or indeed, other important areas of classroom life. However, one should bear in mind the fragility of one's assumptions and from time to time explore and question them, as we have done in this chapter.

References

Adams, R.S. and Biddle, B.J. (1970) *Realities of Teaching*, Holt, Rinehart & Winston, New York

Barnes, D. (ed.) (1969) *The Language, Learner and the School*, Penguin, Harmondsworth

Bloom, B.S. (1956) *Taxonomy of Educational Objectives*, McKay, New York

Brown, G.A. (1978) *Microteaching: Programme of Teaching Skills*, Methuen, London

Corey, S. (1940) 'The Teachers Out-talk the Pupils', *School Review, 48*, 745-52

Delamont, S. (1976) *Interaction in the Classroom*, Methuen, London

Dunkin, M.J. and Biddle, B.J. (1974) *The Study of Teaching*, Holt, Rinehart & Winston, New York

Flanders, N. (1970) *Analyzing Teaching Behavior*, Addison Wesley, New York

Floyd, W.D. (1960) *An Analysis of the Oral Questioning Activities in Selected Colorado Classrooms.* Unpublished doctoral dissertation, Colorado State College

Gall, M.D. (1970) 'The Use of Questions in Teaching', *Review of Educational Research, 40*, 707-21

Hargie, O.D.W. (1978) 'The Importance of Teacher Questions in the Classroom', *Educational Research, 20*, 99-102

——, Dickson, D. and Saunders, C. (1981) *Social Skills in Interpersonal Communication*, Croom Helm, London

Kerry, T. (1982) *Effective Questioning*, Macmillan, London

MacNamara, D. (1980) 'Teaching Skill: The Question of Questioning', *Educational Research, 23.2*, 104

Pate, R.T. and Bremer, N. (1967) 'Guiding Learning Through Skilful Questioning', *Elementary School Journal, 67*, 417-22

Rosenshine, B. (1971) *Teaching Behaviours and Student Achievement*, National Foundation of Educational Research, Slough, England

Smith, B.O. and Meux, M. (1970) *A Study of the Logic of Teaching*, University of Illinois, Illinois

Stevens, R. (1912) 'The Question as a Measure of Efficiency in Teaching', *Teachers College Contributions to Education, no. 48*, Columbia, New York

Taba, H. (1966) *Teaching Strategies and Cognitive Function in Elementary School Children*, San Francisco State College

Thanarrootoo, S. (1981) *Why Ask Questions?* Unpublished MEd minor dissertation, University of Nottingham

Tisher, R.R. (1970) 'The Nature of Verbal Discourse in Classrooms and the Association between Verbal Discourse and Pupils' Understanding', in W.J. Campbell (ed.), *Scholars in Context*, Wiley, Sydney

Turney, C. (ed.) (1973) *Sydney Microskills Series 1*, University of Sydney, Sydney, Australia
—— (ed.) (1975) *Sydney Microskills Series 2*, University of Sydney, Sydney, Australia
Wragg, E.C. (1973) 'A Study of Student Teachers in the Classroom' in G. Chanan (ed.), *Towards a Science of Teaching*, National Foundation of Educational Research, Slough
Wragg, E.C. (1980) 'Learning to Think' in J. Nichol (ed.), *Developments in History Teaching*, Exeter University School of Education, Perspectives 4.
Wright, C.J. and Nuthall, G. (1970) 'The Relationships between Teacher Behaviours and Pupil Achievement in Three Experimental Science Lessons', *American Educational Research Journal, 7*, 477-91

6 EXPLAINING AND EXPLANATIONS

G.A. Brown and S. Armstrong

The art of explaining is a neglected area of research in teacher education, yet explanations are used daily by all teachers in all subjects. My wife, the late Sheila Armstrong, and I were intrigued by the problems surrounding explaining and explanations, hence we explored for the Teacher Education Project the characteristics of explaining, to investigate whether it was possible to improve the explanatory skills of student teachers, and to develop instructional materials which would be of assistance to student teachers and young teachers. The materials that were developed are described in Brown and Hatton (1982) and Brown (1981). A technique for examining the structure of explanatory lessons is described in Brown and Armstrong (1978). In this chapter we discuss briefly the earlier work on explaining and then describe the experiment and the results of our studies of explaining.

The Nature of Explaining

The term explaining is derived from explanare, to make plain (Turney 1975). At its lowest level the process of explaining involves presenting sets of facts or simple instructions. Higher levels of explaining go beyond facts to consider relationships between facts and to consider reasons, motives and causes.

Smith and Meux (1970) in their perceptive study of transcripts of explanatory lessons state that 'to explain is to set forth an antecedent condition of which the particular event or process to be explained is taken as the process'. This definition of explaining is rather narrow. It is certainly not a helpful description of the process of explanatory teaching. As Martin (1970) points out, the process of explaining involves an explainer, a problem to be explained and a set of explainees. The explainer has to take account of the problem and of the existing knowledge and skills of the explainees. The goal of explaining is to provide understanding to others.

Martin's view stresses the importance of intentions. For her, explaining is essentially a task verb like shooting or fishing. For Thyne (1963), one of the few British authors to discuss explanatory teaching, explaining is an achievement verb.

> If the teacher really has explained something to his class, they will understand it, and if they do not understand it, despite his efforts, what purported to be an explanation was not an explanation after all.

Martin's work is part of a tradition concerned primarily with analysing intentions and processes of explaining (Bellack, Hyman, Smith and Kliebard, 1966; Ennis, 1969; Smith and Meux, 1970; Hyman, 1974), whereas Thyne is almost a forerunner of the process-product researchers (see Dunkin and Biddle, 1974).

In the study reported in this chapter we used both approaches. Both are necessary if one wants to extend one's understanding of the art of explaining. We transcribed and analysed explanatory lessons, we used direct observation, and we measured pupil outcomes. We explored the characteristics of explaining, the structure of various explanatory lessons and their relationships to pupil learning.

The working definition of explaining that we adopted was: explaining is an attempt to provide understanding of a problem to others. It follows from this definition that explaining involves taking account of the problem in relation to a set of explainees. The explainer has to present or elicit a set of linked statements, each of which is understood by the explainees and which together lead to a solution of the problem for that particular set of explainees. These linked statements may be labelled as 'keys' since they unlock understanding.

Clearly, for the explainer to be able to carry out the task of explaining he or she must be able to analyse the implicit questions in the problem to be explained. Thus, the problem 'How do local anaesthetics work?' involves the implicit questions 'What is a local anaesthetic?', 'How are nerve impulses transmitted?' Answers to these questions have to be appropriate for the explainees if the explanation is to be successful. Part of the training given to the student teachers was concerned with analysing problems to be explained and choosing appropriate keys.

Characteristics of Explaining

A review of the literature (see, for example, Verner and Dickinson,

1968; Turney *et al.*, 1975; Gage and Berliner, 1975; Brown, 1978a, 1978b) revealed that, not surprisingly, good explanations are clearly structured and interesting. However, clarity and interest are complex notions which involve, amongst other things, the use of structuring moves such as framing statements which delineate sections of the explanation, focal statements which highlight its essential features and the use of carefully chosen examples. Whilst it is easy to offer the advice 'Be clear and interesting', it is less easy to provide detailed hints and guidelines which will help a young teacher to provide clear, interesting explanations.

The main characteristics of explaining, which are summarised in Figure 6.1, were identified in the literature, in discussions with teachers from local secondary schools and from the study of explaining which we undertook.

Figure 6.1: Planning Strategies and Performance Skills in Explaining

Planning strategies	
Analyse topic into main parts, or 'keys'	
Establish links between parts	
Determine rules (if any) involved	
Specify kind(s) of explanation required	
Adapt plan according to learner characteristics	
Basic skills	
Clarity and fluency	through defining new terms
	through use of explicit language
	through avoiding vagueness
Emphasis and Interest	by variations in gestures
	by use of media and materials
	by use of voice and pauses
	by repetition, paraphrasing or verbal cueing
Using examples	clear, appropriate and concrete
	in sufficient quantity
	positive and negative where applicable
Organisation	logical and clear sequence
	pattern appropriate to task
	use of link words and phrases
Feedback	opportunities for questions provided
	understanding of main ideas assessed
	expressions of attitudes and values sought

Types of Explanation

The literature on explaining abounds with typologies of explanations (Swift, 1961; Bellack *et al.*, 1966; Ennis, 1969; Smith and Meux, 1970; Hyman, 1974). We decided to adopt a simple robust typology which would be relatively easy to use and understand by student teachers, but which was related to the work of earlier researchers (see Figure 6.2). Our typology consists of:

The interpretive:	which clarifies, exemplifies or interprets the meaning of terms (What is . . .?)
The descriptive:	which describes a process or structure (How is . . .? How does . . .?)
The 'reason giving':	which offers reasons or causes. the occurrence of a phenomenon. (Why is . . .?)

This typology, like the working description of explaining given earlier, provides a basis for the analysis of explanations and for activities concerned with the preparation, design and structuring of explanations.

Figure 6.2: A Typology of Explanations

After Hyman, 1974	After Smith and Meux, et al, 1970	After Brown, 1978b
Type I: Generalisation — specific instance *empirical* The effects of pressure on the volume of gas	*empirical-subsumptive* Seasonal changes on mammals	*reason-giving*, answering the question 'Why?' Why does the volume of a gas decrease as pressure increases? Why do certain mammals hibernate in winter?
probablistic Relation between lung cancer and smoking	*judgemental* Causes of higher crime rate in urban areas	Why do heavy smokers have a greater risk of contracting cancer? Why is there more crime in inner city areas?
non-empirical A verb agrees with its subject	*normative* The proper use of knives and forks	Why do we say, 'he runs', but 'they run'? Why do we put a fork in the left hand?

Figure 6.2 (cont'd) A Typology of Explanations

Type II: Functional		*interpretive*, answering the question, 'What?'
purpose The motives behind Lord Jim's actions	*teleological* Birds of prey as efficient hunters	What led Lord Jim to become the strange character he was? What uses do talons and curved beaks serve in birds of prey?
function Unions and their members	*consequence* Inflation and our money	What can unions do in an industrial dispute? What are the effects of a high inflation rate on currency?
Type III: Serial		*descriptive*, answering the question, 'How?'
sequential Making a sponge cake	*sequential* Constructing a perpendicular to a given line	How do you make a light sponge? How can a perpendicular be constructed using compass and ruler?
genetic Differences between cats and dogs	*mechanical* The operation of a car engine	As animals, how do cats differ from dogs? How does the internal-combustion engine work?
chronological Events leading to the war in Vietnam	*procedural* Conducting a formal meeting	How did colonial history lead to the Vietnamese war? How does the chairman lead a meeting?

The Experimental Studies

Instructional materials and procedures were developed and piloted in an experimental 2-day course on explaining for a PGCE biology group during the academic year 1975-6 (n = 30). A pre-test/post-test experiment was carried out with the 1976-7 intake of PGCE biology students (n = 27). Biology was chosen partly because the experimenters had taught physiology or psychology, and partly because biology has affinities with both arts and science subjects.

For these experiments ten biology topics were identified from the Biological Sciences Curriculum materials (see Figure 6.3), and the materials were given to the students. Students were required to teach two of these topics to groups of approximately twelve 11 to 12-year-old pupils in two 10-minute lessons. Half of the group were given training in explaining between teaching the two lessons. The remainder were given training after they had taught their two lessons. The training consisted of brief presentations and activities, structured video feedback and an instructional booklet. The experiment was so arranged that no student saw any other student's lesson on the same topic, and each group of pupils was taught each topic only once. The lessons were video recorded. Soon after each lesson the pupils were asked a series of multiple-choice questions on the lesson content, and required to complete a rating form of their reactions to the student teachers. The multiple-choice questions asked the pupils to recall information and to apply it to solve simple problems. The training programme takes approximately two days.

Figure 6.3: Topics for Explanatory Lessons

Interpretive explanations
 What are phyla?
 What is a biome?
 What is a fossil?
 What is ecological succession?

Descriptive explanations
 Where does the energy of the living world come from?
 How do streams become polluted?
 How do environmental factors influence the number of plants and
  animals in a particular area?
 How are animals protected against the dangers of drying out?

Reason-giving explanations
 Why are there no polar bears at the South Pole?
 Why is soil considered to be an ecosystem?

The video recordings were transcribed and the transcripts were analysed. Variables derived from the analyses were related to the pupils' learning outcomes and reactions to the lessons. Two independent observers also viewed the videotapes, which were presented to them in random order.

In addition to the statistical analyses undertaken, the principal investigator also explored the characteristics of the transcripts of each of the topics, and she compared the most and least successful lessons on each topic. This type of analysis is more akin to literary criticism than to statistical methods (Barnes, 1976). It provided interesting and insightful observations of the characteristics of different types of explaining and explanations.

Readers not especially interested in the statistical analyses might like to pass over the next few pages to the section 'Some Studies of Transcripts' on page 134, which gives an account of the lessons of the most and least successful explainers. The statistics in the following section are a little difficult for those not used to such analysis, and they involve mainly analysis of variance and cluster analysis. A description of the techniques used can be found in Youngman (1979).

Some Experimental Results

Three major statistical analyses were undertaken. The particular questions we were interested in were:

What are the characteristics of good explanations?
Can explanatory skills be improved through a 2-day course?
Are there important differences between the types of explanation?

All the analyses are based upon the 48 lessons which were video-recorded and transcribed. (Three students withdrew from the PGCE course during the week in which the experiment took place.) The pupil outcomes and reactions were adjusted for topic difficulty using the formula:

$$CM = cm \pm (GM - GMT)$$

CM = adjusted class mean, cm = raw class mean, GM = grand mean, GMT = grand mean of topic.

This formula is recommended by Gage *et al.* (1972). It minimises differences between classes which are due to topic difficulty, thereby yielding a more accurate measure of the effects of teaching.

The two independent observers were trained and then asked to provide global ratings in structure and presentation. They used the transcripts and the video recordings. The correlation between their combined ratings was 0.87. Intra-observer reliability based upon the first ten lessons viewed with a 14-day gap between sample was 0.86 and 0.83.

The Characteristics of Good Explaining

The criterion measure for good, average and poor lessons was set as the top 25 per cent as measured by pupil outcomes, the middle 50 per cent and the bottom 25 per cent. Other criteria used were the pupil reactions and the independent observers' scores of structure and presentation.

Table 6.1 sets out the main results. Tukey and Scheffé tests were used to compare the groups (Youngman, 1979). Not surprisingly, there were very highly significant differences on all of the criterion measures. These results indicate strongly that direct observation by trained observers can provide a useful, indirect measure of pupil learning.

Only the process variables with a probability level of 0.1 or less are shown in the table. The first five of these are concerned with the keys or major sections of the explanation. The keys are presented in the table in ascending order of cognitive demand. This procedure is based on the work of Tisher (1970) and Bloom (1956). The full set of keys is shown in Figure 6.4

Figure 6.4: The Set of Keys

Cognitive level	
1	Stating, defining, describing, classifying, designating
2	Comparing, descriptive explanation, interpretive
3	'Reason-giving', causes, motives
4	Conditional inferring
5	Evaluating

The good explainers tended to make higher cognitive demands on their pupils although the average group used conditional inferring (If . . . then . . .) more frequently (level 4). No group used evaluative keys (level 5). The poor group used significantly more causal keys (level 4), and the good group used significantly more comparing keys (level 2). Pupils volunteered statements and questions more frequently in the poor lessons (Pupil informs) but not significantly so.

The good group used framing statements and focusing statements most frequently. The poor group used focusing statements more than the average groups. Pauses and incomplete sentences occurred less often in the good groups and incomplete summaries more frequently in the poor group.

The incidence of some of the individual variables in the sample was

Table 6.1: Characteristics of Explaining

Variables	F ratio	Good		Average		Poor		Notes
		Mn	SD	Mn	SD	Mn	SD	
Criteria								
Pupil outcome	19.71**	36.95	2.34	32.89	2.85	29.92	2.62	a
Pupil reaction	13.9**	45.61	2.38	42.11	2.50	39.8	3.11	a
Combined	65.83**	82.56	2.55	75.00	2.71	69.81	2.68	a
Presentation	10.24**	5.67	1.75	3.96	1.06	3.08	1.55	a
Structure	7.75***	6.00	2.12	4.25	1.16	3.50	1.61	a
Combined	9.18**	11.68	4.03	8.21	4.02	6.58	2.84	a
Process								
No. of keys	2.34$^+$	6.25	1.23	5.21	1.41	5.67	1.23	
Stating	2.28$^+$	0.42	0.64	0.67	0.99	1.33	1.49	
Classifying	2.74$^+$	1.00	2.74	0.79	1.86	3.33	4.87	
Comparing	4.33**	2.67	3.06	0.92	1.32	0.67	0.75	b
Causal key	6.29**	2.75	1.96	1.50	1.22	3.50	1.89	c, f
Conditional inferring	2.50$^+$	2.50	1.76	3.54	2.41	1.83	2.07	
Pupil informs	2.37$^+$	0.08	0.28	0.88	1.72	1.62	2.46	
Frames	2.98*	5.75	3.88	3.58	2.33	3.42	1.98	b
Foci	9.43**	4.08	5.63	6.04	3.41	12.50	8.57	b
Pauses	5.43**	0.25	0.13	1.37	1.58	2.42	2.14	b, c
Incomplete sentences	2.98*	2.17	1.82	5.04	4.18	3.58	2.43	
Incomplete summary	3.55*	0.08	0.28	0.0	0.0	0.25	0.43	e

F ratio at 2, 45 d.f.

$^+$ = 0.1 level.

* = sig. at 0.05 level, ** = sig. at 0.01 level, *** = sig. at 0.001 level.

Notes: a. All groups significantly different from each other.
b. Good group significantly different from others.
c. Poor group significantly different from others.
d. Good group significantly different from poor group.
e. Poor group significantly different from average group.
f. Middle group significantly different from others.

Figure 6.5: Cluster Solution

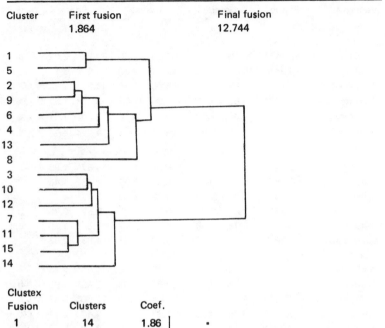

Clustex Fusion	Clusters	Coef.	
1	14	1.86	
2	13	2.29	
3	12	2.30	
4	11	2.66	
5	10	2.90	
6	9	2.91	
7	8	3.36	
8	7	3.61	
9	6	3.71	
10	5	4.41	
11	4	4.60	
12	3	6.12	
13	2	6.37	
14	1	12.74	

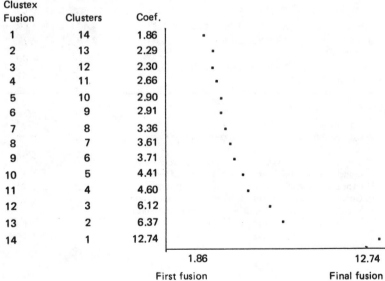

Table 6.2: Better and Weaker Lessons

Variables	Standardised means		Raw means	
	Better	Weaker	Better	Weaker
Criteria				
Pupil outcome	0.38**	−0.45	34.55	31.52
Pupil reaction	0.28*	−0.33	43.35	41.29
Combined	0.44**	−0.52	77.90	72.80
Presentation	0.51**	−0.61	5.08	3.27
Structure	0.58**	−0.68	5.65	3.41
Combined	0.58**	−0.68	10.73	6.68
Process				
Number of keys	0.34**	−0.44	6.57*	4.75
Number of types of keys	0.29*	−0.35	2.77	2.09
Describing	−0.26**	0.31	9.81	11.73
Designating	−0.24$^+$	0.28	0.86	1.15
Classifying	−0.35**	0.41	0.35	2.82
Comparing	0.50*	−0.35	1.88	0.59
Reason-giving	0.42**	−0.50	3.27	1.09
Causal	0.33*	−0.39	1.42	0.41
Framing	0.32*	−0.37	5.00	3.00
Focusing	0.22$^+$	−0.26	8.31	6.41
Incomplete summary	−0.30*	0.36	0.00	0.18
Use of examples	0.43**	−0.51	7.92	5.23
Use of aids	0.57**	−0.68	7.96	5.54
Joke or puzzle in opening	−0.34**	0.40	0.00	0.23
Elicited example	−0.26*	0.31	3.69	6.41
Use of 'Any questions?'	−0.26*	0.31	0.15	0.41
Rhetorical questions	0.26$^+$	−0.30	8.69	5.73
Probing elicit	−0.27*	0.32	1.69	3.45

$^+$ = 0.1 level, * = 0.05 level, ** = 0.01 level

low, and therefore as individual items they were likely to be poor discriminators. However, when considered *in toto* the individual variables might prove to yield very different profiles for good and other lessons. We therefore cluster analysed (see Youngman, 1979) the 50 process variables which had yielded probabilities of less than 0.3 on the analysis of good, average and poor lessons. We also included the criterion variables, but these were masked so they did not influence the profiles.

Figure 6.5 shows the dendrogram plot. A two-cluster solution seemed most appropriate. The first of these contained eleven 'poor' lessons, six below the mean of the average group, three above its mean and two 'good' lessons. The second cluster consisted of ten 'good' lessons, seven above the mean of the average group, six just below the mean and one 'poor' lesson. The teacher of the 'poor' lesson received very favourable reaction scores but poor learning outcomes. In other words he was very popular with the pupils, but he did not teach them anything.

The two clusters were considered to be sufficiently distinctive to merit the labels 'Better' and 'Weaker' explanations. Table 6.2 sets out the major differences between the two clusters. Both standardised and raw scores are presented in the table.

The better explanatory lessons differed significantly from the weaker lessons on fifteen variables. Better lessons had more keys and more types of keys. In other words they varied the cognitive demands on the pupils, and they used higher levels of cognitive demand more frequently.

Better lessons contained more framing and focusing statements, and they had fewer incomplete summaries. More frequent use of examples and of audiovisual aids were made in the better lessons and less use of jokes, 'can you give me an example?' probing elicits an 'any questions?'. The better lessons did however contain more rhetorical questions. These were usually used as attention-gaining devices in the early stages of a new key.

The Effects of Training

As a first step in the analysis of the effects of training we examined the distribution of poor, average and good lessons across the experimental conditions. Six of the 12 good lessons and only 2 of the poor lessons occurred in the post-training lessons of the experimental group. The results are shown in Table 6.3.

Table 6.3: Lessons and Training

| | Experimental | | Control | |
	Pre	Post	Pre	Post
Poor	4	2	2	4
Average	6	3	8	7
Good	1	6	3	2

The criterion measures were then analysed to check there were no significant differences between the 'pre-training' lessons of the experimental and control group and to compare the scores of the experimental and the control groups on the 'post-training' lessons. The results are shown in Table 6.4. They indicate that the training programme was effective with this group of PGCE students.

Table 6.4: Pre-test and Post-test Differences on Criterion Variables

| | Pre-test | Control n_1 | | Experimental n_2 | |
		Mn	SD	Mn	SD
Pupils	Reaction	43.37	1.98	42.86	2.73
	Outcome	32.13	3.52	30.16	3.41
	Combined	75.50	4.34	73.03	4.34
Independent observers	Structure	4.00	1.35	3.64	1.61
	Presentation	4.55	1.62	3.91	1.56
	Combined	8.55	2.81	7.55	3.03
	Post-test				
Pupils	Reaction*	40.30	3.79	43.30	3.67
	Outcome*	33.80	2.50	35.21	3.77
	Combined*	74.18	4.93	78.52	6.56
Independent observers	Structure*	3.82	1.70	5.20	1.35
	Presentation*	4.18	1.61	5.55	1.83
	Combined*	8.00	3.05	10.88	3.04

$n_1 = 11$, $n_2 = 13$

* = sig. at 0.05 level.

Analysis of the process variables did reveal some significant differences between the experimental group and control group in their pre-test lessons. The experimental group asked fewer questions and used the blackboard less frequently to highlight a point. They hesitated more frequently in mid-sentence. In the post-training lessons these differences disappeared. The experimental group had significantly fewer hesitations, used more focusing statements and more reason giving keys. These variables are closely associated with 'better' explanations. Other differences were not significant, but in general they favoured the experimental group.

The effects of the training programme has left us with a conundrum. In terms of pupil learning, pupils reactions and independent observers' scores, the training programme was successful. In terms of the low inference process variables studied, the programme yielded few significant differences between the experimental and control group on the post test. These results may be due to the low incidence of some of the variables studied. Alternatively, it may be that in evaluating a training programme one should use high inference variables rather than fine-grained variables (see Rosenshine and Furst, 1973).

Types of Explanations

Differences between the interpretive, descriptive and reason-giving explanatory lessons were explored using analysis of variance. There were no significant differences on the criterion variables nor in the number of keys used. The interpretive explanations contained more different types of keys than the other explanations, fewer causal keys and more interpretive keys, although the incidence was not high. The mean length of sentence was highest in the interpretive explanations. The lessons based on descriptive explanations were more likely to open with examples, to contain sentences beginning with 'so . . .' The reason-giving explanations contained fewer hesitations and shorter sentences. More stating, more reason giving and more conditional inferring occurred in the reason-giving explanations. In other words the range of cognitive demand was greater in the reason-giving lessons.

The differences between the types of lessons shown in Table 6.5 should not be considered as solely due to the type of explanatory lesson being tackled. Not surprisingly, the student teachers varied in their approach to the explanatory topics. To explore this issue further we examined the structure and content of the transcripts.

Some Studies of Transcripts

One of the authors studied each of the lessons taught using SAID (Brown and Armstrong, 1978) supplemented by her observations of the opening key sections and endings of the lessons. She viewed the

Table 6.5: Types of Explanation

Variables	F ratio	Interpretive		Descriptive		Reason-giving		Notes
		Mn	SD	Mn	SD	Mn	SD	
No. of types of keys	3.38*	3.00	0.87	2.20	0.87	2.17	1.28	a
Stating	3.04*	0.69	1.36	0.45	0.67	1.42	1.11	c
Classifying	2.43[+]	2.75	4.47	1.30	2.67	0.08	0.28	
Descriptive	1.34	1.50	2.57	3.70	5.07	2.67	2.90	
Interpretive	8.21**	0.50	0.50	0.10	0.30	0.00	0.00	a
Reason-giving	2.88[+]	1.50	1.46	2.10	2.17	3.58	3.07	c
Causal	3.44*	0.25	0.45	1.40	1.71	1.17	1.28	a
Conditional inferring	9.60**	1.12	1.38	4.00	2.43	8.25	1.23	c
Opening with examples	4.14*	0.25	0.43	0.70	0.46	0.42	0.49	b
Role example	3.58*	0.31	0.46	0.60	0.66	0.08	0.28	b
'so ...'	3.50*	9.06	5.06	13.9	6.57	9.83	4.44	b
Rephrasing	2.83[+]	4.32	2.96	2.35	1.65	4.00	3.37	
Hesitation	4.66**	11.37	10.36	6.85	8.44	2.00	2.16	c
Mn sentence length	3.42*	21.23	4.90	17.25	5.52	17.20	3.46	a

[+] = 0.1 level, * = 0.05 level, ** = 0.01 level.
Gp sizes 16, 20, 12 respectively.

Notes:
a. Interpretive
b. Descriptive   significantly different
c. Reason-giving

lessons and read the transcripts. She grouped the lessons according to topic and compared highest and lowest-scoring lessons for each topic. She then grouped the topics into interpretive, descriptive and reason-giving explanations, and provided various tentative generalisations for the teaching of various topics.

It is only possible to provide a few examples of her approach in this chapter, but it is hoped to produce a monograph which will contain a full report of the project on explaining.

In the sections that follow one example of each type of explanation and a summary of each type is given.

Interpretive Lessons

The lesson topics which require interpretive explanations were: What are phyla? What is a biome? What is ecological succession? and What is a fossil?

What is Ecological Succession? This topic was one of the most challenging for the student teachers as the subject was completely new to the pupils. The teachers were faced with the problem, as they were in the lesson on phyla, of deciding how much it was necessary for the children to know in order to understand the process of ecological succession.

The high-scoring lessons were the simple ones which described the process in words with which the children were familiar and to which they could relate. The low-scoring lessons introduced so many new ideas that the children became confused. This is illustrated in the examples given in the comparison of high and low-scoring lessons.

Analysis of Highest-scoring and Lowest-scoring Lessons

The lessons which received the highest and lowest overall scores on this topic had the following features:

Orientation

High-scoring

> *T:* Well, first, of all I wonder if you could tell me what this is?
> *P:* A piece of concrete.
> *T:* Yes, it's a piece of concrete, a slab of concrete, out of my garden. Now, if I wanted to plant a tree or a shrub on here what would you say was missing?
> *P:* Soil.
> *T:* Yes, the soil. And today I want to start by talking about some plants that can grow straight on to a rock.

Low-scoring   No orientation

Keys

High-scoring
1. Which plants can grow straight on to rock?
2. How do mosses replace lichens?
3. Which plants replace mosses?
4. What is this process called?
5. What other examples of ecological succession are there?

Low-scoring
1. In what two ways can we group organisms?
2. Which organisms are consumers?
3. Which organisms are producers?
4. What is it called when we group organisms that depend on each other together?

5. What do we call it when one community takes over from another?
6. How does ecological succession take place on a bare rock?

Summary

| High-scoring | Unfinished |
| Low-scoring | Unfinished |

Comparison of Highest-scoring and Lowest-scoring Lessons

In these two lessons, the highest-scoring and the lowest-scoring, the selection of material was yet again a crucial factor. The teacher in the low-scoring lesson said that he felt that there was too much to explain in 8 minutes. He assumed that in order to explain ecological succession the children must understand the differences between taxonomies and ecology, and between consumers and producers. That this was not necessary was shown by the simple approach used in the high-scoring lesson, in which the teacher blended imagination and fact, an approach which was also successful in the highest-scoring lesson on pollution (see below. 'I want you to imagine that this is a big piece of rock; (holding large stone) a bare rock in the countryside'.

The teacher in the high-scoring lesson made particularly good use of his visual aids. Having passed around lichens he asked: 'Can you tell me what the shape is like? . . . Is it very tall off the ground? . . . Would you look to see if there is much soil underneath?

The pattern of keys in the high-scoring lesson was the one which proved successful in the highest-scoring lesson on biomes. The teacher used the rule/example/rule pattern advocated by Rosenshine, and shown by him to lead to greater pupil achievement. In this case the pattern was incomplete as the lesson was unfinished, but the teacher led up to his definition of ecological succession (rule), asked for other examples of ecological succession (example), and as his lesson plan showed, intended to finish the lesson with a restatement of the definition (rule).

The failure of the low-scoring lesson can again be accounted for by the choice of material covered rather than by poor presentation. This was also the case in the lessons on 'What are phyla?' There was too much information at too difficult a level for 12-year-olds. The teacher had not taken the age of his pupils sufficiently into account when he planned the lesson, nor did he pick up the non-verbal cues from the class, as he mentioned the word 'organism' 46 times without realising that the children were not familiar with the concept.

The main differences between the high-scoring and low-scoring lessons were therefore attributable to the choice of material at the lesson-planning stage. The teacher in the high-scoring lesson went from the known or familiar (moss, grass, trees) to the unknown (the term 'ecological succession'). The teacher in the low-scoring lesson moved at rapid speed from the unknown to the unknown (organism, consumers, producers, communities, succession). The choice of content and the level of presentation again seemed to be crucial factors in deciding the success or failure of the lesson.

Descriptive Lessons

The topics which required descriptive explanations were:

How do environmental factors influence the number of plants and animals found in a particular area?

Where does the energy of the living world come from?

How do streams become polluted?

How are animals prevented from drying out?

Drying Out. This was one of the most popular topics with both student teachers and pupils, and the structuring of the material presented no major problems. Presentation skills were an important factor influencing pupil achievement rather than selection of appropriate content at the appropriate level. The most difficult part of the explanation was the question of the surface area of the animal in relation to its weight. The best attempt was the following:

> Now, it's also very bad if animals get too wet. Now, when you are in a bath and you get out of the bath you're very wet aren't you? And the first thing you do is grab hold of a towel. Now, all over us is a film of water. And this film of water is about one-fiftieth of an inch thick. Very thin. But it's spread all over our surface. Well, we've got big bodies — well when you're my age, you know, and it's spread all over me. And it weighs — if I were to collect it all up and put it in a bucket it would weigh about a pound. Right? Weigh a pound. Little animals, they have the same film of water over them one-fiftieth of an inch thick, but because they are small and haven't got a very big

surface area it feels very heavy to them. And mice, if mice get wet the weight of water on them is nearly the same as their own weight and they can hardly move. So you know, it's pretty bad for a mouse to get wet.

This topic gave the teachers plenty of opportunity for the use of visual aids. In two of the lessons the teachers used a sponge and a plastic bag as an example of a protective covering which prevented water loss. But although they had the same idea, their presentation was quite different as the following two extracts show:

(Lesson A)

T: There are a lot of animals that don't stay in water all their life, aren't there? Can you think of how they — if you think of a sponge and we're saying it can't stay in water all the time. Can you think of how we could stop it from drying out?

P: Put water on it now and again.

T: We could put water on it now and again. Can you think of any other ideas? What could we do to the sponge to stop it drying out? Supposing you wanted to take a sponge away with you on holiday and you wanted it wet 'cos you weren't sure whether you were going to get any water. What would you do with it? Yes?

P: Wrap it up in something.

T: You'd wrap it up in something. Yes. What sort of thing can you think you'd wrap it up in? Yes?

P: Polythene.

T: Yes. We could put it in a polythene bag. There we are (produces polythene bag and puts sponge in it) there's a polythene bag. Now, animals, well, we don't have polythene round us do we? But we do have things round us to stop us drying up. We have our skin, don't we?

(Lesson B)

T: Listen a minute. I'm going to show you — I'm going to show in this bag. It's got a wet sponge in it and that is like the inside of a mealworm. Can you see on the inside of the bag?

P: It's leaking.

T: I hope not. Is it? What can you see on the inside of the bag?

P: Water.

P: Drops.

T: Water. You feel the outside of that bag. What is it?

P: Nothing.

T: Nothing?

P: Dry.

T: Dry. So how do you think the mealworm stops itself from losing water? How do you think — if it's wet inside and dry on the outside — how do you think the mealworm stops itself from losing water?

P: Because the condensation inside cools him down.

T: No, we're talking about how he stops himself from losing water.

P: Gets too hot.

P: Overdoes it.

T: Yes, but what do you think the polythene bag's like? What do you think it's like? What do you wear in wet weather?

P: A mackintosh.

T: A mackintosh.

P: Polythene.

T: Polythene, that's right. So how do you think the polythene bag stops?

P: It stops the water getting in.

T: And out! The polythene bag acts like a waterproof coat doesn't it?

P: But the sponge soaks it up.

T: The sponge soaks it up so the water's held in the tissues in the mealworm, isn't it?

In lesson extract A the teacher used higher level of questioning than in the second extract, where most of the questions required a descriptive reply. Although both teachers used a sponge and plastic bag it was perfectly clear to the listener in extract A what the teacher was referring to. In lesson extract B the teacher moved between the sponge and the mealworm, and finally combined the two in the sentence 'the sponge soaks it up so the water's held in the tissues in the mealworm isn't it? In extract B the teacher accepted several inconsequential answers, but rejected outright a thoughtful reply to her question on how the mealworm stops itself from losing water.

One of the lessons on this topic with the highest reaction scores was given by a male student teacher with an obvious talent for acting. He occupied the centre of the stage for the entire lesson, asking only four questions, but keeping the class's attention with his animal impressions, in particular of a St Bernard with a steaming tongue. Another of the lessons had a tiny experiment (the children liked this word) in which the children blew on one hand and then licked the back of the other hand before blowing on that. The second hand felt much colder than the first and was a neat way of showing that we sweat in order to keep cool.

Analysis of Highest-scoring and Lowest-scoring Lessons on Water Loss

The lessons which had the highest and lowest overall scores on this topic had the following features:

Orientation
High-scoring

> *T:* Now, I wonder what you would think if a man was to walk through that door now and say to you 'Did you know that half of your body came out of a tap? Do you think he's a bit funny? What would you think? Would you think anything? You shook your head, what would you think if a man came in and said half your body came out of a tap? (laughter). Do you think he was telling the truth?
>
> *P:* He was right.
>
> *T:* Because nearly all of your body has water in it. That's quite good isn't it? He wasn't far out, the man, was he? Didn't really come out of a tap but water comes out of a tap and you've got a lot of water in your body. In fact, half of your body is made up of water. It doesn't mean to say all your legs are water because it's all mixed in together, isn't it? But about half your body is made up of water. So we've got water inside our body.

Low-scoring

> *T:* Right. Today we're going to talk about the danger of animals drying out. Why might it be dangerous for animals to dry out?

Key Points
High-scoring lesson

1. How much water do different animals lose?
2. How do different animals lose water?
3. What must animals that lose water do to replace the water?
4. How do insects protect themselves from losing water?
5. Why do some animals need to be dry and some animals need to be wet?

Low-scoring   1. What are these animals?
                     2. How do they lose water (unfinished)
                     3. How do you lose water?
                     4. How do locusts stop themselves losing water?
                     5. How do mealworms stop themselves losing water?
                     6. How do animals get water?
                     7. How do gerbils get water?

Summary
High-scoring   So there (indicating transparency) we have two
                     groups. Animals which like water because they need
                     it and animals which don't like water.

Low-scoring   Unfinished

Comparison of Highest-scoring and Lowest-scoring lessons

The highest-scoring lesson on this topic was planned and executed in a
purposeful way. The lesson was well structured, with the children
contributing to the lesson within the structure provided by the teacher.
The teacher had prepared a transparency with the heading 'animals that
like water'. As the children provided examples of these the teacher
added them to the transparency. The teacher used the overhead projec-
tor very skilfully, adding to prepared transparencies and showing only
the parts of the transparency about which he was talking.

A great deal of time and effort had obviously been spent in the
preparation of the lesson which received the lowest score, but the
teacher had failed to anticipate the reaction of the pupils when, right at
the start of the lesson, she placed a gerbil in a cage and several petri
dishes of dead locusts on the table. She never really gained control
again, and was constantly interrupted with comments about the unplea-
sant smell and questions about how the locusts were killed. The only
other lesson in which locusts were used was much more under control
of the teacher. She had already established rapport with the class before
producing the locusts, and although there was a certain amount of noise
and confusion it was all contained within the same key. After the children had seen the covering of the locusts they were removed. The live
specimens did not have the unfortunate smell of the locusts in formalin,
and an additional disadvantage of the preserved ones was that the outer
covering had become soft and did not show to advantage.

Apart from the visual aids the main feature of the lowest-scoring
lesson was the large number of questions which were asked by the

teacher. There was constant verbal interaction throughout the lesson, but the teacher's questioning skills were not highly developed and at least two of the keys were abortive. This lesson, with over 30 questions in 8 minutes exemplified Hargie's observation (1980) when reviewing questioning techniques, that the frequency with which some teachers ask questions is probably proof that no great number of 'thoughtful' answers are expected.

Reason-giving Explanations

The reason-giving topics were 'Why are there no polar bears at the South Pole?' and 'Why is soil considered to be an ecosystem?'

Soil as an Ecosystem. The student teachers tackled this topic in two different ways. In the better lessons (those with high achievement scores) the teachers defined an ecosystem and then showed how soil fitted the definition. In the less successful approach the student teachers described soil and its component parts, and concluded that such a system was called an ecosystem.

The teachers who used the second approach did not in fact answer the question which was asked, and in this way simplified their task. An examination of the key points which this group used shows that they discussed the living and non-living things in the soil, and concluded that such a system is called an ecosystem. They failed to explain why soil could be regarded as an ecosystem or how the non-living and living things interacted. The question they were answering was 'What is an ecosystem?' For example, one lesson ended in this way: 'This is what is known as an ecosystem, where all animals and plants are living all mixed up together in the soil. Any questions?'

In this particular lesson the teacher had had some good ideas. She had used children to demonstrate the freeze-thaw action and had shown the class the water-holding properties of soil by pouring water on beakers of sand and soil, but she had failed to answer the central question. Out of the nine lessons given on this topic, five answered the question 'Why is soil considered to be an ecosystem?' and four lessons answered the question 'What is an ecosystem?' It is interesting to note that the five lessons which answered the question asked were given by teachers who had been trained in explaining. The four teachers who failed to answer the question had not been trained in explaining. It seems from this that training in explaining makes the teacher think more carefully about the question he is trying to answer.

One of the lessons on this topic had the following thought-provoking conclusion:

T: Now, I'll leave you with one thought. You normally think of bacteria as nasty things that give you germs and diseases don't you? But what would happen if there weren't any at all in the world? Can you imagine what would happen? Thinking of our ecosystem? If there weren't any bacteria? Yes?

P: There wouldn't be any soil or anything.

T: Well, there wouldn't be any soil or goodness in the soil. Yes.

P: All the bodies would pile up.

T: All the bodies would pile up and there wouldn't be any room for anyone to live, would there? There wouldn't be any room for all these big animals and plants because the world would be full of dead bodies and dead plants.

Analysis of Highest-scoring and Lowest-scoring Lessons on Soil as an Ecosystem

The lessons which received the highest and lowest scores on this topic had the following features:

Orientation

High-scoring   Well, my name is Mrs. H. and today I'm going to look at the soil and the reason why scientists call the soil an ecosystem.

Low-scoring   Right. In this lesson we're going to talk about something I'm sure everyone will see every day, sometimes you'll walk on it, and your mothers might get quite annoyed. And although we see it every day I bet none of you ever think about it very often. It's something that's very important. Although we might think it is quite simple, it's something that plants couldn't do without as they wouldn't be able to grow without it, and if the plants couldn't grow without it and there weren't any plants we couldn't live without it either. So it's very important. I wonder if anyone can think what I'm talking about?

P: Air

T: No, not air, something we walk by or sometimes we walk on.

P: Mud.

T: Mud, that's it, mud. Another name for mud?

P: Soil.

T: Soil, that's it.

Keys

High-scoring   1. What is soil made of?
                 2. What is this system called?
                 3. What are the mineral components?
                 4. What is the decaying matter?
                 5. What are the living organisms?

Low-scoring   1. What are the non-living things?
                 2. What are the living things?
                 3. What is this system called?

Summary
High-scoring   Unfinished summary
Low-scoring   No summary

Comparison of Highest-scoring and Lowest-scoring Lessons on Soil as an Ecosystem

These two lessons displayed different structures which seemed to lead to differences in reaction and recall. The high-scoring lesson defined an ecosystem in an early key, whereas the low-scoring lesson did not introduce the concept until the final key. In the interpretive explanations definitions given near the beginning of explanations were also more successful than definitions given at the end of explanations.

The major difference between the high-scoring and low-scoring lessons was that the high-scoring lesson answered the question asked whilst the low-scoring lesson did not. The low-scoring lesson had an interesting orientation (given above) and some imaginative analogies, as for example, the air surrounding each particle of soil being the same as the air surrounding tennis balls in a bucket, but the lesson failed to answer the question 'Why is soil considered to be an ecosystem?' This failure to answer the question to be explained appears to be the major difference between the high-scoring and low-scoring lessons. However, this question was a difficult one, involving as it did a reason-giving explanation based in part upon a hidden interpretive question.

Summary of Analysis

The analysis of the interpretive lessons highlighted the importance of the selection of the appropriate content. Simple lessons with only one or two new concepts scored more highly than lessons in which the pupils were introduced to a large number of ideas, even when those new ideas were carefully linked.

Three out of the highest-scoring lessons used the rule/example/rule pattern which Rosenshine found effective (Gage *et al.*, 1972). This pattern was not used in the highest-scoring lesson on phyla. Nor was this pattern found in the highest scoring lessons in descriptive and reason-giving topics. It may be that the rule/example/rule model is more appropriate for interpretive explanations than for other types of explanations.

In the descriptive lessons the keys selected by the student teachers were almost identical. The order of keys did not seem to be crucial, although there were structural weaknesses in the poorer lessons. But by far the greatest differences were in the presentation of the key points and in the use of questions.

The main differences between the better and weaker reason-giving explanations was that the poorer lessons did not answer the central question. The better lessons in both topics stated the problem and the principles relatively early in the lessons and proceeded to elicit and give examples. However, this procedure was not rule/example/rule but rather example/rule/example.

Concluding Remarks

This chapter has given an outline of the study of explaining and explanations. In the study we used deliberately a combination of experimental methods and descriptive evaluative techniques so that we could explore the characteristics of good explaining, the effects of training, and we could provide meaningful examples of various strategies of explaining. The experimental work and the analysis of transcripts has provided us with valuable insights into the nature of explaining which will be of use to teachers and researchers.

The analysis of the keys of a lesson enables one to study the structure of a lesson, and almost without exception the lessons which yielded high pupil-achievement scores had a more well-defined and appropriate structure. These lessons could also be characterised as more stimulating in that they made a wider variety of cognitive demands upon the pupils, whilst at the same time building upon the pupils' existing knowledge.

It was also clear from this study that it is possible to help students

to analyse explanations and thereby prepare and give better explanatory lessons. What is less clear is how that training affects the low-
inference variables of explanatory teaching. It is likely that minute
changes in these variables produces a markedly different pattern of
teaching. Further study of this issue is required.

The study of types of explanations and the analysis of transcripts
revealed differences between the types of explaining. The well-known
rule/example/rule model seemed to be most appropriate for interpretive
explanations but less appropriate for other types of explanation. The
question 'What counts as good explaining?' now requires translating
into 'What counts as good interpretive, good descriptive and good
reason-giving explanations?'

References

Barnes, D. (1976) *From Communication to Curriculum*, Penguin, Harmondsworth
Bellack, A.A., Hyman, R.T., Smith, F.L. and Kliebard, H.M. (1966) *The Language
of the Classroom*, Teachers College Press, New York
Bloom, B.S. (1956) *Taxonomy of Educational Objectives*, Longman, New York
Brown, G.A. (1978a) *Microteaching: Programme of Teaching Skills*, Methuen,
London
—— (1978b) *Lecturing and Explaining*, Methuen, London
—— (1981) *Explanatory Teaching in Biology*, University of Nottingham
—— and Armstrong, S. (1978) 'SAID: A System for Analysing Instructional
Discourse', in R.W. McAleese and D.R. Hamilton (eds), *Understanding Class-
room Life*, NFER, Slough
—— and Hatton, N. (1982) *Explaining and Explanations*, Macmillan, London
Dunkin, M.J. and Biddle, B.J. (1974) *The Study of Teaching*, Holt, Rinehart &
Winston, New York
Ennis, R.H. (1969) *Logic in Teaching*, Prentice-Hall, Englewood Cliffs
Gage, N.L. *et al.* (1972) Chapter 9 of I. Westbury and A. Bellack (eds), *Research
into Classroom Processes*, Teachers College Press, New York
—— and Berliner, D. (1975) *Educational Psychology*, University of California
Press, Berkeley
Hargie, D.D.W. (1980) *An Evaluation of a Microteaching Programme*, PhD thesis,
Ulster Polytechnic
Hyman, R.T. (1974) *Teaching: Vantage Points for Study*, Lippincott Press,
New York
Martin, J.R. (1970) *Explaining, Understanding and Teaching*, McGraw-Hill, New
York
Rosenshine, B. and Furst, N. (1973) 'The Use of Direct Observation to Study
Teaching', in R.W. Travers (ed.) *Second Handbook of Research on Teaching*,
Rand McNally, Chicago, pp. 122-83
Smith, B.O. and Meux, M. (1970) *A Study of the Logic of Teaching*, University
of Illinois Press
Swift, L.F. (1961) 'Explanation, in B.O. Smith and R.H. Ennis (eds), *Language
and Concepts in Education*, 179-94 Rand McNally, Chicago
Thyne, J.M. (1963) *The Psychology of Learning and Techniques of Teaching*,
University of London Press

Tisher, R.P. (1970) 'The Nature of Verbal Discourse in Classrooms and Associa-
   tion between Verbal Discourse and Pupil Understanding in Science' in W.J.
   Campbell (ed), *Scholars in Context*, Wiley, Sydney
Turney, C. (ed.) (1975) *Sydney Microskill Series 2*, University of Sydney,
   Sydney, Australia
Verner C. and Dickinson, G. (1968) 'The Lecture: An Analysis and Review of
   Research', *Adult Education, 17*, 85-100
Youngman, M.B. (1979) *Analysing Social and Educational Research*, McGraw-
   Hill, London

CLASSROOM ORGANISATION AND LEARNING

T. Kerry and M.K. Sands

The purpose of the Teacher Education Project in investigating mixed-ability teaching was to aid student teachers to handle such classes more effectively. In the period 1976-80 when the investigation was in progress, few practising teachers had had anything but a brief period of *ad hoc* experience in this form of organisation, and so the Project found itself also with an in-service role. This chapter describes in outline some of the researches which were to underpin the Project's *Focus* series of practical skills workbooks, published by Macmillan. Some of the work is more fully reported in Sands and Kerry (1982).

Data were collected by a combination of questionnaire and case-study methods. In 1977 a number of teacher trainers in universities were asked to act as observers, and each completed a sizeable study of a teacher chosen by him or her as an effective practitioner in the relevant subject area. Twenty-one such case studies were completed. Each consisted of a period of observation in the teacher's classroom, a lengthy interview with the teacher about practice and philosophy, and another similar interview with the teacher's head of department in order to gain a middle-management perspective of mixed-ability teaching in operation. In addition to the 21 detailed case studies which emanated from this research phase, a semi-structured questionnaire was sent to headteachers of 70 schools used by the Nottingham University School of Education for teaching practice placement. Heads from 40 schools responded. In 1980, three years later, a similar questionnaire was mailed to the 40 respondents, and 39 replied, thus enabling the picture of the development of mixed-ability teaching to be updated. Much of what follows is based upon these data, though additional researches into teachers' use of group work and into the education of bright pupils and slow learners are described at appropriate points in the account. Table 7.2 shows the use of mixed-ability teaching in the 30 non-selective schools in the sample.

The first major discovery of the Teacher Education Project was the mismatch between the underlying *philosophy* of mixed-ability teaching and its *practice*. Work by writers such as Kelly (1975, 1978) would lead one to believe that a mixed-ability organisation allows a teacher to cater for the needs of each individual pupil, and that to do this, group work and individualised learning are common. We found that definitions of 'mixed ability' varied. In some schools the mix excluded remedial pupils; in others classes were selected at random from a year's intake. But in some schools a systematic attempt was made to assess pupils' abilities and to spread the most and least able throughout all classes. We have even discovered (since this research) one school where able pupils were put into an 'A' band, and the mix achieved after this creaming process.

However pupils were allocated to classes, and often it was on the basis of friendship choices, once in the classroom it was common for the teacher to use hidden streaming methods. Where this did not happen teachers reported that friendship pairs or groups usually consisted of pupils of similar ability; or that able pupils were made to act as teachers' aides or pupil-teachers to serve the needs of the slower learners. Furthermore, it was clear from the case studies that, whatever the theory, genuine group work was rarely used and was of a limited nature (this will be taken up again later). Whole-class teaching predominated.

In a separate but related piece of research known as the Sherwood Project, Kerry (1982a) found that, in a study of five first-year, mixed-ability classes in large comprehensive schools, whole-class teaching consistently took up a major proportion of all teaching time. These results are set out in Table 7.1.

Table 7.1: Proportions of Time (in Percentages of Total Lesson Time) Spent on Whole-class Teaching, Group Work and Individualised Learning in Five First-year, Mixed-ability Classes in Comprehensive Schools

School	Whole class	Group work 1*	Group work 2**	Individualised learning
Will Scarlet	64	36	0	0
Huntingdon	58.1	16.9	8.7	16.3
Robin Hood	49.1	26.7	14.6	9.6
Friar Tuck	71.8	2.4	4.8	21
Alan Adale	71	0	4.9	24.1

* 1: organisational group work, i.e. friends sitting together but working on essentially whole-class tasks.

** 2: educational group work, i.e. where pupils are actively engaged in a task requiring co-operation and pooling of resources to produce the end-product.

Source: Kerry, 1982c.

The earlier work discovered, too, that teachers used two kinds of group work: organisational groups in which the members of a group although seated together were working individually and simultaneously on identical tasks, and educational group work in which the group was responsible for the collective completion of a co-operative and common task or piece of learning, and all members of the group pooled their resources to complete the task. If the figures for whole-class teaching and organisational group work quoted in Table 7.1 are added together, it will be seen that most mixed-ability teaching is undifferentiated in the sense that it fails to provide for the specific needs of individual pupils or of several pupils with similar needs. Indeed, in practice, teaching is clearly aimed at classes, not at pupils, which seems to be a denial of the spirit of mixed-ability organisation.

Teachers in the case studies articulated the purposes of whole-class teaching as these: to start off work, to introduce a new topic, to motivate pupils, to transmit factual information, to cover a particular topic all pupils need to share, and to consolidate work covered individually or in groups. They justified the large amount of time spent on this teaching mode by pointing out that pupils do not care to learn on their own all the time, that learning needs a structure not available in other modes, and that it is the most economical way to use teacher time. While balance between modes was important to the teachers, the nature of this balance was dependent upon the teacher's own philosophy, the background of the pupils and the quantity and suitability of available resources.

This paucity of educational group work led Sands to conduct follow-up enquiries, using an observation schedule devised by the Project co-ordinator, to discover exactly how classroom groups were used by teachers. This research is summarised below, and fuller accounts can be found in Sands (1981a, 1981b).

The aim of the three studies undertaken was to try to determine what most teachers understood by the term 'group work', to see the extent of its use, the teaching skills involved in it, and how and why teachers used groups in their classes. How were the groups chosen, by self-selection or by the teacher? What kind of work was it expected could be done in groups, did a group get on with its work, or was there a considerable amount of time off task? What kinds of pupil-pupil and teacher-pupil interactions were there in groups?

It was found that group work was not common. Where it did occur in a lesson it was usually the first type of group work given earlier in this chapter: members of the group seated or standing together, but working individually on the same task. Clearly, there were external factors (for example, size and layout of room, furniture, length of lesson and size of class, available resources and ancillary help) which affected the extent to which groups could be used. Other factors were the teacher's own skill and teaching style, and what one might call the 'class personality': whether or not the pupils in it were thought to be committed and motivated and could work quietly and sensibly. The most successful group-work lessons were those where the teacher showed skill in handling and understanding of groups, where he or she gave a positive lead to a lesson before the group work began, and follow-up where the group experiences were pooled and discussed, occurred.

As one might have expected, the teacher was regarded differently by the pupils during group work from when a whole-class lesson was going on. He or she was seen, and behaved, more as a consultant and facilitator than as an instructor. The role was an active (and tiring) one as work was monitored and directed, information gathered and processed, questioning and explaining carried out with speed and at different levels, while groups were controlled, motivated and supervised.

What were the groups asked to do? What kinds of task were being performed? Firstly, tasks set were fairly straightforward. In science the pairs (rarely more than two) followed instructions or a work-sheet as they proceeded through a piece of practical work, recorded the results and cleared up. Individual writing up usually followed. In other subjects a group might be following a work-sheet or booklet together and jointly producing answers, making a cooked dish or meal, designing and producing a piece of art work; or working on a group project involving a literature search and the selection and amalgamation of different types of material.

In 90 per cent of the lessons observed each group was given the same task. Occasionally this was given at three different levels of understanding and/or language so that similar content or skills were covered by all groups but at a different pace and to different depths. In some science lessons the science topic under study was presented as a programme of practical work which could be tackled by several different approaches using different work-cards, again appropriate for varying levels of ability.

In one study time-on-task was recorded for a number of groups. The result showed that most groups were working most of the time. In only 5 per cent of the observed groups were group members working for less than half the time. The talk between group members was mainly related to the work in hand, and was never at a particularly high level. Simple questions were asked, instructions were repeated, straightforward comments made. A certain amount of chat went on, and, if not excessive, probably played an important part in keeping the group working together.

The size of groups was frequently two. Many groups were allowed to select their own members and therefore were long-lasting, consisting of friends of the same sex and with a similar outlook, usually of the same ability. Where a group formed consisting of pupils of widely differing ability, the teacher reported that its members might lose patience with each other and re-form in another group.

What then of the teacher's aims for group work? We have reported findings where very little group work was discovered. When it was found, it proved to be a relatively impoverished model, where the tasks given were relatively low level, the resources were rarely adapted to a wide spread of ability, and the interactions which took place within the group were commonplace. Teachers told us that groups were used in mixed-ability classes as a way of dealing with the broad spectrum of ability, achievement and even motivation within the class. Children could find success and perhaps independence within a group which might escape them both as a member of a whole class and if working individually. Conversely, they would learn to co-operate, help each other to learn, as well as gain practice in the use of language.

It could be that the interactions between pupils within the group were simply a consequence of the straightforward tasks set. Even in the problems which could have been posed in an enquiry-based approach to practical work in science, groups were rarely or never asked to indulge in any serious thinking. No higher-level thinking skills nor creative imagination were demanded of them. This could perhaps be interpreted as reasonable foresight on the part of the teacher, as the verbal comments overheard were all low level. Kempa (1979), who made detailed studies of group interactions in science lessons over the course of a year, reported that what he refers to as Cognitive Level II discourse (which includes higher-level cognitive skills) was rare, even when teachers particularly stressed this aspect. As with our findings, the talk which was concerned with the work in progress was entirely Cognitive Level I discourse. Kerry (1981) also working with broad-banded science lessons, reported the same, pointing out that most of the teacher-pupil interactions were about procedure and that many opportunities for stimulating thought in pupils were lost. Even if, as Eggleston, Galton and Jones (1976) point out, one would expect many more simple cognitive transactions than those at a higher level because of the need to build a solid base to the pyramid before using the acquired knowledge to form abstractions, there are still so few as to cause concern.

For mixed-ability teaching the implications of the findings are fairly dire, although not unexpected. The tasks set were by and large the same for all the groups. Some children proceeded rapidly and with ease, others floundered. In some classes extension work (although sometimes simply more of the same) was available for bright pupils.

The pessimistic view of group work gained by observations such as those discussed above is countered to a certain extent by the knowledge that group work of a high level is possible using skill and careful planning. Although in total only a fraction of the appointments made with teachers to observe lessons containing groups resulted in such high-level group activity, there were nevertheless some excellent examples.

These comments, relating to the limited and impoverished use of groups in mixed-ability classes, are paralleled in other recent reports where the teaching modes in use with mixed-ability classes are analysed and discussed. The findings of the Reports by HMI (1978, 1979) were supported by those of Reid, Clunies-Ross, Goacher and Vile (1982) for the NFER mixed ability research project. In the latter many of the teachers' comments reported reveal that their teaching is geared to the middle of the ability range, and that class teaching aimed at this level is inevitably prevalent.

If there is a mismatch then between teachers' idealistic aims for group work and the reality, if group work fails to contribute effectively as a teaching technique in the handling of mixed-ability classes, and if what goes on inside a group fails to match up to one's hopes for the interactions at various levels, the development of leadership and responsibilities, the exchange of ideas and discussion between its members, why are groups used at all? The science lessons we observed and the work of Galton, Simon and Croll (1980) give perhaps a useful pointer to a possible answer. In the primary school classes studied by the Leicester research team, group work was used by the teachers principally as an organisational device. Again, group work was found frequently to consist of children seated in groups but working alone, with group interactions playing little part in the completion of the task. In secondary school science lessons where expensive sets of apparatus and other materials are involved, and no doubt in other curriculum areas too, the ideal would be for individual practical work. But if children work in groups one needs less material, and group work here too could be being used to accommodate to the prevailing circumstances rather than as a teaching device which uniquely develops certain skills.

So far the picture of mixed-ability lessons is of largely undifferentiated work in a whole-class teaching mode, with group work rarely used effectively and usually pressed into service only as an organisational device. The cognitive level of verbal transactions during group work has been described as low; and the same would apply to those in whole-class contexts too. This phenomenon is documented at length elsewhere (Kerry, 1982b, 1982c; Sands and Kerry, 1982), and the theme will not be elaborated here. However, for the sake of completeness some mention should be made of the other possible teaching mode: individualised learning.

In the case-study research few teachers advocated individualised learning. The picture was confirmed by the Sherwood study. However, two advantages were stressed: its potential as a means to cater for extremes of the ability range, and the opportunity it afforded pupils to proceed at their own pace. Typically, individualised learning was commonest where work-cards or textbooks were used, for example in mathematics, where pupils could follow a scheme of work at an appropriate pace, using the teacher as consultant. Reasons given for not using the individualised mode more often were: the inability of slower pupils to read work-sheets or instructions and to direct their own work, the dangers inherent in pupils choosing inappropriate directions of work, and the removal of teacher initiative in the structuring of classroom learning.

The foregoing discussion has thrown some doubts upon the quality of thinking in mixed-ability classes (aspects of this theme are taken up again in Chapter 8), and also upon the ability of this form of organisation to cater for pupils at the two extremes of the ability range. It is to this latter subject that we now turn.

During the case-study interviews, the nominated effective teachers were asked to describe the problems which they had with bright pupils and slow learners in their classes. The results, along with some reported solutions to these articulated problems, can be seen as Figures 7.1 (bright pupils) and 7.2 (slow learners). Even these effective teachers experienced problems caused by extremes of ability within one class, and were also quite often at a loss as to how to deal with them. In the case of the slow learners they isolated some 22 individual problems, found solutions to all but 4, and generally agreed about the core problems: poor reading and comprehension ability.

Figure 7.1: Teachers' Reported Problems in Dealing with Bright Children in Mixed-ability Classes, and Their Reported Solutions to the Problems

1. Reported problem	Reported solution
1. Fast pace of working compared with rest of class (6 occurrences)	Provision of new, valid and challenging work (once) Additional work (once; teacher adds 'an easy problem to cope with'). Extra material to work through (e.g. worksheets, problems, experiments (once)) Extra material (once; teacher adds 'not too serious a problem') Extension work (once) No solution offered (once)
2. Bright held back by slower pupils	No solution offered (teacher adds 'not serious problem at first-form level')
3. Failure to reach potential because they easily look good in mixed ability classes	Individual contact with teacher to extract best from each child
4. Failure to stretch them because slow pupils demand teacher's time	No solution offered
5. Boredom	Having enough material available to stretch the brighter pupils
6. Frustration at being held up by rest of class	No solution offered
7. Provision of occasional extension work or extra work (twice)	Set additional homework and let pupils demonstrate their achievements to rest of class. (One teacher comments 'this is not a successful solution')
8. Need to extend bright pupils	More thought has to be put into worksheet to occupy the ablest
9. Provision of extra reading	No solution offered
10. Maintaining progress	Use of lots of apparatus and additional work
11. Need teacher's help too frequently	No solution offered

Figure 7.2: Teachers' Reported Problems in Dealing With Slow Learners in Mixed-ability Classes, and Their Reported Solutions to These Problems

Reported problem	Reported solution
1. Slow pace at which these pupils work	Remedial cards — but the pupils still need attention and this is NOT a fully effective solution
2. 'Dragging their feet'	More teacher attention
3. Lack of time, e.g. to give practice in reading skills	—
4. Poor reading ability (6 occurrences)	Reading with the pupils, to the pupils. Putting slow pupils with a pupil who can read better. Intensive individual attention where possible (and it often isn't). Putting instructions, etc. on tape
5. Inability to read instructions	—
6. Inability to follow instructions	Press pupils individually to re-read and explain to the teacher
7. Inability to understand instructions and worksheets	Teacher must devote more time to explanations
8. Understanding and starting set work	Individual attention to pupils in early stages
9. Short memories	Give extra revision (French teacher)
10. Short attention span	Provision of extra materials helps
11. Short concentration span and problems in understanding complex explanations directed at whole class	'Suppress the slow' or 'speak to the bright pupils separately'
12. Difficulty in writing	Encourage pupils to write précis from worksheets
13. Pupils' written work — knowing what to say and how to say it	Individual attention and help from teacher
14. Lack of books and resources suitable for both age and ability	Make up deficiency with teacher attention (not a satisfactory solution)
15. Level of classwork too high for least able	Special work at slow learners' level and plenty of teacher attention
16. Pupils have difficulty in choosing work units	Teacher must give help to them to choose within their own capabilities
17. Sustaining motivation	Jump to new work to sustain interest

Figure 7.2 (cont'd) Reported Problems in Dealing With Slow Learners in Mixed-ability Classes, and Their Reported Solutions to These Problems

Reported problem	Reported solution
18. Maintaining progress and interest	Use a lot of apparatus
19. Keeping morale high because this group is slowest and least successful always	—
20. Behavioural problems caused by boredom	Use a lot of apparatus
21. Giving individual attention to pupils whenever possible	'I try. Not always successful, but I'm working on it'
22. Need for continual attention from the teacher to	
assist with practical work	—
assist with reading	—
answer questions	—

With bright pupils, teachers were less able to discern problems and less able to cope with them. In only 7 of the case studies did the effective teacher attempt to diagnose and meet the needs of the ablest pupils in the class. There was a general feeling that it is 'not too serious' to fail to cater for able pupils; and one teacher put the blame for there being a problem at all on to the shoulders of the pupils themselves, who simply 'worked too fast'.

Though the causes of the problems of slow and bright pupils in mixed-ability contexts were different, the symptoms were similar: work quickly finished, boredom leading eventually to lack of motivation, and disruption (more common among the slow). Teachers were aware of the need to give more individual time and attention to both groups, but were unable to do so. There simply was not any more available.

Nor was provision at a school level much more effective than in the individual classrooms. Analyses of the headteachers' questionnaires completed in 1977 and in 1980 showed that almost no special provision was made to stimulate able pupils until they passed the hurdle of GCE 'O' level and passed into the sixth form (Kerry, 1980a). For slow learners, some schools had found withdrawal or partial withdrawal helpful (and there were examples of good practice in remedial provision); but in many cases there was simply a series of different experimental approaches within a given school over the three years with no clear idea about what kind of education was really most suitable for this group. Where mixed ability scored was that it split up pupils who might otherwise form 'sinks' or 'ghettos' (the heads' words): so discipline tended to be easier (Kerry, 1982a).

At this juncture enough has been said to establish that many mixed-ability classes are in the whole-class mode, with mainly undemanding and undifferentiated work aimed at, or a little below, the middle of the ability range. This is a rather negative picture, and the time has come to balance the perspective with a description of the gains which were seen to come from mixed-ability grouping.

In our research teachers pointed to the strengths and advantages of mixed-ability organisation. Social aims were frequently quoted. Though these were often vague, a finding shared with HMI (1978), it was clear that the teachers wanted pupils to work co-operatively, to learn from one another, to avoid being labelled, and to interact across ability levels. In the process teachers felt that pupils gained in self-respect and therefore in self-confidence. In terms of learning, self-pacing was valued by our respondents. There was a general belief that, in the mixed-ability context, slow learners learned more, were more mature and less disruptive. But mixed-ability teaching produced gains for the teachers themselves. They played different roles from those of traditional class teaching: facilitator and consultant rather than director and instructor. They had to rethink curriculum content and teaching method. Team teaching sometimes resulted. The distance between teacher and pupil seemed lessened in this form of organisation.

On the other hand there were hurdles to be jumped. With a range of ability to cater for preparation time was greatly increased; and schools had to find a great many more resources, particularly of the textbook and audiovisual varieties.

One characteristic of the successful teacher of mixed-ability classes which emerged was flexibility. The teachers themselves defined this as the skill to use a variety of teaching modes within one lesson, to vary the pace and style of approach within a lesson, to use a range of audio-visual media, and to encourage a variety of pupil activities to progress simultaneously.

In the case studies of lessons given by effective teachers the observers noted particularly the informality of relationships between teachers and pupils, the involvement of pupils in learning and in decision-making, and the skill of the teacher in controlling several activities at once.

Some of the lessons analysed showed that mixed-ability classes could be handled in an interesting and effective way. There were, however, weaknesses in the approach. Too much reliance was put upon work-cards (Wragg, 1978). Too few teachers were able to articulate clear aims and philosophies (HMI, 1978). To succeed, schools needed good back-up facilities and resources (Schools Council, 1977; Ingleson, 1982). Mixed-ability teaching should be regarded as an *advanced* set of teaching skills: as a beginner the young teacher would do well to master basic steps first (Kerry and Sands, 1982a, 1982b).

Table 7.2: Analysis of Mixed-ability Teaching by Subject

	1st yr	2nd yr	3rd yr	4th yr	5th yr
Maths	18	8	4		
Physics	3	2	5	2	2
Chemistry	3	2	5	2	2
Biology	1	2	5	2	2
Combined Science	19	16	4	2	2
English	19	16	9	5	4
French	18	9	3	1	
German	2	1	1	1	
History	8	8	11	1	1
Geography	9	9	11	2	2
Humanities	10	9	5	6	6
Classics	1	1			
Religious Studies	12	10	11	9	9
Arts, Crafts, Metal/Woodwork, Creative Arts	17	16	12	4	4
Drama, Sound and Movement	4	4	3	2	2
Music	16	14	11	3	3
Physical Education	12	9	7	6	6
Technical Studies	5	5	3		
Design	3	3	3	3	3
Home Economics	4	4	3		
Inter-disciplinary Enquiry	2	2			
Environmental Studies				1	1
Social Education				2	2
Computer Studies				1	1
Careers				1	1
Total number of schools in the sample using mixed-ability teaching in the year indicated (out of 30 comprehensive schools)	23	21	17	15	15

When this research began mixed ability teaching was on the crest of the educational wave: its use was spreading and it appeared that it would soon be at the high tide of educational organisation. But the tide ebbed, and, probably because of some of the shortcomings outlined in this chapter, the use of a mixed-ability organisation is now commonly restricted to the early years of the comprehensive school.

Table 7.2 examines the distribution across year groups of mixed-ability organisation in 30 East Midlands schools. In most subjects mixed ability gives way after year 2 to some form of banding, or to setting as public examinations draw near. It seems likely that mixed-ability teaching may suit some curriculum areas such as religious education (Kerry, 1980b) more than others (maths and modern languages) (Reid, 1982). Probably, as with most educational fashions, its strengths have now been harnessed and its weaknesses probed. It will find its natural level in a 'mixed economy' of school organisation.

During the late 1970s a good deal of research effort was put into exploring the pros and cons of mixed ability. One approach, typified by the Banbury Report (Newbold, 1977), attempted to compare pupils taught by mixed-ability and more conventional means according to examination performance. This method is almost inevitably doomed to failure. The Hawthorne effect, and variables such as the relative competencies of individual teachers defy such comparative studies. The NFER study (Reid *et al.*, 1982) tended to parallel the findings reported here, even in matters of detail. HMI (1978) noted the discrepancy between philosophy and practice, and went on to wonder at the vagueness of what appeared to be ubiquitous 'social aims'. Studies of individual subject areas (Schools Council, 1977; Torbe, 1979) were mostly concerned to provide practical hints either about classroom teaching or about departmental organisation. A summary by Kerry of research on the topic of mixed-ability teaching can be found in Cohen, Manion and Thomas (1983).

References

Cohen, L., Thomas, J. and Manion, L. (eds) (1983) *Educational Research in Britain 1970-1980,* NFER-Nelson, Windsor

Eggleston, J.F., Galton, M.J. and Jones, M.E. (1976) *Processes and Products of Science Teaching,* Macmillan, London

Galton, M.J., Simon, B. and Croll, P. (1980) *Inside the Primary Classroom,* Routledge & Kegan Paul, London

HMI (1978) Department of Education and Science, *Mixed Ability Work in Comprehensive Schools,* HMSO, London

—— (1979) Department of Education and Science, *Aspects of Secondary Education in England*, HMSO, London

Ingleson, S. (1982) 'Creating Conditions for Success with Mixed Ability Classes', in M.K. Sands and T. Kerry, (eds), *Mixed Ability Teaching*, Croom Helm, London

Kelly, A.V. (1975) *Case Studies in Mixed Ability Teaching*, Harper & Row, London

—— (1978), *Mixed Ability Grouping: Theory and Practice*, Harper & Row, London

Kempa, R.F. (1979), 'Study in Curriculum Implementation in the Classroom', in P. Tamir (*et al.*) (eds), *Curriculum Implementation and its Relationship to Curriculum Development in Science*, Israel Teaching Centre

Kerry, T. (1980a) 'Provision for Bright Pupils in 40 Schools: Three Years' Progress', *Cambridge Journal of Education, 10*, 3 134-43

—— (1980b) 'RE: a Suitable Case for Mixed Ability?', *British Journal of Religious Education, 3*, 2, 46-52

—— (1981) 'Thinking in Science Lessons', *School Science Review, 63*, 223

—— (1982a) 'Providing for Slow Learners', *Special Education: Forward Trends, 8*, 4, 9-11

—— (1982b) 'The Demands made by RE on pupils' Thinking', in J. Hull (ed.), *New Directions in Religious Education*, Falmer Press, Lewes, Sussex

—— (1982c) 'Teachers' Identification of Exceptional Pupils and their Strategies for Coping with them', PhD thesis, University of Nottingham

—— and Sands, M.K. (1982a) *Mixed Ability Teaching, Focus* series, Macmillan, Basingstoke

—— and Sands, M.K. (1982b) *Handling Classroom Groups, Focus* series, Macmillan, Basingstoke

Newbold, D. (1977) *Ability Grouping*, NFER, Slough

Reid, M, Clunies-Ross, L, Goacher, B and Vile, C. (1982) *Mixed Ability Teaching – Problems and Possibilities*, NFER-Nelson, Windsor

Sands, M.K. (1981a) 'Group-work: Time for Re-evaluation?', *Educational Studies, 7*, 2

—— (1981b) 'Group-work in Science: Myth and Reality', *School Science Review, 62*, 221

—— and Kerry, T (eds) (1982) *Mixed Ability Teaching*, Croom Helm, London

Schools Council (1977) *Mixed Ability Teaching in Mathematics*, Evans/Methuen, London

Torbe, M. (1979) 'Success in Learning', *Forum, 21*, 3

Wragg, E.C. (1978) 'Death by a Thousand Workcards', *Times Educational Supplement* 3 November

8 ANALYSING THE COGNITIVE DEMAND MADE BY CLASSROOM TASKS IN MIXED-ABILITY CLASSES

T. Kerry

In Chapter 7 there was a description of the Teacher Education Project's research into aspects of mixed-ability teaching. It emerged from this general survey of current practice that teachers saw exceptional pupils, both bright and slow learners, as the source of a number of classroom problems. Clearly, these pupils required some kind of special treatment: in Warnock (1978) terms they had 'special educational needs' of varying kinds. The underlying philosophy of mixed-ability teaching is that each child, not simply the most and least able, can be given appropriate attention rather than being lumped crudely with others as 'A' stream, 'remedial' or 'average'. So it seemed logical to suppose that from a practical teaching point of view teachers were evolving 'strategies' to cope with the varying needs of pupils at the extreme ends of, and across, the ability range in mixed-ability classes. A research and development project such as the Teacher Education Project was interested to investigate these practical procedures in order to extract some implications for teacher training, both initial and in-service.

It was also possible to construe the same problem from a different perspective: that of cognitive or developmental psychology. The most frequently cited work in stage theory of cognitive development is that of Piaget (1972). Piaget's work has been shown to have relevance to an understanding of children's learning in a variety of curriculum areas by a variety of subject specialists — in RE by Goldman (1964, 1966), in history by da Silva (1972) in geography by Rhys (1972), in science by Harlen (1978) and Shayer (1970). According to this theory, although cognitive development is viewed as a continuum, children pass through clearly observable stages in their ability to understand complex ideas and solve problems. The pre-operational and concrete operational stages give way at about the age of 12 years to the formal phase in which youngsters can cope with increasingly abstract ideas. The passage from concrete to formal thinking does not take place instantly, indeed the transition may happen much earlier for some people than others, and it will occur earlier for the more able. In the first year of a

163

comprehensive school a teacher facing a mixed-ability class will be presented with some able children who have passed into formal thinking some time before, some who have just made or are in the process of making the transition, and others who are in or must be nurtured towards a stage of readiness to cope with concepts and abstract ideas.

Both a study of practical teaching and a scrutiny of educational theory, then, alert the teacher or teacher trainer to the fact that, when pupils enter mixed-ability classes in the comprehensive school, the demands made upon them must develop and extend their intellectual or cognitive abilities. Does this happen in practice?

This last question is deceptively simple. To answer it the researcher has to be able to observe and try to measure the thought processes which take place in the classroom. Thoughts are essentially invisible events, but in a public learning situation such as classroom lessons there are visible manifestations of the thought process. Teachers talk, and that talk can be assessed for cognitive demand and for the signals it puts out to pupils about their own expected levels of thinking. Teachers ask questions, and those questions can be recorded and analysed as described in Chapter 5. When pupils respond, or initiate, their contributions can likewise be analysed for thought-level: whether they are regurgitating facts, dealing in concepts, or exploring abstract notions.

A study of teacher talk, teachers' questions and pupils' responses, analysed for cognitive-level, would tell the observer a great deal about the quality of thinking which takes place in classrooms. It would also omit a large and important area of classroom cognitive life: the task which had been set. Almost all the manifestations of thinking in classrooms can be divided either into the three oral components listed above or into tasks set by teachers and responded to by pupils. For a more complete picture of classroom cognitive life the observer would have to record and analyse all three oral components and all the classroom tasks, classifying each according to appropriate measures of cognitive demand. This data collection and analysis was carried out in five first-year comprehensive school classes during the Teacher Education Project, and this chapter reports some of the findings from the research, which was code named the Sherwood Project.

Information about teacher talk, teacher questions and pupil response in the five classes studied has been reported elsewhere (Kerry 1982; Sands and Kerry, 1982). What follows is a précis which can be compared with the findings about tasks set in these classes. These last are described in rather more detail in the second half of this chapter.

The Project adopted five first-year mixed-ability classes in comprehensive schools and studied the teacher talk, teachers' questions and pupils' responses in a representative sample of lessons in eight curriculum areas: RE, French, science, history, mathematics, English, geography and music. In all the study involved a look at work by 36 teachers and 135 pupils during 213 lesson hours in five schools which were endowed rather above the average in terms of equipment, resources and catchment area.

Teacher talk commonly occurred in relatively brief units of a few sentences (typically, punctuated by teachers' questions, pupils' responses or task activity). Each of these units was coded by the observer for level of cognitive demand as follows:

TO management talk
T1 information, data-giving
T2 conceptual-level talk, reasons, explanations
T3 abstract ideas, laws, generalisations

Similarly, each teacher question was coded for cognitive demand, though a more appropriate coding system for questions depended upon the work of Bloom (1956) and Turney (1973, 1975) and contained seven categories:

Q0 management questions
Q1 recall   } Lower order
Q2 simple comprehension

Q3 application
Q4 analysis   } Higher order
Q5 synthesis
Q6 evaluation

Question types Q0 to Q6 do not make up a strict hierarchy; but Q1 and Q2 represent lower-order thought operations and Q3-Q6 can be grouped together as higher-order events.

Pupil responses and initiations to the teacher were also coded using a system similar to that employed for teacher talk, and borrowing an underlying framework from Gallagher (1970):

R0 management level
R1 information level
R2 concept level
R3 abstract level

Incorrect responses (RW) were also coded, as were fleeting inter-changes between pupil and teacher which had a social rather than a managerial or learning significance (Code C).

This produced a 17-category coding system to measure the cognitive-level of classroom verbal exchanges. Table 8.1 shows the results of this investigation for each of the five schools in the sample, and the overall proportions of each cognitive category across the whole study period. One way of conceptualising the findings from this research is to group together all those transactions which have to do with management (management talk by the teacher (T0), management questions (Q0), and management responses including social contacts (R0, 6)) and to express them as a percentage of the total transaction. Likewise T1, Q1, Q2 and R1 transactions, as a group, represent trading of factual infor-mation; and codes T2, T3, Q3, Q4, Q5, Q6, R2 and R3 have to do with the stimulation of higher-level thinking. The result of this grouping of data produces the result shown in Figure 8.1.

Table 8.1: Breakdown of Classroom Transactions in Five Mixed-ability Classes Analysed by Type and Level of Cognitive Demand

	TO	T1	T2	T3	Q0	Q1	Q2	Q3	Q4	Q5	Q6	C	R0	R1	R2	R3	Rw	Total (%)
Will Scarlet	15.1	16.3	1.3	0.02	1.9	7.2	5.1	1.1	0.2	0	0	21.5	8.2	14.2	4.9	0.02	2.5	100
Huntingdon	14.5	15	1.2	0	3.8	10.1	4.3	0.5	0.08	0	0	21.3	8.4	16	3	0	1.6	100
Robin Hood	17	6.3	2	0	2	7.5	3	1	0.3	0	0.1	36.6	3.7	15.4	3.8	0.2	1.1	100
Friar Tuck	29	17.3	1	0	3.3	12.7	0.5	0.02	0.03	0	0	9.5	6.8	17.3	0.03	0	2.5	100
Alan Adale	29.4	11.7	1.06	0.02	5.4	12.2	0.4	0	0.6	0	0	15	9.3	12.8	0.1	0.01	2.1	100

Figure 8.1: Proportions of Classroom Verbal Transactions Concerned With Managing, Informing and Stimulating in Five First-year Mixed-ability Classes

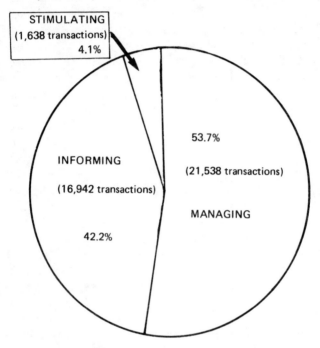

STIMULATING
(1,638 transactions)
4.1%

INFORMING
(16,942 transactions)
42.2%

53.7%
(21,538 transactions)
MANAGING

From Figure 8.1 it seems fair to conclude that for teachers of first-year comprehensive school classes more than half of their oral transactions are taken up by management operations (these are not necessarily to do with discipline and none of the classes observed was badly behaved). The remainder are largely consumed by informing or receiving back information. Very little classroom dialogue allows room for the kind of formal, abstract thinking one might be looking for in average, let alone able, pupils of this age.

When teachers in the sample were asked to nominate their able pupils they did so; but though they perceived them as able they made few attempts to ask these identified pupils' higher-order, more demanding questions or to elicit more abstract responses. One was drawn to the conclusion, therefore, that if cognitive stimulation was indeed taking place in these classrooms, even for the minority of very able pupils, it was not through oral transactions. Though many of the children in these classes were at the stage of readiness for formal thinking there was little indication that teachers were aware of this or were encouraging the process. If this encouragement or opportunity was lacking in oral classroom transactions then it might be coming through that other component of classroom cognitive life, the task.

Throughout the study period in the five sample schools all the tasks set by teachers were recorded by the observer. In all, 640 tasks were set by the 36 teachers. Tasks, then, clearly form an important part of the learning process which pupils experience; and task-setting must be regarded as an important skill for the trainee or experienced teacher. To draw out training procedures from this investigation, the Project needed to discover what kinds of tasks were set and what kinds of cognitive demands they made. The following procedure for data collection and analysis was established. All the tasks set by teachers were recorded and described. Task descriptions were then sifted by two analysts. A series of 'task types' emerged from this preliminary sifting. The types were given appropriate labels using descriptions closely akin to the words the teachers themselves used to set up the tasks (draw, listen, etc.). A basic division was found to exist between high-level tasks (H) and low-level ones (L) with respect to cognitive demand. From this two-fold division and using labels already mentioned, a category system was developed (L1-L12; H1-H6). Within the broad divisions L and H, the numbered order does not necessarily represent a hierarchy, however. This produced a proforma for analysing classroom tasks (ACT) which, along with typical task descriptions for each category, is shown in Figure 8.2.

Figure 8.2: Analysis of Classroom Tasks (ACT) Proforma

Low-level tasks

Code	Description	Example
L 1	Disciplinary tasks	Write six reasons why you must not run round the classroom
L 2	Administrative tasks	Move classroom furniture to make more space; collect or pack away equipment
L 3	Drawing or colouring task	Commonest examples were of copying maps from atlases or colouring pictures to illustrate written work. These tasks took little thought, but some manual skill.
L 4	Copying or writing headings	Teachers frequently gave the instruction 'put a heading'; copying directly from blackboard or text was included here
L 5	Reading aloud	In all subjects teachers were inclined to ask pupils to read passages round the class. This category was extended to include singing together, repeating phrases from a tape-recorder, or playing musical instruments one note at a time in direct imitation of the teacher
L 6	Silent reading; listening or watching	Teachers often asked pupils to be a passive audience (to a record, a demonstration experiment). Pupils also read silently, often to allow time for slower workers to catch up
L 7	Memorising	Learn lists of vocabulary in a language or dates in history
L 8	Revising or taking revision test	This category was reserved for those occasions when a teacher used the word 'revision' in a description of the task
L 9	Carrying out an experiment (exactly following a demonstration); or making simple observation of results	Many science lessons began by a teacher demonstrating and then pupils either observing the result or doing an exact replication of the experiment
L10	Simple cloze, comprehension or note-taking	These tasks involved the pupils in understanding or make a précis of simple data already supplied by textbook, worksheet or teacher

Figure 8.2 (cont'd) Analysis of Classroom Tasks (ACT) Proforma

Code	Description	Example
L11	Reinforcing	A common set of tasks involved practice in a skill already learned, e.g. pupils, having learned about fractions last week, were given 20 examples of addition of fractions to perform. This category was used to include such tasks as logging results from experiments, matching French sentences to descriptive pictures, putting actions to words in foreign language songs, and doing corrections to previous work
L12	Looking up, finding out information	This category was used only for looking up simple factual information (data) such as finding out a date or what happened in a particular incident. If the data were applied or used the appropriate higher-level task category was used instead

High-level tasks

Code	Description	Example
H1	Imaginative tasks	This category included what is often termed creative writing. Typical examples were: write a shape poem about fire; or, write a serial story called The Great Adventure
H2	Collecting evidence, problem solving, deducing and reasoning tasks	Devise some questions you want answers to such as a) does temperature make a difference? b) which detergent product washes best? c) is biological powder better?
H3	Application tasks	Tasks in this category ask pupils to use knowledge gained in order to perform in a new situation. In a French lesson pupils were asked to use recently acquired words for foods to devise a menu and order a meal in a restaurant
H4	Analysis tasks	In an experiment about water and its reaction to temperature pupils were asked to find out why, in one piece of apparatus, water levels dropped on heating before rising (as expected) because of expansion. Analysis tasks ask pupils to differentiate between facts and hypotheses, to find patterns and clarify relationships

Figure 8.2 (cont'd) Analysis of Classroom Tasks (ACT) Proforma

Code	Description	Example
H5	Synthesis tasks	Synthesis involves organising ideas to make a new statement, developing plans to test ideas and discovering relationships or proposing changes or improvements, e.g. 'write a letter from the Emperor telling the people of Britain why the Romans have decided to leave'
H6	Evaluation tasks	These tasks require pupils to appraise, assess or criticise according to justified criteria. Writing book reviews or an assessment of a character in a novel would be included here

Once the analysis system had been established it was possible to look closely at the patterns of task being set in the five schools. These are shown in Tables 8.2, 8.3 and 8.4. In addition, the teaching-mode (whole class, group work or individualised learning) context of the task was recorded, and these are given in Table 8.5.

From these four tables it is possible to draw a number of conclusions. Task-setting is a relatively frequent operation in most classes, with an average of 4.3 tasks per 80-minute double lesson over the five sample schools. When the tasks are classified using the ACT proforma the picture is suprisingly consistent from school to school. Though teachers at Robin Hood school set more tasks than others, the balance between the tasks which make higher-order cognitive demands and those on the lower level is fairly uniform. Only Friar Tuck school is slightly out of line at 9 per cent of higher-order tasks; the rest vary between 15.3 and 18.1 per cent of total tasks set.

If the tasks are divided into subject areas we discover that distribution between higher-order and lower-order tasks varies considerably from one subject to another — see Table 8.6. Integrated studies, English and science make sizeable cognitive demands; while RE and geography make above one-tenth of this demand.

Table 8.2: Number of Lessons Observed, and Number of Tasks Identified in Each Lesson, by School and Subject Area

	Will Scarlet	Huntingdon	Robin Hood	Friar Tuck	Alan Adale	Total	Average number of tasks per subject lesson
RE	2 (5, 6)	—	4 (16, 12, 24, 7)	4 (4, 0, 5, 4)	—	10 (83)	8.3
French	4 (6, 4, 1, 6)	5 (3, 4, 7, 7, 3)	4 (7, 9, 5, 7)	4 (2, 3, 7, 6)	4 (5, 7, 4, 3)	21 (106)	5.0
Science	4 (3, 3, 3, 3)	3 (3, 4, 6)	4 (11, 6, 5, 4)	4 (2, 4, 5, 5)	4 (6, 2, 6, 6)	19 (87)	4.6
History	4 (6, 8, 5, 3)	—	4 (7, 6, 7, 7)	2 (6, 6)	—	10 (61)	6.1
English	4 (5, 2, 5, 2)	5 (2, 6, 2, 2, 1)	4 (4, 7, 5, 3)	4 (3, 8, 1, 4)	4 (2, 2, 3, 3)	21 (72)	3.4
Mathematics	4 (4, 8, 2, 4)	5 (1, 0, 3, 2, 1)	4 (3, 5, 3, 2)	8 (1, 1, 1, 1, 4, 1, 5, 3)	4 (7, 12, 3, 2)	25 (71)	3.2
Geography	4 (4, 1, 1, 2)	—	4 (1, 3, 4, 3)	2 (2, 3)	—	10 (24)	2.4
Music	4 (6, 2, 3, 3)	4 (4, 7, 6, 2)	4 (6, 6, 3, 5)	4 (2, 4, 6, 3)	4 (7, 3, 4, 7)	20 (89)	4.5
Integrated studies	—	9 (0, 1, 2, 6, 3, 1, 6, 6, 5)	—	—	6 (1, 3, 2, 1, 1, 1)	15 (39)	2.6
Total lesson tasks (Total talks)	30 (116)	31 (106)	32 (203)	32 (112)	22 (103)	147 (640)	
Average number of tasks per lesson school by school	3.8	3.4	6.3	3.5	4.7	Overall an average of 4.3 tasks per lesson across all subjects and schools	

Note: Figures in parentheses denote number of tasks in each lesson.

Table 8.3: Breakdown of Classroom Tasks Set in Five Mixed-ability Classes According to the Categories in the ACT Proforma

Will Scarlet

L1	L2	L3	L4	L5	L6	L7	L8	L9	L10	L11	L12	Total	
—	16	16	24	1	3	6	7	—	11	10	1	95	= 81.9%

H1	H2	H3	H4	H5	H6	Total		Total tasks
3	12	3	0	0	3	21	= 18.1%	116

Huntingdon

L1	L2	L3	L4	L5	L6	L7	L8	L9	L10	L11	L12	Total	
1	13	10	17	9	9	—	3	1	2	19	3	87	= 82%

H1	H2	H3	H4	H5	H6	Total		Total tasks
10	—	6	1	0	2	19	= 18%	106

Robin Hood

L1	L2	L3	L4	L5	L6	L7	L8	L9	L10	L11	L12	Total	
—	24	42	12	14	9	1	2	5	5	37	17	169	= 83.25%

H1	H2	H3	H4	H5	H6	Total		Total tasks
8	7	9	2	2	3	31	= 15.3%	203*

*3 tasks unclassified (1.4%)

Friar Tuck

L1	L2	L3	L4	L5	L6	L7	L8	L9	L10	L11	L12	Total	
—	8	7	26	14	14	3	—	2	1	23	3	101	= 91%

H1	H2	H3	H4	H5	H6	Total		Total tasks
2	1	2	2	3	0	10	= 9%	111

Alan Adale

L1	L2	L3	L4	L5	L6	L7	L8	L9	L10	L11	L12	Total	
—	17	12	20	10	7	2	1	2	2	13	1	87	= 84.5%

H1	H2	H3	H4	H5	H6	Total		Total tasks
3	2	—	—	1	10	16	= 15.5%	103

Table 8.4: All Tasks in All Study Schools Analysed by Cognitive Demand

	L1	L2	L3	L4	L5	L6	L7	L8	L9	L10	L11	L12	Total	
	1	78	88	100	48	42	12	13	10	21	102	25	540	*
	0.1	12.1	13.7	15.6	7.5	6.5	1.9	2.6	1.7	3.2	15.8	3.8	85%	lower-level tasks
	H1	H2	H3	H4	H5	H6	Total							
	26	22	20	5	6	18	97							
	4.0	3.4	3.1	0.8	0.9	2.7	14.9%	higher-level tasks					Total tasks = 640 (100%)	

Note: *Three tasks were unclassified due to lack of adequate information.

The reason for this is not too hard to find. In integrated studies the interdisciplinary approach lends itself to making connections and relationships. These usually involve pupils in either empathic tasks (H1) or evaluative tasks (H6); and such tasks apparently feed into and out of the subject matter with ease. English too is dominated by the need to empathise – this is especially true of English literature or of 'creative' writing. For science the approach is different: here collection of evidence, deduction and reasoning (H2) are paramount. Again, the subject matter itself tends to condition the kind of task set.

But if this is so, how can RE be so low in cognitive demand? By its very nature religion is about the most abstract idea we possess; and the whole of religious language is a conceptual minefield. Yet doubtless this is precisely why the tasks set are lower order. To make the subject intelligible teachers had to side-step the real issues and reduce topics to a lowest common denominator: everyday life in Palestine or a map of Paul's route from Tarsus to Antioch. Perhaps something similar is true of geography. At all events, the evidence of Table 8.6 is that, in cognitive terms at least, it might be preferable if integrated studies were to replace the individual subjects of RE, geography and history in the earliest years of the comprehensive school. For although history ranks fourth in cognitive demand according to Table 8.6, the commonest single task in history lessons is L3; and if we look at the complete breakdown of tasks in Table 8.4 we discern that the most frequent overall are:

L11 reinforcing and practising already acquired skills   15.8 per cent
L4   copying or writing headings   15.6 per cent
L3   drawing or colouring   13.7 per cent

Both L11 and L4 tasks are more frequent than *all* higher-order tasks put together: which should cause both teachers and trainers to pause for thought.

Table 8.5: Teaching-mode Context of Classroom Tasks in Five Mixed-ability Classes

Type of school (+ total tasks)	Whole-class context	Group-work context	Individualised learning context
Tasks in five 1st-year secondary mixed-ability classes (640)	588 (91.9%)	36 (5.6%)	16 (2.5%)

Table 8.5 leads to another important discovery: *tasks seem to be aimed at classes not pupils*. Not only are 91.9 per cent of all tasks set in a whole-class context, but a detailed study of the exceptions showed that less than a handful were set specifically to provide differentiated work for pupils whom teachers considered to be amongst the most or least able in their classes.

Table 8.6: Distribution of Higher-order and Lower-order Tasks Set in Five First-year Comprehensive Classes Analysed by Subject Area

	Higher-order (per cent)	Lower-order (per cent)
Integrated studies	41	59
English	33.3	66.6
Science	23	77
History	11.5	88.5
French	11.3	88.7
Maths	8.9	91.1
Music	6.7	93.3
RE	5	95
Geography	4.2	95.8

Before drawing together the implications of the research findings reported in this chapter, it is worthwhile to dispose of one possible objection to the procedure adopted for task analysis. It could be suggested that a task set by the teacher was often ambiguous with respect to cognitive demand, and capable of interpretation at a variety of levels by pupils of different abilities. The analysis carried out using the ACT proforma was done on tasks as set by teachers rather than from pupils' responses to the tasks, so there may be room for error. However, in placing a task in an H or L category, the procedure was to assign it according to the highest possible demand it made. Thus, a workcard containing 19 factual revision questions, and one only which demanded empathy, would be classified H1 on the strength of the potential of the 20th question. Furthermore, examples of pupils' written responses to tasks were collected to ensure that they were interpreting ambiguous tasks along lines which accorded with the observer's categorisation of those tasks. If anything, therefore, there is an *over-estimate* of the amount of higher-level task setting.

To summarise these findings about classroom tasks set in first-year mixed-ability classes one has to conclude that most task-setting provides undifferentiated work for pupils who differ widely in ability; that such task-setting contradicts the underlying philosophy of individual growth in mixed-ability classes; that few tasks make adequate cognitive demands on the able, in many cases not even on the average pupils, and that much time is spent on tasks which are simply trivial.

Early in this chapter it was suggested that almost the whole of the cognitive life of classrooms could be observed in the two processes of verbal transaction and task-setting. Now we have discovered that in the schools studied only 4.1 per cent of verbal transactions and 14.9 per cent of tasks made what we felt able to call stimulating demands on pupils. The finding is not dissimilar to the one about teachers' questions mentioned in Chapter 5, that only one question in five was of a higher order. Many readers will find this unpalatable. Some may allege that the research methodology is at fault (they may devise a better one), that the interpretation is erroneous (but an alternative is hard to see), and that the schools were untypical (they were, in that they were probably more favoured than most). Exhausting these possibilities, others will argue that the analysis we have employed is too mechanistic, that teaching is intuitive, and that personal relationships in school are more important than the tasks set. A few may seize on the findings with glee as a way of denigrating the comprehensive system. This would be a very foolish conclusion indeed in the absence of any comparative measures for other forms of school organisation, or of data gathered in a similar way in schools in former times.

It would be better to face the possibility that a rigorous reappraisal of the tasks teachers set is necessary. The challenge is for trainee and experienced teachers to be able to analyse and reflect on the tasks they ask children to undertake, to consider the demands they make on the pupils and whether these are worthwhile and appropriate as well as sufficiently exacting and stimulating.

References

Bloom, B.S. (1956) *Taxonomy of Educational Objectives*, Longman, London
Da Silva, W.A. (1972) 'The Formation of Historical Concepts Through Contextual Cues', *Birmingham Educational Review, 24*, 3, 197-211
FOCUS Books, (DES) *Teacher Education Project Workbooks*, 1981, 1982, Macmillan Education, Basingstoke
Gallagher, J.J. (1970) 'Three Studies of the Classroom' in J.J. Gallagher, G.A. Nuthall and B. Rosenshine (eds), *Classroom Observation*, AERA Monograph No. 6, Rand McNally, Chicago
Goldman, R. (1964) *Religious Thinking from Childhood to Adolescence*, Routledge & Kegan Paul, London
—— (1966) *Readiness for Religion*, Routledge & Kegan Paul, London
Harlen, W. (1978) 'Matching the Learning Environment to Children's Development: the Progress in Learning Science Project', in A. Floyd (ed), *Cognitive*

Development in the School Years, Croom Helm, London

Kerry, T. (1982) 'Teachers' Identification: of Exceptional Pupils and their 'Strategies' for Dealing with Them', PhD thesis, University of Nottingham

Piaget, J. (1972) 'Human Development', translated in A. Floyd (ed), *Cognitive Development in the School Years*, Croom Helm, London

Rhys, W.T. (1972) 'Geography and the Adolescent', *Birmingham Educational Review, 24*, 3, 183-96

Sands, M.K. and Kerry, T. (1982) *Mixed Ability Teaching*, Croom Helm, London

Shayer, M. (1970) 'How to Assess Science Courses', *Education in Chemistry, 7*, 182ff

Turney, C. (1973) *Sydney Microskills Series 1*, University of Sydney, Sydney, Australia

—— (1975) *Sydney Microskills Units Series 2*, University of Sydney, Sydney, Australia

Warnock, M. (1978) *Special Educational Needs* (The Warnock Report), HMSO, London

9 THE NATURE OF THE NEW TEACHER'S JOB

M.B. Youngman

When planning teacher training courses it is useful to know what new teachers have to do when they begin their professional career. Teaching is probably the one job that the majority of people would claim to know most about. Rather ironically, when the practitioners have been asked to describe their work, accurate information has been considerably harder to achieve. The Clegg Commission, which looked at teachers' salaries in 1981, encountered so much difficulty in obtaining usable job descriptions that it abandoned the attempt altogether. At the individual level, formal job descriptions are so rare as to be exceptional. Where efforts have been made to identify the nature of teaching, the focus has tended to be selective, concentrating on the teacher-pupil interaction, or on the duties of key personnel (headteachers, heads of department, pastoral tutors especially). No-one would want to diminish the value of such studies, but to assume their full value it is essential that it should be possible to place them in context. Only one broad-based British study of the complete teaching span is currently available (Hilsum and Strong, 1978), and even that has its inevitable limitations. Clearly, there is ample scope for further study of the content of secondary school teaching. Furthermore, it would be very useful if such a study could provide a context within which some of the more selective investigations could be interpreted. In these circumstances a particularly productive line of development consists of establishing a methodology which can then be used to extend available information. The remainder of this chapter outlines a project to design a self-report job description instrument; it then proceeds to describe some of the findings arising from applications of the instrument, especially in as far as these findings elucidate the nature of the new teacher's job.

A Structure of Teaching Activities

The NFER teachers' day study (Hilsum and Strong, 1978) used observational data collection, and its analysis was based on a classification devised by the research team. Both of these features of the methodology have their limitations. Observation is time consuming and complicated; it can rarely be employed by practitioners without considerable training. Imposed classifications of data are useful when consensus regarding their validity exists, but in teaching there is widespread disagreement over content and form. For these reasons it was felt that a simpler data-collection method was needed, and as far as possible treatment of the data generated should avoid pre-determined categories. Full details of the solution to these quests cannot be given here, but extended accounts are available (Youngman, 1979, 1982). The essence of the method was a long checklist of actual teaching tasks or tactics which was assembled from lengthy interviews with teachers. Responses from a pilot sample of 232 teachers were classified using cluster analysis. It was then possible to construct a checklist, the final version of which had 115 items, and analyse the responses of teachers who completed it.

The structure consists of fourteen teaching activities, a summary of which is presented in Figure 9.1. Each activity comprises between six and thirteen teaching behaviours whose association is defined by actual occurrence within jobs, not by some kind of theoretical similarity or assumed correspondence. Activity 1 (*exercise-based teaching*) for example, comprises the following seven behaviours or operations, listed below with the actual number of the item on the full checklist.

    1 listen to pupil's performance of oral task
  15 require memorisation of selected topics
  29 set tests to assess learning from homework
  43 require pupils to write corrections
  57 ask pupils to read silently to themselves
  71 require pupils to read aloud or talk to the class
  85 use oral exercises

The activity's name attempts to summarise the range of content, but that name should be seen only as a convenient label. All use and analysis of the checklist retains the nature of all the items in each activity. In this particular case the name *exercise-based teaching* highlights the use of recurrent tests and tasks, although there is also a noticeable bias towards oral work such as prevails in languages or English teaching.

Activity 11 (*manage teaching*) covers a very different aspect of the teaching job, but still the emphasis is on what is actually done by the teacher, not on attitudes or expectations. The thirteen constituent items are:

Figure 9.1: Activity Outlines

Brief descriptions of the 14 teaching activities identified in analyses of checklist responses. The scoring form gives the lists of all the operations constituting each activity.

Activity	Samples of content
1. Exercise-based teaching	set tests, require note-taking, use oral exercises, use written exercises, require corrections, use silent reading
2. Resource-based teaching	operate a/v equipment, obtain special materials, allow pupil choice, contact organisations, book equipment or rooms
3. Supervise equipment use	clean equipment, devise safety rules, demonstrate correct usage, permit equipment use, check equipment condition
4. Provide pupil work	write information on board, set and mark exams, set written work, explain assessments, use textbooks
5. Assess pupil adjustment	contact parents over problem, acquire information on pupil, suggest transfer of problem pupil, select for special teaching
6. Pastoral administration	write pastoral reports, discuss pupil with pupil or parents, check notes and excuses, request pupil reports, file pupil information
7. School administration	oversee student timetables, bank cash, assign tutors, organise distribution of DES/UCCA forms, liaise with media, oversee external exam arrangements
8. Exam administration	select exam candidates, compute estimated marks, submit lists of entries, collate exam work, produce mock external exam
9. Construct syllabus	monitor subject developments, update syllabus, order inspection copies, identify teaching topics, determine timing of topics
10. Control teaching supplies	order materials or books, record expenditure, prepare estimates, consult staff on expenditure, establish financial priorities
11. Manage teaching of others	select exam board, liaise with FE/HE, allocate staff, compile room timetable, monitor teaching of other staff, write references for staff
12. Manage staff	chair staff, meetings, evaluate staff teaching ability, reprimand staff, delegate tasks to staff, serve on school policy group, deal with other staff's problems

Figure 9.1 (cont'd) Activity Outlines

13. Supervise trainees	write reports on students or probationers, discuss teaching with trainee, observe trainees, assess trainee performance
14. External liaison	contact educational psychologist, liaise with social workers, write court reports, liaise with EWO, contact police or probation service

   11 select examining board
   25 check testing and marking of other teachers
   39 liaise with department in further or higher education
   53 compile timetable for student teacher
   67 participate in the selection of new staff
   81 write references for staff
   93 compile documentation on student or probationer in difficulty
100 compile room timetable
105 allocate staff to classes
108 arrange for staff to attend courses
110 maintain record of marks of other staff
112 explain option-choice arrangements to staff
114 decide allocation of rooms to staff

The 14 activities cover teaching, pastoral, administrative and managerial functions, enabling more than simple classroom studies of teachers to be made. Most of their content reflects traditional views about the content of teaching, but it is interesting to note some of the less conventional features. For example, the absence of assessment or discipline might seem to question the structure's completeness. What has happened is that these components of teaching have been subsumed within other activities because they tend to be performed in association with the operations forming those activities. The exercise-based teaching activity listed in full above clearly contains assessment tasks. Other behaviours associated with assessment appear in the *exam administration* or *provide pupil work* activities. The virtue of this feature of the 14-activity structure is that it incorporates the realistic occurrence of these behaviours, thereby extending the discriminatory power of the instrument. Bearing in mind the difficulties experienced by many investigators in trying to distinguish between the contents of various teaching roles, this increased discrimination should prove productive in examining the new teacher's job.

The Samples Used in the Investigation

The main study employed two separate samples of secondary school teachers. The first (n = 232) was administered a pilot version of the instrument, whilst the second (n = 133) completed the developed version. Both samples were selected to represent the complete span of teaching activity, and indeed they compare very favourably with current DES statistics on teacher characteristics. There is no reason to believe that findings from these samples would not be mirrored in the population at large. Various sub-divisions within each sample were analysed to identify differences in work patterns, but for the purpose of the present discussion only the experience classification is relevant. The sub-groups involved are shown in Table 9.1.

Table 9.1: Sub-groups Used in the Main Study

Experience	Pilot sample	Main sample
Probationer	24	7
2-5 years	69	29
6-15 years	99	62
16 or more years	40	35
Total	232	133

In view of the smallness of the probationer contingent in the main sample it will be necessary to consider results from both samples, although the activity structure does show slight differences between the two administrations. The major difference is in degree rather than kind since the final developed version is based on 115 items as opposed to the 245 operations used in the pilot study. As far as interpretation goes, the effect of the reduction is to produce a more discriminating structure so that differences between various teacher categories are more easily detected.

A further sample to be referred to in the following discussion does not involve experienced teachers at all. It consists of a large PGCE group (n = 166) recording their experiences on teaching practice. This might seem somewhat tangential to the central concept of the new teacher, but it does offer valuable information on at least two counts. First, it helps complete the experience span, since it is possible to interpret this one-term practice as akin to the very early stages of the probationary year. Secondly, and more constructively, it enables a comparison to be made between what might be expected of the new teacher in his first year and what he is introduced to in his practice term. These issues will be elaborated later, but at the moment it is sufficient to outline and justify the samples used. Any limitations inherent in a PGCE sample should be fairly obvious. They are not representative of all trainee teachers, because the pattern of their training differs from that of BEd students, and they are older than other students on teaching practice. However, this particular sample should be reasonably representative of PGCE students, so long as certain specialist areas (music, RE and PE for example) are discounted.

The New Teacher's Job

There is little point in repeating information that is available in more detail elsewhere (Youngman, 1979), and therefore the emphasis here will be on interpretation rather than statistical analysis. The essence of this interpretation is in Figure 9.2, where the activity profiles for the two teacher samples and the PGCE sample are presented. Further justification for playing down the importance of statistical findings stems from the smallness of the probationer group in the main sample. Statistics based on a sample of seven have only limited reliability, and for that reason it is essential to interpret this group's results in relation to trends across all four experience groups, and with regard to equivalent result for the larger pilot sample probationer group. Basic statistics and between-groups significance tests are available from the main report (Youngman, 1979) if required. Nevertheless, it must be emphasised that the validity of these findings should not be under-estimated. The two samples are quite separate, the overall sample sizes are not small, and analyses of trends are very effective in overcoming limitations arising from necessarily small sub-groups.

Figure 9.2 is almost self-explanatory. For each activity the first (dotted) column records the activity usage level for the PGCE sample, the second block represents the main sample, the third is the pilot. The probationer sub-groups are in black. The activity-usage score is the percentage of that activity's operations used by the individual. The full vertical extension for each column represents 100 per cent usage. The complete absence of a column (see activity 7, main sample probationer group, for example) indicates an average score of zero, and that in turn means that *no* member of the group performs *any* of the operations comprising that activity.

Figure 9.2: Activity Profiles for Different Experience Groups

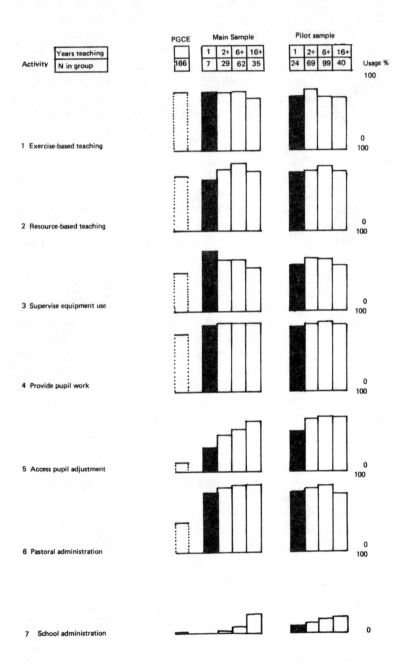

Figure 9.2: (contd)

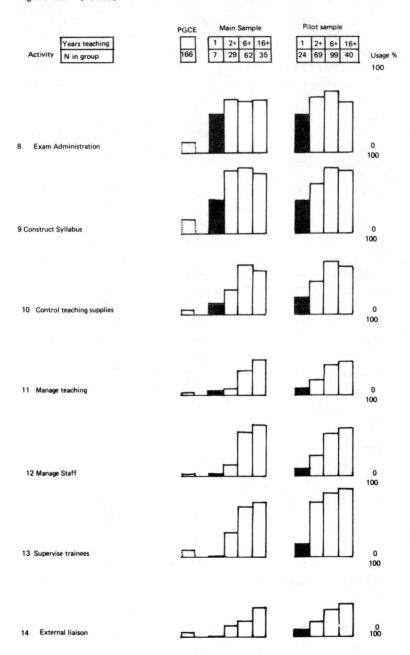

Activities 1-4: Classroom-based

These four activities cover those tasks normally associated with class-room teaching. Apart from 3 (supervise equipment use) usage is uni-formly high with little indication of any variations for the four experi-ence lengths. Where there is a hint that probationers might operate differently (notably resource-based teaching and supervise equipment use for the main sample), there is no confirmation in the larger pilot sample. Since even the PGCE sample records comparable levels on three of these four activities the conclusion must be that the probationers' range of classroom-teaching activities is similar to that of the more experienced teachers.

Activities 5-6: Pastoral

These two activities are differentiated predominantly by the seriousness of the incidents covered. Pastoral administration encompasses those everyday requirements that would feature in most teachers' duties, and this is reflected in the similarity of the usage levels across the experience groups. The lower score for the PGCE group is in accord with the normal assumption that these students are not expected to be involved in form-tutor duties or report-writing. Within the assess pupil adjustment activity are less common eventualities such as parental contact and selection for special teaching. These are responsibilities that do tend to be allied with particular posts, and consequently some relationship with experience could be expected. The results confirm this although the pilot sample effect is not so strong. It does seem that this is an area where probationers are not so heavily involved as their colleagues.

Activities 7 and 8: School and Exam Administration

The immediate impression gained from the profile for activity 7 (school administration) is the very low usage regardless of teaching experience. This is because the activity covers functions almost exclusively alloca-ted to deputies and heads so that the experience classification hides the true discrimination. None of the probationers in the main sample per-forms any of the constituent tasks although the pattern is not so extreme for the pilot sample, largely a consequence of changes in the definition of the activity rather than sampling variations. Exam administration (activity 8) does not discriminate between the more experienced teachers, but it is an area where probationer teachers show lower involvement.

Activities 9-11: Departmental

These three activities do cover responsibilities directly related to departmental organisation, but all the remaining activities (9-14) show strong associations with experience. The broad definition of activity 9 (construct syllabus) produces moderately high scores for most teachers, but there is a clear indication that the new teachers are less involved than the rest. For the other two departmental activities (control teaching supplies and manage teaching) the overall usage patterns are lower, with the probationers recording very low scores. Their involvement in manage teaching is negligible.

Activities 12-14: Management

As one would expect, the new teachers have little or no experience of the tasks covered by these three activities, and even teachers with under six years service are only involved in activity 13 (supervise trainees). The slight contradiction apparent in the score for the PGCE group on activity 13 is explained by the fact that they discuss and observe each other's teaching.

In spite of a well-established folklore claiming baptism by total immersion, the picture emerging here suggests that probationers do operate a restricted range of teaching activity, if they are to be compared with all teachers. Indeed, even their most recently appointed colleagues (those with under six years teaching experience) show a greater involvement in the majority of the activities identified here. This finding should not be particularly surprising in view of the way responsibility posts usually do carry extra tasks or duties. Furthermore, the three-tier organisation of schools, whereby departmental and school responsibilities tend to be superimposed on the basic class-teaching function, does serve to exaggerate scale-point differences.

There is, however, an alternative interpretation of the activity patterns shown here, and it does change the emphasis of the conclusion. Although the classroom-based activities comprise only about one-third of the total number, their demands cannot be quantified so easily. As regards breadth they cover a wide range of different tasks and tactics, and it could legitimately be argued that those four activities (five, if pastoral administration is included) cover proportionately much more than one-third of the teaching repertoire. Then again, the differences between these activities are much greater than between, say, some of the managerial activities, putting even more strain on the novice teacher. Certainly at the classroom level there is little evidence of a reduced involvement by the probationer teacher. Since this situation has to be accommodated, how far does the main teaching practice assist in the process?

The Postgraduate Teaching Practice

From the evidence of Figure 9.2 it is reasonable to offer the general conclusion that the PGCE students do operate an even more restricted range of activities than the first-year teachers. This is particularly the case for those parts of the job that are not continuous, for example syllabus construction or exam administration. The generalisation is less acceptable for the classroom-based activities, where the differences between the PGCE profiles and those of the other teachers are so small as to be irrelevant.

The PGCE sample is a large group, and consequently the inevitable variation around the average profile includes sizeable numbers of students.

Table 9.2: Activity Usage Patterns for the PGCE Sample: Number of Students Recording Each Activity Score

Number of items ticked	Activity*													
	1	2	3	4	5	6	7	8	9	10	11	12	13	14
0	0	2	27	0	77	6	152	89	67	122	110	104	117	146
1	0	4	30	0	45	14	11	43	35	33	41	43	29	10
2	2	11	19	4	16	30	1	15	29	9	12	12	13	4
3	7	15	20	19	10	38	2	8	19	0	1	3	5	3
4	14	27	15	32	10	21	0	3	3	1	2	4	0	3
5	14	42	26	38	4	21	0	2	8	0	0	0	1	0
6	31	36	29	45	1	16	0	5	2	1	0	0	1	0
7	34	29		28	2	8	0	1	2		0	0		
8	37			1	7	0		1			0	0		
9	27				4	0					0	0		
10					1						0	0		
11											0	0		
12											0	0		
13											0	0		

*Numbered as in Figure 9.2

Table 9.2 offers more detail on this variation by recording the number of students obtaining all possible activity scores. So 27 (16 per cent) indicated that they performed all nine of the operations comprising the exercise-based teaching activity. The importance of being aware of the spread of involvement is immediately apparent from the supervise-equipment-use activity. A third of the sample (57 students) register virtually no involvement, whilst at the other extreme a quarter (45 students) perform at least five of the six constituent tasks. And this must be interpreted against the background of a sample with no explicit emphasis on practical subjects. Variation on the other widely occurring activities is nowhere near so marked, although the noticeable spread does point to the need to consider individual differences in the teaching practice experience. The very low usage on the more senior activities in turn restricts the amount of variability recorded, but again there is no unanimity. Even on the most exclusive activity, school administration, 14 students indicate some involvement. There are six instances where item 98 (pay cash into bank) is ticked, and four for item 49 (receive and distribute DES/UCCA forms). Three other items, liaise with local press or media, oversee timetables of all student teachers, and arrange exam invigilation, attract three responses each. The pattern of these particular items suggests that the students' involvement in this activity is at a predominantly personal level: their interpretation of the items is different from the way the full-time teachers would react. In general (as has already been hinted for the supervise trainees activity), apparently unexpected involvement by the PGCE students is perhaps more a function of the instrument not being fully suited to their special situation, rather than their being highly involved in these teaching activities.

Summary and Implications

The final picture confirms and contradicts the assertion that probationers invariably are thrown in at the deep end of teaching. They might be thrown in, but it is rather a smaller pool in which they have to swim, since most of the administrative and managerial responsibilities do not come their way. Nevertheless, to continue the metaphor, it is possible to drown in a very small pool, and this particular one, the classroom, is notoriously hazardous. The major consolation is that much of the classroom-based work will have been encountered during the teaching practice term. Certainly the first four activities feature strongly in the majority of the PGCE students' experiences. The most noticeable omissions in the PGCE practice are the two pastoral activities (assess pupil adjustment and pastoral administration) and the exam-administration activity. If it is felt desirable that the teaching practice should reflect as much as possible of the actual teaching demands then these two areas would be candidates for further development of the students' experience.

One area that could arouse some speculation is syllabus construction (activity 9). One viewpoint might be that probationers record significantly lower involvement than all other teachers (Figure 9.1) and therefore it need not concern teacher trainers. A more forward-looking stance would be that very soon after the first year all teachers seem to be highly involved in this activity, yet the PGCE practice incorporates a minimal amount of this aspect of teaching. The conclusion must be that at the moment this ability is acquired on the job, rather than being developed beforehand. Whether this is the most effective way is very much a matter for discussion by all concerned.

The remaining teaching activities show the gradual increase in involvement that almost invariably corresponds to formal responsibility or status. This has interesting implications for in-service training of teachers, but relates only peripherally to initial teacher training. Taken together these characterisations of the young teacher's job do seem to offer useful insights into the way training and induction mesh into the complete teaching activity. The simplicity of the methodology, a relatively quick and valid checklist, should commend itself to anyone wanting to elaborate on the outline offered in this preliminary study.

References

Hilsum, S. and Strong, C.R. (1978) *The Secondary Teacher's Day*, NFER, Windsor
Youngman, M.B. (1979) *Analysing Teachers' Activities: Technical Report*, Social Science Research Council, London
—— (1982) 'A System for Describing Teachers' Jobs', *Educational Studies, 8*, 23-32

10 TRAINING SKILFUL TEACHERS: SOME IMPLICATIONS FOR PRACTICE

E.C. Wragg

The HMI report *The New Teacher in School* published in 1982, reached the conclusion that the majority of the 294 probationer teachers in their sample had been well trained, but that many were dissatisfied with some aspects of their training, and that nearly one in four were in some respects poorly equipped with the skills needed for teaching. This last assertion does not accord with the ratings of heads of schools who felt nearly 90 per cent were competent, and, since it was based on only two observations of each new teacher, must be regarded with some scepticism (Wragg, 1983). Nevertheless, whether there is general satisfaction or not, it is essential that teacher training should be conceived in such a way as to nurture the talents of new recruits. Then they may develop into highly skilled professional people with sharp insight into classroom life and a sustained appetite for improving their own teaching and their pupils' learning.

Most of the research described in the previous chapters has relevance for teacher training. The study of student teachers on teaching practice in Chapter 2 showed that most problems of discipline encountered were of a minor kind, usually a level of general chatter which the student found too loud, rather than an act of violence, a confrontation or a serious threat of insurrection. The study of first encounters in Chapter 3 raises several matters to do with class management. Experienced teachers did not hesitate to come on strong, be larger than life by exaggerating their authority, their preciseness or even, in some cases, their real or feigned eccentricity. Student teachers, especially those taking the PGCE course, identified strongly with the pupils, were reluctant to become socialised into the 'hard teacher' stereotype. In Chapter 4 it was shown how well pupils understood classroom processes, and how skilfully they could predict the behaviour of their teachers, recalling vividly in interview events which took place in lessons earlier in the year. They even, when commenting on the photographs of classroom scenes to which their own teachers had reacted, used phrases to describe what would happen which were, in some cases, nearly identical to those used by their teachers.

These three studies of class management, first encounters and pupils' views, as well as the research described in other chapters, raise a number of issues relevant to teacher training courses. There seem, for example, to be few opportunities during many training courses for forethought about first encounters, yet the evidence of our study suggested that these are very important moments in a young teacher's career. Trainees should be sensitised more to the factors affecting first lessons, including the expectations of pupils, and be made aware of the huge collective effort which took place at the beginning of the school year and to which they were not a party. They need to understand the extent to which teachers may have defined territory, established rules and developed certain kinds of relationship for good or ill.

Many students, identifying as they do with the pupils, wish to establish a different kind of relationship from that which they inherit. They will need more help than they often get in negotiating this with their pupils, especially if their early attempts encounter hostility or resistance. In training this can involve preliminary reflection on the kind of relationship they hope to establish, the steps they might have to take when they meet their classes, and the likely reaction of the pupils they are going to teach when this is known. Once they are in school they need to analyse the process in which they find themselves engaged, otherwise it is too easy to veer from one extreme to another. Some students, intent on establishing a relaxed relationship with children but meeting some initial difficulties, find themselves yelling for silence all day and filling out the very stereotype they sought to avoid. It is at this point that the model we tried to establish in the Teacher Education Project, of students working with fellow students, teachers and tutors to analyse and modify what they do, comes into its own.

When students do more than one teaching practice they need to reflect back on, perhaps having documented them at the time, their first lessons, and consider how they might begin their next school assignment. Interviews with BEd. students in Chapter 3 showed that this reflection was sometimes very crude in nature, being little more than a determination not to be 'caught out' next time. Again, careful analysis, perhaps by keeping a diary on the first practice and then reflecting on what occurred and what can be learned, is most useful. It does seem odd that tutors and teachers often give students a very long period in which things may 'settle down'. Laudable though it may be to allow them to establish relationships and a classroom climate on their own and without interference, in a few cases there will be serious consequences.

In view of the smaller numbers currently in training, students should not have to begin their professional experience overwhelmed by very difficult classes. Our evidence suggests that handling the customary naughtiness met on teaching practice may be sufficient of a challenge. To have to teach classes with which even very experienced teachers have difficulty would prevent many student teachers from being able to establish positive relationships. Students on the other hand who profess an interest in working in those schools where class management is especially difficult should be given some opportunity of undertaking a tougher assignment at the training stage. All students need the experience of coping with at least one class where they have some problems if they are not to be professional cripples at the beginning of their career.

If pupils are as knowledgeable and insightful about classroom processes as we suggest in Chapter 4, perhaps there should be much more discussion with them about teaching and learning. Although many schools now include 'study skills' as part of their curriculum, few raise with pupils the matters discussed when teachers themselves meet to talk about teaching. When interviewed during the project about group work, for example, teachers often spoke about how the bright help the less able, how important personal and social development takes place when children wait their turn or listen to others.

Unfortunately, actual observation of groups shows that the reverse often happens: some pupils criticise or demoralise their fellows, dominate the group or fail to listen. Schmuck and Schmuck (1975) describe how the teacher can sensitise children working in groups to the processes involved, and capitalise on their natural insights to make them partners in learning rather than merely the recipients of teaching. When classes are badly behaved it might be possible for pupils and teachers to analyse together why relationships are poor. Sadly, those teachers with ineffective class management are the very ones who are least likely to be able to do this, and it may need another person to join them, a professional tutor, head of department or deputy head, with all the threat that offers to the teacher's sense of personal and professional competence.

Experiments involving children in talking about what have often been teachers' professional secrets may be preferable to the traditional tendency to leave students or experienced teachers who are having discipline problems to flounder on with little support. Those few teachers, like the Mr Baker described in Chapter 4, who try to establish, in his case with little success, the powerful dominance more common in Victorian times, might need to reflect on the substantial social changes of the last few decades.

Whereas a hundred years ago children left school at 12 and reached physical maturity at 16 or 17, being effectively children for the first four or five years of their working life, today the position is almost exactly reversed. With the advent of youth training schemes, full-time education and training for most persists until at least the age of 17, yet many reach physical maturity at 13 or 14 and are in some respects more like adults for the last three or four years of their schooling. In this context the kind of relationship Mr Baker appeared to desire seemed a sad anachronism to his pupils.

In many teacher training courses there is still too little attention paid to such important basic classroom skills as questioning and explaining. Yet there have been a number of studies recently which offer a great deal of information about these skills, even if the evidence does not point unequivocally to the use of any single style. Furthermore, they are skills which lend themselves especially to discussion and practice in training. Students can note down the written and oral questions asked by teachers they observe or by their fellow students. They can plan and discuss key questions for groups they are teaching, analyse transcripts of lessons to work out the kind of thought or action being elicited by different sorts of question or by sequences.

Though many experienced teachers have often given considerable thought to their questioning, others have fallen into a routine of asking largely data-recall questions which may be unexacting for many of their pupils. Slower-learning children are perfectly capable of responding to higher-order questions, especially if the teacher sequences them carefully. This was shown by some of the teachers described in Chapter 5, and was the subject of some remarkable research by the late Hilda Taba at San Francisco State College. She produced teaching modules (Simon and Boyer, 1968) showing how social studies teachers could ask questions that moved up from simple recall to grouping, labelling, predicting, making inferences and establishing generalisations. Sadly, she died just as her work was beginning to grasp the imagination of a number of teachers and trainers.

In view of the very large number of questions that many teachers ask, it is important that trainee teachers reflect on the context and the nature of the topic during which questioning takes place, the demands questions place on pupils, the appropriateness of the language of questions to the individual or group concerned and the effect of questions on subsequent activity and learning. Experienced teachers can also benefit from analysing their own style of questioning, as did the teachers who took part in our study

George Brown and Sheila Armstrong showed in Chapter 6 that a well-conceived training programme in explaining led to the students in the experimental group not only being more highly rated by observers, but also producing higher test scores from pupils. That students in training as well as experienced teachers can learn to give more telling explanations is especially important when one remembers that pupils frequently put a high value on teachers' ability to explain things clearly, and develop a sense of frustration when the explanations are confusing.

It is not difficult in training programmes, either for novices or for experienced teachers, to let them explain certain concepts, principles or events to each other or to a group of children, and then analyse an audio or video recording of the explanation. Nor is it impossible to combine this with a simple test of recall or interviews with individual pupils to see what they have understood from the explanation. In addition, it is a good safe environment in which people can reflect on the kind of explanation they have given, the extent to which it was helped by diagrams, pictures, questions from the teacher or pupils, examples and illustrations.

Some of the work done by Trevor Kerry and Margaret Sands described in Chapters 7 and 8 has considerable implications for teacher training. There seemed to be much less confidence amongst teachers about how best to teach bright pupils and slow learners in mixed-ability classes than in any other aspect of professional work we studied during the project. Most mixed-ability teaching was to the whole class, and some schools made almost no use at all of co-operative group work. Teachers had had to learn the skills of teaching children of widely varying ability with very little, or often no release from their teaching duties to allow them to attend courses, assemble materials or visit other schools.

Even the teachers we studied who were regarded as successful found it very exacting to teach a mixed-ability class well, and were less sure about their teaching of bright pupils than about other aspects. Developing stimulating extension work for those who finish early, or find a group task simple, requires considerable time and ingenuity, and teachers who handle mixed-ability classes skilfully should be given some release from their duties to work with their colleagues and with trainee teachers, and to devise more materials and ideas.

Trevor Kerry's finding that the demands of many of the tasks set by teachers were relatively slight is also one that gives cause for concern. Again it requires immense professional skill to create or elicit from pupils tasks which are not only appropriate to the age, intelligence, previous experience of the child and the field being studied, but which extend the imagination and stimulate thought and action. Much of human learning may require repeats and rehearsals of what has gone before, and may also perhaps need to be unintimidating and reassuring, but if too much is in that category which makes but modest demands on the learner, then classroom life becomes tedious and fails to fire the enthusiasm.

Teachers in training can profitably analyse the tasks set by experienced teachers or by fellow students, and this is another activity which can be set up during a training course without a great deal of difficulty. It is also one which has immediate and positive payoff. When novices and experienced teachers work together to analyse process in this way then all may benefit. The students discover how they might better structure pupils' learning, the teachers put their own or a student's practice under the microscope and modify it for the better in the light of what they learn from the analysis, and not least the pupils may in future hopefully be the recipients of more stimulating assignments from teachers, or may themselves develop a bigger stake in what they do if they are party to the consultation process, as they should be.

The analysis of the teacher's job by Mick Youngman in Chapter 9 shows how young teachers are not expected to fulfil all the management functions for which some senior teachers have responsibility, but they are expected to do most other things. His finding that trainees on the PGCE course were not as involved in syllabus construction, pastoral and examination work as teachers in their first job, suggests that these aspects might in future be brought in much more during teaching practice.

Some schools already invite trainees to undertake form tutoring under the supervision of an experienced teacher, and some allow students into meetings which are concerned with the syllabus or with examinations. If many young teachers are now being expected to assume responsibility for these important assignments, in some cases from the earliest days of taking their first post, it suggests that much higher priority should be given to ensuring that all trainees obtain supervised experience of pastoral care and syllabus construction during teaching practice, and this should not be too difficult for supervising tutors and teachers to arrange.

One overwhelming conclusion from much of the work we did during the Teacher Education Project, whether it was research or the development of training ideas, was that when teachers and students analyse their own and each other's teaching the dividing line between in-service and initial training becomes so thin as to be almost non-existent. Indeed, if student teachers did not exist, one very effective way of influencing the practice of experienced teachers in a school would be to invent them. When at Nottingham University Professor Jim Eggleston trained several heads of science departments to use his Science Teaching Observation Schedule (Dreyfus and Eggleston, 1979) to analyse the lessons of students doing teaching practice in their school, many reported benefits to themselves. As one said, 'You can't very well sit in a student's lesson looking out for questions which invite children to formulate and test their own hypotheses, without wondering how often you do that sort of thing yourself.'

Since many teachers enjoy helping to develop the skills of new teachers and also benefit themselves from such work, much more thought must be given to training them effectively for this sort of assignment. It became very clear during the Teacher Education Project that the teachers involved were fascinated and excited by the scrutiny of their own and other people's practice. They would have welcomed a proper training course which we were not able to give them. Yet the cost of their travel, or substitute teaching for them when they are away from school, would be negligible compared with the long-term benefits to the profession.

I once talked about classroom processes and the work of the project at a conference of professional tutors in Avon. They were extremely enthusiastic about their work, and I received several letters from them telling of what they had done as a result of the session. At Priory School, Weston-super-Mare, for example, David Oldroyd, with the strong support of the head and staff, produced his own training materials for his colleagues which allowed them to scrutinise and discuss their own classroom practice.

During the project we worked with schools who so much enjoyed analysing the teaching of students they found time to do a similar exercise with their own colleagues. It is astonishing that many teachers never see another at work, nor are themselves seen by a professional colleague for ten, twenty years or even a whole professional career. Surgeons, by comparison are quick to share their skills or disseminate new techniques so that the profession collectively can use and improve them.

Despite one or two incompetent teachers encountered during the study of over 1,000 lessons, we were in general very impressed by the professional skills of many of the teachers we saw. It was disappointing to feel that, as a witness to classroom life, one was privileged, because few other people are able to go to several schools and see the skill which our best practitioners possess. Some of the teachers who most excited the imagination were sometimes even reluctant to talk about their professional expertise, and did not want to seem to be boasting in case their colleagues disapproved. It seems difficult to imagine Dr Christian Barnard keeping heart transplant techniques to himself in case his fellow surgeons thought he was showing off.

We learned a great deal about classroom life during the Teacher Education Project in an incidental way. One of the frustrations of classroom reaearch is that you see things happening which are not quite central to your study, or which you are not able to pursue in a systematic way, but which are nevertheless important. We found it very difficult, for example, to discover secondary school classrooms where we could study group work. Even when we went to schools which told us they made extensive use of group work we found either that little in fact took place, or that it often involved children sitting together but not working as a group. Yet there is an assumption that group work is a fundamental part of secondary school life.

This is another reason why training in the analysis of classroom processes is so important for teachers, especially professional tutors or deputy heads with special responsibility for the curriculum. At Nottingham University there have been courses for deputy heads of secondary schools for a number of years in which they have had to analyse one department in the school by attending meetings, looking at syllabuses, interviewing staff and watching each member teach. Not only did the deputies handle the exercise skilfully, but their evaluations showed it was one of the most profitable and informative professional tasks they had ever undertaken. It was an effective way of using a supportive insider to see the extent to which practice matched intentions, and issues like the one on group work frequently surfaced.

Another incidental finding occurred during the periods when we studied individual children at work. Our main purpose was often to obtain some rough-and-ready index of how many appeared to be involved in their task, and we therefore spent periods of time watching each pupil in the class for 20 seconds, or studying certain target children for longer periods.

It soon became clear, even allowing for the frailty of data on involvement because of the difficulty of deciding whether a pupil is really tuned into his task or not, that there was a huge disparity in time spent on the task in hand, not only between the classrooms of different teachers, but also within the same room. One of the advantages of doing individual pupil studies, however superficial, is that it forces the observer to concentrate on one pupil and disregard other distractions. When one observes a lesson with no particular focus, the eye wanders naturally to whatever catches its attention, and this may be a piece of bad behaviour, a noise, laughter, a movement, the teacher doing something significant or an outsider entering the room.

Studies of individual pupils reveal that many of them work on unperturbed through all kinds of distraction. Even in lessons where there was considerable disruption there would often be 20 pupils out of 30 who played no part in it, and much of this we were able to document. However, it was most striking, if galling, that we were not able to devote more attention to this alone, that some pupils consistently seemed to devote over 90 per cent of their time to their work, and yet others gave it only 3 or 4 minutes out of the lesson.

I do not offer this as 'hard' evidence, and it needs the proper kind of intensive study devoted to it by several investigators such as Good and Brophy (1978), the California Beginning Teacher Evaluation Project (Denham and Lieberman, 1980) among many others. Nevertheless, it was shown in Chapter 1 that teaching is a sustained activity rather than a short sprint, and that pupils may have 1,000 lessons in a major secondary school subject like maths or English between their first and fifth years. Imagine, therefore, the cumulative difference between someone spending 1,000 times 30 minutes on whatever pupils are expected to learn, and another only devoting, say, 5 minutes each lesson. It does help to explain some of the substantial difference in learning between pupils of apparently comparable ability who have, in theory, been through the same programme. It also underlines the need for training in class management not to be seen purely as a repressive set of whole-class teaching techniques, but rather as a sensitising of teachers to the classroom life of each individual pupil.

By focusing in the Teacher Education Project on certain skills, we are aware that this raises several important matters, and indeed sometimes arouses strong feelings. Not the least of these is the one raised first in Chapter 1, whether these skills should be learned in part or as a whole. The extreme part-learning stance is taken by some supporters of competency-based teacher education who believe that the teaching can be atomised into hundreds of discrete mini-acts which can be systematically learned and appraised, and the extreme holist stance is adopted by those who contend that teaching is an art, and to seek to segment it is to destroy it. This view is expressed in striking form in Goethe's early poem *Die Freuden*, which tells how he pursues a dragon-fly and dismembers it to discover its beauty, only to be left with a crumpled heap of lifeless parts in his hand.

My own belief, for what it is worth, is that if one tries to break down teaching through too fine a sieve it not only becomes silly but makes the student or teacher self-conscious. I once saw a micro-teaching session where the supervisor was analysing a video recording with a student and telling her to smile more as he would be looking out for this feature in the re-teach lesson. There was indeed a greater incidence of what was arguably 'smiling' in the second lesson, but it carried as much conviction as a party political broadcast. To smile with sincerity people need to feel genuinely pleased. It is probably better to say to the student, 'Why not listen more carefully to the pupils' answers, they are often very interesting.' Ensuing smiles, if they occur, may be more spontaneous.

On the other hand it is, I find, false to expect that if the general development of the person is sound, then all the skills of teaching will emerge of their own accord. There is now a useful literature on teaching skills. There are reflections and exercises one can undertake in a positive attempt to improve the practice of some aspect of teaching. We have concentrated on class management, mixed-ability teaching, questioning and explaining as key skill areas, but this is not to imply either that there is nothing else, or that we have exhausted these aspects.

In training one can concentrate on a particular aspect of teaching whilst not excluding others. Thus, the emphasis in one training session may be on explaining. A teacher may be videotaped explaining something to a group of children and then the video may be played back and analysed. It would be foolish indeed to restrict one's attention only to the act of explaining. It might, for example, rule out the use of questions because that was next week's topic, which would be an absurd stance to adopt. During the explanation no doubt questions will occur, and quite possibly the pupils if they are bored will misbehave, which will in turn raise matters to do with class management. The aim in such a training session should, therefore, be to give prominence to one aspect of teaching skill and proper attention to such others as naturally occur. In that way the art of teaching can be nurtured, and such science as exists from empirical studies can be fed in if thought to be germane.

Nor should the study and development of classroom skills be seen in opposition to the established modes of teaching educational theory. Teaching skills do not replace psychology, sociology or philosophy. Each rather enhances the other. My own inclination has increasingly been to move much more towards an inductive approach to the teaching of educational theory. When students go to classrooms with a set of assignments, things to look for, questions to ask heads and teachers, teaching ideas to try out, pupils to talk to and so on, they collect in a slightly hit-or-miss way an enormous amount of valuable empirical data. A good theory course can start by trying to make sense of what students report, and then elicit key constructs which may or may not be endorsed in the traditional literature. In this respect I am not so much on the side of Erasmus and those classical humanists who believed that instruction should precede experience, but more in accord with the empiricists like Comenius who argued that we should study the heaven, the earth, oaks and beeches before books.

In the early stages of a training course, therefore, the emphasis can be on collecting sense data, experiences, impressions, with the trainers and teachers using their own knowledge to structure these in such a way that they are valuable and fruitful rather than pointless or random. Subsequently, debriefings can ensue which will usually produce a great deal in common with established precepts in the foundation disciplines, about pupil learning or failure to learn, motivation, language, social class, home and school, curriculum, teaching strategies, learning styles, choice, child development, school organisation. Stones (1979) has shown how some of what is known in psychology can be applied with a proper degree of rigour, the classroom being like an experimental laboratory. Subsequent courses which cover theory in a more systematic way will, if all has gone well, find their studies and reflections more closely related to practice, and will thereby engage the student's commitment much more firmly than has sometimes been the case in the past.

Furthermore, the theory will receive much more rigorous scrutiny. Generations of trainee primary teachers in the 1930s, 1940s and even 1950s and beyond were told firmly by many teacher trainers that children should not be taught to read until they were 6½. This was based on statements by such as Morphett and Washburne (1931) that children were not ready to read until they had obtained a mental age of 6 years 6 months. It was bunk, and students engaged in the sort of inductive experience-led early training I have described above would have reported countless examples to show it was not true. With an inductive approach bad theory is likely to be seen off.

The danger, however, is that too close a concentration on current practice in the early stages of training leads to an ultra-conservative style of preparation based on imitation. This is where good theory comes into its own, because it will challenge students to question current practice, to experiment with their teaching skill, to take sensible risks in order to improve practice.

The logical consequence of all this, too, is that teaching skill should affect the class of degree in an undergraduate professional course like the BEd. At Exeter University we have made the final teaching practice grade a classified degree mark which is part of the finals profile, as is a school-based project which students do in their final year to hone their professional skills to the very limits of their capability. During assessment one must, of course, recognise the many factors which influence teaching practice, which are not so variable during the written 3-hour paper when all, in theory, work under the same conditions. These include whether the school is an easy or hard one in which to teach, whether the teachers and tutors were supportive or not, and a host of others. If we are serious about teaching skills being important, however, then we must allow them to influence a BEd. degree class, even if this is not a straightforward matter to implement.

Our intentions in the Teacher Education Project were modest as we described in Chapter 1. In 1963 the American researcher Ned Flanders wrote of his disappointment at the lack of congruence between theory and practice and the relatively low value accorded to the act of teaching itself:

> To be understood, concepts in education must be efficiently conceptualised to gain insight. With most present practices, the gorge between theory and practice grows deeper and wider, excavated by the very individuals who are pledged to fill it.

Since that time there has been a move towards recognising the importance of teaching skill. Our principal intention in the project was both to investigate teaching skills via the research described in this book, and also to influence practice not only through the training materials we piloted and produced which are listed in Appendix A, but to help, along with others working in this field, to shift the balance of training courses for new and experienced teachers more in the direction of developing skilful teaching.

We encountered a heartening degree of interest and support. The enthusiasm of teachers, HMI, advisers, heads, deputies, teachers' centre wardens and most teacher trainers for information about and ideas for skill development was colossal. A small number of teacher trainers were hostile, sometimes for very well-argued reasons, occasionally I suspect because it can be a threatening concept. After all, any project that is about the development of teaching skills by implication appears to be suggesting that training institutions do not do this sort of work in their existing courses.

In one of our evaluations we went to a college where some of the staff said they had no need of any ideas on teaching skills because topics like class management, questioning and explaining were covered. Interviews with students told a different story. They felt there was almost nothing about skills in the course. One student in interview about her course put it this way:

> Yes all these things are mentioned, that you need to ask questions that pupils understand, that mixed-ability classes are difficult to teach, or that group work is important. But the operative word is 'mentioned'. You have to actually practise skills and then analyse them if you are going to get anything out of it.

Most of our own research into classroom teaching has not been restricted to one single subject area. There is a need for much more research into the use and effects of various teaching strategies in quite specific contexts. In the teaching of different subjects, particularly modern languages, history, geography, expressive arts, and more recently introduced elements of the curriculum like health education, media studies, personal and social development, political education or microelectronics, there is still precious little published work describing observations of classroom teaching and learning, and more research is essential. Teachers and trainers can take our findings and those of others working in the field, and try to relate them to the situation in which they work. Applying the result of enquiry to the teaching of specialist subjects was the principal purpose behind the second series of teacher education training materials listed in Appendix A.

It is sometimes assumed that anyone can train teachers, hence the frequent proposal that all one need do is to place students for longer periods in a school and then the teachers will automatically teach them how to teach, or that one invite a good practitioner out of school to talk to students. There is a craft to training teachers which it takes time to acquire, and both teachers and teacher trainers, however experienced, can learn a great deal about teaching skills and how to support others who are developing their art. If teaching children is one of the most important responsibilities that a society can ask some of its members to undertake, then the challenge to nurture the professional skills of the new generation of trainees and sharpen those of the present cohort of practising teachers must be an equally vital assignment.

References

Denham, C. and Lieberman, A. (eds) (1980) *Time to Learn*, National Institute of Education, Washington

Dreyfus, A. and Eggleston, J.F. (1979) 'Classroom Transactions of Student Teachers of Science', *European Journal of Science Education, 1*, 3, 315-25

Flanders, N.A. (1963) 'Intent, Action and Feedback: a Preparation for Teaching', *Journal of Teacher Education, 14*, 251-60

Good, T.L. and Brophy, J.E. (1978) *Looking in Classrooms*, Harper and Row, New York

HMI (1982) *The New Teacher in School*, HMSO, London

Morphett, M.V. and Washburne, C. (1931) 'When Should Children Begin to Read?' *Elementary School Journal, 31*, 496-503

Schmuck, R.A. and Schmuck, P.A. (1975) *Group Processes in the Classroom*, William C. Brown Co., Dubuque, Iowa

Simon, A. and Boyer, E.G. (eds) (1968) *Mirrors for Behavior*, vol. 5, Research for Better Schools, Philadelphia

Stones, E. (1979) *Psychopedagogy*, Methuen, London

Wragg, E.C. (1983) 'Headlines Which Failed to Tell the Whole Story' *Times Higher Education Supplement*, 20 May

APPENDIX A

Teacher Training Materials

On the development side of the Teacher Education Project all training materials were tested out in draft form. Each trial booklet contained a tear-off evaluation slip, which student teachers, teachers, tutors or whoever else used it, were invited to fill in. A second and trial version was then piloted and again evaluated. On this occasion visits were made to institutions who were heavy or light users of the materials, and tutors and students were interviewed. In addition, a one-in-ten random sample of users of some of the booklets was written to and comments were solicited. In all some 15,000 copies of trial materials were tested out. Feedback was obtained only, one way or another, from about 10–15 per cent of the users.

Teacher Education Project – Training Materials – Books, Workbooks, Slides

1981
C.R. Sutton (ed.) *Communicating in the Classroom* (Hodder and Stoughton)

FOCUS workbooks (Macmillan)
1981
E.C. Wragg *Class Management and Control*
T. Kerry *Teaching Bright Pupils in Mixed Ability Classes*

1982
P. Bell and T. Kerry *Teaching Slow Learners in Mixed Ability Classes*
T. Kerry and M.K. Sands *Mixed Ability Teaching in the Early Years of Secondary School*
T. Kerry *Effective Questioning*
G. Brown and N. Hatton *Explanations and Explaining*
T. Kerry and M.K. Sands *Handling Classroom Groups*
T. Kerry *The New Teacher*

Subject Specialist Series

1984

K.E. Selkirk *Teaching Mathematics*
J.D. Nichol *Teaching History*
T. Kerry *Teaching R.E.*
J.A. Partington and P. Luker *Teaching Modern Languages*

1985

M.K. Sands *Teaching Science*
C. Daniels and U. Hobson *Teaching Home Economics*
F.H. Molyneux and H. Tolley *Teaching Geography*
P. King *Teaching English*

Colour Slides

Three sets of slides and accompanying notes were produced during the Project under the topics:

(1) Class Management and Control (Primary)
(2) Class Management and Control (Secondary)
(3) Handling Classroom Groups

Details of these can be obtained from

  Trans-Ed Copying Services
  15 Lady Bower Close
  North Hykeham
  Lincoln LN6 8EX

APPENDIX B

Nottingham Class Management Observation Schedule Used in Chapter 2

			For computer use	
Name of teacher:	Code		C1, 2	
Name of school:	Code		C3	
Sex of teacher:	Female	☐ 1	C4	blank
			C5	
	Male	☐ 2		

Lesson details

			C6	instance code
Subject of lesson	Science	☐ 1		
	Mathematics	2		
	Humanities	3		
	English	4		
	History	5	C7	
	Geography	6		
	Foreign language	7		
	Other	8		
Class year group	First	☐ 1		
	Second	2		
	Third	3	C8	
	Fourth	4		
Lesson observed	First	☐ 1		
	Second	2		
	Third	3	C9	
	Fourth	4		
	Fifth	5		
	Sixth	6		
Stage of term	Period A	☐ 1		
	Period B	2	C10	
	Period C	3		

Description of deviant act

1. *Time of act: lesson activity*

	1	2	3	4	5		
Teacher active (solo)						1	
Teacher-pupil interaction (whole class)						2	
Pupils working and teacher monitoring						3	C11
Pupils working and teacher not monitoring						4	
Block transition involving movement of class						5	
Block transitions not involving movement of class						6	

For computer use

2. *Task involvement of class*
High involvement (20 or more pupils) — 1
Most pupils involved (11-20 pupils) — 2
Some pupils involved (4-10 pupils) — 3
Few pupils involved (0-3 pupils) — 4

C12

3. *Number of pupils involved in deviant act*
No deviant act — 1
1 pupil — 2
2-4 pupils — 3
5 or more pupils — 4

C13

4. *Type of deviant act* (yes(tick) = 1   no(blank) = 2)

(i) Pupil talk which is:

Excessively noisy	1/2 C14
Irrelevant to task	1/2 C15
Insulting to teacher	1/2 C16
Insulting to pupil	1/2 C17
Interrupting teacher	1/2 C18
Interrupting pupil	1/2 C19
Provoking laughter	1/2 C20
Disobedient or defiant	1/2 C21

(ii) Involving materials or equipment

Damage	1/2 C22
Inappropriate use	1/2 C23
Wasting	1/2 C24
Being without	1/2 C25
Taking without permission	1/2 C26

(iii) Movement

At wrong time	1/2 C27
At wrong speed	1/2 C28
To wrong place	1/2 C29
Involving contact with other pupils	1/2 C30
Refusal to move	1/2 C31

(iv) Non-verbal

Physical aggression	1/2 C32
Fidgeting	1/2 C33
Illicit eating or drinking	1/2 C34
Appearance: clothing, dress	1/2 C35
Not appropriate to task	1/2 C36
Cheating or copying	1/2 C37

(v) Other — 1/2 C38

For computer use

5. *Mildness-seriousness of act*
   - Mild — 1
   - More serious — 2 C39
   - Very serious — 3

Teacher response

6. *Whether or not response is made*
   - Teacher responds — Yes — 1 C40
   - No — 2

7. *Timing of teacher response*
   - Teacher responds before escalation of deviance — 1 C41
   - Teacher responds after escalation of deviance — 2

8. *Type of teacher response*
   (i) Verbal
   - Order to cease — 1/2 C42
   - Reprimand — 1/2 C43
   - Threat of punishment — 1/2 C44
   - Statement of rule — 1/2 C45
   - Humour — 1/2 C46
   - Involves pupil(s) in work — 1/2 C47
   - Praise or encouragement — 1/2 C48
   - Other — 1/2 C49

   (ii) Non-verbal
   - Gesture — 1/2 C50
   - Facial expression — 1/2 C51
   - Proximity — 1/2 C52
   - Touch — 1/2 C53
   - Dramatic pause — 1/2 C54
   - Other — 1/2 C55

   (iii) Punishment
   - Extra work — 1/2 C56
   - Pupil moved — 1/2 C57
   - Confiscation — 1/2 C58
   - Detention — 1/2 C59
   - Physical — 1/2 C60
   - Ridicule — 1/2 C61
   - Another teacher involved — 1/2 C62
   - Other — 1/2 C63

9. *Teacher response made to*
   - Whole class — 1
   - Group of pupils — 2 C64
   - Individual pupil — 3

10. *Pupil(s) named or not* Named Yes   1   C65

No   2

11. *Target*

Target of teacher responses is correct   1

incorrect   2   C66

inapplicable   3

12. *Teacher appears*

Calm   1

Agitated   2   C67

Angry   3

13. *Duration of teacher response*

Teacher response is brief   1

sustained   2   C68

Reaction of deviant pupil(s)

14. *Verbal response*

Pupil silent   1

Accepts or agrees with teacher response   2

Justifies action   3   C69

Altercates or protests   4

Other   5

15. *Pupil action*

Deviance ends   1

Deviance lessens   2

Deviance sustained   3   C70

Deviance escalates   4

16. *Deviancy during observation period*

Low deviancy (1 act only)   1

Medium deviancy (2, 3 or 4 acts)   2   C71

High deviancy (5 or more acts)   3

For computer use

Footnote: In addition to this schedule observers used part III of Appendix C and also made field notes in each lesson.

APPENDIX C

Observation Instrument for First Encounters Study in Chapter 3

PART I. PRELIMINARY DATA

Date . . . .

1. Observer's Name. . . . . Code. . . . . .
2. Name of teacher/student. . . . . Code. . . . . .
3. Name of school . . . . Code. . . . . .

4. Sex of teacher/student

Male	01
Female	02

5. Teaching experience

5 years +	01
2-5 years	02
Under 2 years	03
PGCE	04
B.ED	05

6. Lesson subject

Art	01	German	10
Biology	02	History	11
Chemistry	03	Humanities	12
Classics	04	Maths	13
Drama	05	Music	14
English	06	P.E.	15
French	07	Physics	16
General science	08	R.E.	17
Geography	09	Other	18

7. Year group

First	01
Second	02
Third	03
Fourth	04
Fifth	05
Sixth	06

213

8. Grouping   ability: High   [ ] 01

                                        Medium   [ ] 02

                                            Low   [ ] 03

                                        Mixed   [ ] 04

9. Lesson time in day   First   [ ] 01

                                            Last   [ ] 02

                                        Other   [ ] 03

10. Length of lesson   minutes . . . . code . . . . .

11. Teacher's encounter with pupils. (Check with teacher, asking if necessary, how many lessons have you had with this class now)

First	[ ]	01	Seventh	[ ]	07
Second	[ ]	02	Eighth	[ ]	08
Third	[ ]	03	Ninth	[ ]	09
Fourth	[ ]	04	Tenth	[ ]	10
Fifth	[ ]	05	Eleventh	[ ]	11
Sixth	[ ]	06	Twelfth plus	[ ]	12

12. Number of lessons observed with particular teacher

First	[ ]	01	Seventh	[ ]	07
Second	[ ]	02	Eighth	[ ]	08
Third	[ ]	03	Ninth	[ ]	09
Fourth	[ ]	04	Tenth	[ ]	10
Fifth	[ ]	05	Eleventh	[ ]	11
Sixth	[ ]	06	Twelfth plus	[ ]	12

PART II: ENTRY INTO ROOM

1. Pupils waiting outside room

yes	☐	01
no	☐	02
Don't know	☐	03

2. Teacher arrives at classroom before majority of pupils

yes	☐	01
no	☐	02
Don't know	☐	03

3. First audible words to class verbatim . . .

4. Teacher's words to obtain attention

5. Teacher's other behaviour for obtaining attention (comment on *salient* characteristics)

Voice
(e.g. rough, strident)

yes	☐	01
no	☐	02

Posture
(e.g. arms folded)

yes	☐	01
no	☐	02

Movement
(e.g. goes toward someone)

yes	☐	01
no	☐	02

Eyes
(e.g. engages X in eye contact)

yes	☐	01
no	☐	02

Facial expression
(e.g. smiles, scowls)

yes	☐	01
no	☐	02

Waiting
(e.g. 5 seconds)

Yes	☐	01
no	☐	02

Gesture
(e.g. points)

yes ☐ 01

no ☐ 02

Other

yes ☐ 01

no ☐ 02

6. *Pupils*

noise ceases ☐ 01

noise lessens ☐ 02

noise remains at same level ☐ 03

no noise ☐ 04

7. *Entry* Describe the actual entry to the classroom of:
(a) *The teacher* (e.g. chatting to pupils, giving directions, indicating where pupils may sit etc.)

(b) *The pupils*

8. *Setting up the task* (how the teacher sets up the substance of the lesson)

9. *Involvement in the task* (at three stages in the lesson)
Complete 1st period now.

	1st period	2nd period	3rd period
HIGH			
MEDIUM			
LOW			

PART III

Supplementary Data Sheet (Individual Pupil Study)

Teacher: _____ Date _____ Lesson:_____

Pupil	Seconds on task (out of 20)			Level of deviancy		
	Low 0-6	Medium 7-13	High 14-20	Serious	Mild	None
1						
2						
3						
4						
5						
6						
7						
8						
9						
10						
11						
12						
13						
14						
15						
16						
17						
18						
19						
20						
21						
22						
23						
24						
25						
26						
27						
28						
29						
30						
31						
32						
33						
34						
35						
Total						
	X0	X1	X2	X2	X1	X0
Factor A	0					0
Sum						

Formula $\dfrac{\text{Sum of Factor A}}{\text{Total of Pupils} \times 2} \times 100$ = Involvement or deviancy level

Task Involvement level _____

Deviancy level _____

GO BACK TO QUESTION 9, PAGE 3. COMPLETE 2ND PERIOD.

PART IV: (SUMMARY OF TEACHER'S STYLE)

Manner	1	2	3	4	5	Warm/friendly
Teacher appears	1	2	3	4	5	Confident
	1	2	3	4	5	Businesslike
Lesson is	1	2	3	4	5	Stimulating
Eye contact	1	2	3	4	5	High overall sweep
(withitness) (individuals)	1	2	3	4	5	High contact with individuals
Mobility (teacher changes place in room)	1	2	3	4	5	High mobility
Teacher formality/ informality	1	2	3	4	5	Formal

VOICE

POSTURE

GESTURE

OTHER

Comment on establishing or maintaining rules

Comment on establishing or maintaining relationships

Comment on transitions

PART V: CRITICAL EVENT

Identify one event which you saw occur during the lesson to do with the establishment of rules or relationships, e.g. dealing with deviancy, putting someone at ease.

Say   a) What led up to the event.
         b) What did the teacher do.
         c) What did the pupil(s) do.
         d) What was the outcome of the event.

PART VI: GENERAL COMMENT

(Including the nature of the task, the end of the lesson if significant)

GO BACK TO QUESTION 9, PAGE 3. COMPLETE 3RD PERIOD.

Footnote: Much more space was available for field notes on the actual schedule than is shown here. For example in part II item 5 observers made full notes under each heading (voice, posture etc.) and the yes/no computer code only signifies if any response has been made or not.

APPENDIX D

Pupil Attitude Questionnaire Used in Chapter 4

QUESTIONNAIRE ON TEACHING METHODS

Name: ....
Sex: M/F (Please circle) Year: 1 2 3 4
IMAGINE THAT THE BEST TEACHER IN THE WORLD HAS BEEN SENT TO
TEACH AT YOUR SCHOOL (It might be a man or a woman). In all the following
questions please answer with this teacher in mind. The first three questions
require you to circle the number of the statement you agree with.

1. How would you expect this teacher to introduce him/herself to you?
    1. By telling you his/her name.
    2. By telling you his/her name and something about his/her teaching
       experience.
    3. By telling you his/her name and something about his/her interests and
       hobbies.

2. How would you expect this teacher to be dressed?
    1. Very smartly
    2. Smartly
    3. Casually
    4. Doesn't matter

3. Think of your VERY FIRST LESSON with this teacher. Which one of the
   following would you expect him/her to be?
    1. Efficient, orderly and business like.
    2. Friendly, sympathetic and understanding.
    3. Firm and serious but fair.
    4. Understanding, friendly and firm.

The next set of questions have a five-point scale with which to answer them. On
this scale, the numbers mean:

1	2	3	4	5
STRONGLY AGREE	AGREE	DON'T KNOW	DISAGREE	STRONGLY DISAGREE

What you have to do is to circle the number that corresponds to your opinions on
the following statements. For instance if you disagree with statement 28, your
answer should look like this:
1   2   3 (4) 5.
(Please remember that your answers should be about *the best teacher in the world*).

4. This teacher would expect you to finish all work set by the end of the
   lesson   1   2   3   4   5
5. This teacher would be quick to say something nice when you do well.
                            1   2   3   4   5
6. This teacher would punish people for not getting work done.
                            1   2   3   4   5
7. This teacher would help you to learn a lot in every lesson.
                            1   2   3   4   5
8. This teacher would have lots of fun with you in lessons.
                            1   2   3   4   5
9. This teacher would boss you about.
                            1   2   3   4   5
10. This teacher would always be kind to you.
                            1   2   3   4   5
11. This teacher would let you plan the work for the class sometimes.
                            1   2   3   4   5
12. This teacher would tell you off in front of the rest of the class.
                            1   2   3   4   5
13. This teacher would always laugh at a good joke.
                            1   2   3   4   5
14. This teacher would punish the whole class if necessary.
                            1   2   3   4   5
15. This teacher would make you learn things just because they will be in
    exams.   1   2   3   4   5
16. This teacher would want you to help each other when working.
                            1   2   3   4   5
17. This teacher would always be fair when people misbehave.
                            1   2   3   4   5
18. This teacher would help the slower ones catch up in a nice way.
                            1   2   3   4   5
19. This teacher would let you mark your own tests.
                            1   2   3   4   5
20. This teacher would be interested in *all* your work.
                            1   2   3   4   5
21. This teacher would ask the class what they think about the work before
    setting it.   1   2   3   4   5
22. This teacher would do something else if that's what the class want.
                            1   2   3   4   5
23. This teacher would let you read any book you like if you have some free
    time.   1   2   3   4   5
24. This teacher would expect high standards.
                            1   2   3   4   5
25. This teacher would give you more time to finish work if you asked for it.
                            1   2   3   4   5
26. This teacher would ask you to raise your hand to show how many you got
    right in a test, even if you only got one or two.
                            1   2   3   4   5
27. This teacher would sometimes be too busy to talk to you.
                            1   2   3   4   5

28. This teacher would hit you.

    1   2   3   4   5

29. This teacher would call you by your first name.

    1   2   3   4   5

30. This teacher would be enthusiastic in lessons.

    1   2   3   4   5

31. This teacher would be interested in what you do outside of school as well as in it.

    1   2   3   4   5

32. This teacher would be a good listener.

    1   2   3   4   5

33. This teacher would always get the marking done on time.

    1   2   3   4   5

34. This teacher would live by the same rules that you are expected to.

    1   2   3   4   5

35. This teacher would explain things clearly.

    1   2   3   4   5

The last few questions are to do with your views on various aspects of school life.

36.   Children in school can be grouped in different ways. Circle the number of the way that you think is best.

   1. The brightest children in the A class for all subjects and the slowest children in the E class.
   2. Bright children in the top set for one subject and the slower children in the bottom set (with this method someone could be in the top set for English, but a lower set for Maths).
   3. Children of all abilities in the same class.

37.   Circle one of the following:

   1. Teachers should run schools the way they think fit.
   2. Teachers should run schools but pupils' opinions should be respected.
   3. Teachers AND pupils should run schools.
   4. Pupils should have more say than teachers in the running of schools.

38.   The teacher says that you are going to work in groups. Please circle the number that, in your opinion, is the best size for such a group.

    2   3   4   5   6   7

39.   Children learn things in many different ways. How do you learn best? Below are a number of ways of learning something, each with its own five-point scale. On this scale, one means a very good way of learning, and five is a very poor way. Therefore if you think that reading a book is a good way of learning your answer should look like this:

    1   ②   3   4   5

WAY OF LEARNING	v. good	good	medium	poor	v. poor
1. Using the Library	1	2	3	4	5
2. Practical work	1	2	3	4	5
3. Listening to the teacher	1	2	3	4	5
4. Work cards	1	2	3	4	5
5. Reading a book	1	2	3	4	5

NOTES ON CONTRIBUTORS

Sheila Armstrong was, until her tragically early death, the holder of a SSRC research studentship at Nottingham University School of Education.

Dr George Brown is Director of Teaching Services and Reader in Education at Nottingham University.

Pauline Dooley held a SSRC research studentship at Nottingham University School of Education and is now a Lecturer at the College of St Paul and St Mary, Cheltenham.

Rowena Edmondson is a research assistant at Nottingham University.

Dr Trevor Kerry was the Teacher Education Project Co-ordinator and is Head of Applied Social Science at Doncaster Metropolitan Institute of Higher Education.

Dr Margaret Sands is Senior Lecturer at Nottingham University School of Education.

Dr Kay Wood was a research assistant on the Teacher Education Project and is now a lecturer at Rolle College.

Professor Ted Wragg was Director of the Teacher Education Project and is Director of the School of Education at Exeter University.

Dr Mick Youngman is a Lecturer at Nottingham University School of Education.

INDEX